Ordinary People

Also by the Osbournes:

Bark at the Moon
Offically Osbourne: Opening the Doors to the Land of Oz

Ordinary People

OUR STORY

Ozzy and Sharon Osbourne
with Aimee, Kelly, & Jack
with Todd Gold

MTV BOOKS/POCKET BOOKS
New York · London · Toronto · Sydney · Singapore

POCKET BOOKS, a division of Simon & Schuster, Inc.
1230 Avenue of the Americas, New York, NY 10020

ISBN: 0-7434-6620-9

First MTV Books/Pocket Books hardcover edition January 2004

10 9 8 7 6 5 4 3 2 1

Designed by Jaime Putorti

Manufactured in the United States of America

For information regarding special discounts for bulk purchases,
please contact Simon & Schuster Special Sales at 1-800-456-6798
or business@simonandschuster.com

This fucking book is going to be the death of this family, I swear to God!

—KELLY OSBOURNE

Contents

CONTENTS

I

Lost in the O Zone

Things aren't as complicated as the show is edited to seem. I think everyone in our family can be portrayed as kind of hectic and crazy and not very rational. We're all really kind of basic, pretty much like anyone else's family with the same kind of problems. . . .

—AIMEE OSBOURNE

Ozzy: I'm not ever going to say anything bad about my family, but here's the main thing about the Osbournes: They are all out of their fucking minds. My wife is insane and my kids are insane. I am the one who actually thinks things through.

While they are out doing crazy things, I am home trying to figure out the mysteries of my life. Here's an example. For years, I was always telling Sharon to put something away for a rainy day. She's a spendaholic. I walked around the house saying, "We've got to stop spending all this. The money goes out of this fucking house like water from a pipe. We've got to save for when we get older." I'm not kidding, I was truly worried. I said, "We can make do with what we have. Let's put the next big check away." But my wife would have none of it. Sharon was always cool and calm as she rolled off to Tiffany's, Neiman Marcus, or some other store.

I don't know how she's done it. She must be a genius, or she's been touched by the Man himself, or she's incredibly lucky and taking the rest of us on a ride with her. Sharon and I haven't always had the perfect marriage. We had our ups and downs. There was fighting, infidelity, and drugs. But we weren't one of those couples you whisper about when you're in the kitchen or about to go to bed. "Did you hear? So-and-so's getting divorced." We held on to the horse's reins.

Then the universe tilted a bit. The other day I was driving in Sharon's car, talking to my assistant, Tony. All of our cars have tinted windows except for Sharon's Mercedes. I wasn't aware of it until I said to Tony, "Hey, man, is every single person in Beverly Hills a lousy driver? Or are they all looking at me?" Because we nearly got into a wreck every other block. It was like one of those PlayStation games. People were waving like fucking maniacs, and their cars were just missing ours. I called Sharon and said, "Why are you doing this to me?"

"Come home, Ozzy," she said.

I made it, and a few days later it was something else. We were having a huge party for Sharon's cancer charity. My house was turned into this place I hardly recognized. There were boards over the garden. A dance floor was put up. People were running all over with hors d'oeuvres. Tony Bennett sang in the backyard. I turned around and there was Sylvester Stallone. Elton John. My wife was hanging out with Elizabeth Taylor.

That scene hit me like a fucking brick. I had a problem dealing with it. I made Tony walk into a quiet room, where I said, "Do you see what the fuck is going on out there?" He nodded. "Tony, man, I'm from a working-class background," I said. "I woke up this morning and I thought, I have a house in Beverly Hills, a house in Malibu, I've got three houses in London, plus a farm. I fly around in private jets. And now I have Sir Elton John and Dame Elizabeth Taylor in my house."

"Pretty wild, eh?" Tony smiles.

"Well, then tell me this: How the fuck did this happen?"

"I don't know, Ozzy."

"I don't fucking know, either."

Jack: Privacy?

What's privacy?

I gave that up one afternoon about four years ago when Kelly barged into my bedroom while I was involved in a rather personal bit of business.

"Get the fuck out," I said.

Not that our family hides much of anything. Our personal lives have all been on TV. It's in the press. It's been in the tabloids. It's part of the mainstream pop culture. A stranger can walk into our house and basically know my father gets fucked up, my mom has battled cancer, my sister Kelly has an album out, my other sister Aimee has an attitude, and I'm this totally happening stud, or some facsimile, who made it into rehab by the time I was seventeen. It's cool. We made a deal with the devil to give up our privacy.

Despite the TV series and the press, though, I can attest the Osbourne family still has secrets and thoughts, people, that have not been broadcast publically. Some shit has occurred away from the cameras. Take the very first time I felt the full-on rush of fame and said, "Whoa, what the hell is happening to us?"

It was the summer of 2002, and my mom had been diagnosed with cancer. The shit had hit the fan. My dad was out of it and unable to deal. My sisters were doing their things. Just that we were going through a lot, which is a statement, considering as a family we have dealt with alcoholism and drug addiction, infidelity, abuse, depression, wealth, fame, learning disabilities, weight problems, and dudes who drive up in the front of our house every day and yell, "Ozzy, come out. You rule!"

So my mom decides we're going to the Emmy Awards, the biggest night of the year for television. We had won a special creative Emmy the previous day in a ceremony that wasn't televised. The Emmy Awards were on prime time. They were a big fucking deal black-tie affair. We—meaning Kelly and myself—were informed that while Mom would be wearing half of Harry Winston's inventory of diamonds, we were to make sure we wore clean underwear.

"I'll be the only one showing off the family jewels," my mom joked.

As everyone got ready for the big evening out, I noticed the weirdness start building up. We had gone out to fancy events before, but I never felt the nervousness or tension about looking not just great but phenomenal. I'm sure my mother's cancer had something to do with it. She was thin and fragile. She'd lost weight. You could see the toll the disease had already taken on her, and she hadn't really begun the treatment, which would make her even worse. My dad was drinking in the kitchen, watching television, but a mess from worry and concern.

Then in come the army of stylists, hair and makeup people. They brought dresses and brushes and blow-dryers and bags of lipstick and crap. Our publicist was there. Melinda, our nanny, is running around. There are like a thousand people doing things to help us get ready, and from my vantage the only thing they're helping is to create chaos and confusion. My dad vanishes when things get like that, and my mom's usually in the middle of it. My thing is staying in control, keeping your cool. And no one was cool. As far as I was concerned, they had lost their minds. Everyone's nerves are jacked and I'm getting dressed while people offer various opinions about hair, clothes, and shoes.

Finally I had had enough. I looked around and thought, I have to help everyone get a grip. That's what we need. We need a grip on things. So I called everyone together, asked for a time-out, and said, "A year ago we were blackballed from this town. Now everyone's out of their head. Who the hell do you think we are? We're just going out to a party."

The room fell silent as if I had made time stop. They all looked at me. Then Kelly stomped out of the room and said, "Mind your own business." My mom turned back to what she was doing, and my dad walked back into the kitchen; he wasn't going to the Emmys. Aimee didn't say a word. And suddenly things were the way they always are.

The limo arrived and like any kid going to a major black-tie event I had a last question for my mom. "Should I take a condom?"

Sharon: There comes a time when you wonder whether the fast lane is too fast, whether the limos are going to take you where you want to go, and whether you have chartered the wrong private jet. For me, that occurred a few days after I cheered as Nicole Kidman and Adrien Brody won Academy Awards when Kelly was headed back on tour.

She had flown into L.A. for a round of parties: the different post-Oscar soirees, as well as Elton John's birthday and my own first charity fund-raiser. It was a hectic but fun time. I loved having her home. But then she had to pick her tour back up in Philadelphia. I kissed her good-bye and watched her drive to the airport.

One minute I was the picture of a proud mother, then the next I was as petrified as any parent has ever been. Kelly and her tour manager, her best friend Sarah, had been flying for about twenty minutes when the oxygen masks dropped, things onboard the plane began popping, and one of the pilots—Cher's former "bagel boy" boyfriend Rob Camilletti—announced they were turning back in order to make an emergency landing back in Van Nuys.

She had called me from the plane right before it happened, so when stuff started to go wrong I heard her screaming, "Mommy! Mommy!" Then we got disconnected. That began the worst twenty-five minutes of my entire life. Forget Ozzy. Never mind the cancer. This was pure terror.

It was 1:00 A.M., and I scrambled to find the phone number for the charter company. Nobody picked up. I was going insane.

Finally, the phone rang and it was Kelly, telling me the plane had landed safely at the Van Nuys Airport. I had never been so glad to hear from her or felt such relief.

"Oh Mommy, I'm so scared," she said. "I love you."

"How are you?" I asked.

"We threw up all over the plane."

Kelly and her friend came back to the house. They were still crying and shaking when they walked through the door. Kelly had a hard time imagining herself getting back on a plane. She was like a little girl, traumatized. Late that night, we had a family meeting where all of us, Ozzy included, discussed the next move. The question wasn't just whether Kelly could get up the nerve to go. It was also whether we could go through with it.

We ended up canceling the show in Philadelphia, which she couldn't get to in time, but we decided she would try again because she was scheduled to appear on *Late Night with David Letterman* in New York. I said, "I'll fly with you. I'll be with you the whole flight. I'll stay through the weekend, and we'll have fun in New York."

Late the next night, following Elton's birthday party, we got on another chartered jet and took off. An hour into the flight, one of the hydraulic systems went out and we made an emergency landing in Denver. I couldn't believe it. None of us could. Kelly was screaming on the plane, "Why did I get on a plane again?" The parent onboard, I was shitting and peeing in my pants, as well. All of us on the plane were white-faced.

As we neared the runway, we saw an ambulance and fire trucks. They followed the plane down the entire runway. Then we stopped and all of us burst out in laughter. Nothing else made sense. All we could do was laugh. It was so frighteningly absurd a second disaster could happen to us again. We called Ozzy and told him we had just made another emergency landing, and he started screaming at us.

We just laughed. Manic laughter. While he swore.

"What are you laughing about?" he asked.

"Because this could only happen to the Osbournes," I said. "This is really the Osbournes, the real Osbournes, and there's not a fucking camera in sight!"

II

𝔑ativity in 𝔅lack

———— ⟿ ————

Waggin' it	Missing school, playing truant.
Mucker	A good friend who can be relied on to lend a hand no matter what, who will always *muck in* with you.
Guzzunda	A vessel used in houses lacking an inside toilet. The word describes where it was kept: "The pot guzzunda the bed."
Or roit?	Are you well? Okay?
Point	Large glass of ale, one-eighth of a gallon.

—TRANSLATIONS OF BIRMINGHAM SLANG
FROM *PROPER BRUMMIE: A DICTIONARY OF BIRMINGHAM
WORDS & PHRASES*

Kelly: I don't really know, because I don't like to ask. It makes me sad to know how my dad was treated as a child. He never told me stories about his childhood. Neither would I have wanted to hear them.

Aimee: He was picked on at school. One time he told me how they would take his clothes off, beat him up, and leave him crying. He had learning disabilities. He was made fun of and called stupid. Those kinds of things have an effect. My dad is usually pretty quiet and laid-back. He keeps to himself. But get close to him and you sense his pain. You know he's suffered a lot.

Jack: He once compared his upbringing to the book *Angela's Ashes*. It wasn't that bad, but he said it was close. My dad's been a lot more open with things than my mother. I didn't know much about her family until recently—she used to tell us that her father was dead.

Aimee: We never knew any family history while growing up. When we asked about our grandparents, they said everyone was dead. The stories changed and were exaggerated, but when you're a kid you accept a certain amount of that and then you lose interest. We had no idea they were lying to us.

Jack: It's kind of a stretch to get my mom to talk about things when she was a kid. I mean, she'll talk about things from fifteen up until about twenty-eight, then after we were born. I'm not really expecting this book to say (in a kiddy-show voice), "Well, kids, it's time for us to sit you down," but I kind of want to know what happened in between those years.

Aimee: I don't really think that the book is going to expose anything more that the TV show didn't. Maybe some history and that would be it.

Ozzy: Well, Sharon says I'm going to say things I'm going to regret, but it's good to do the book. It is kind of like a therapy session in a way.

Sharon: For two years we've been on air and people think they know us intimately? *I* didn't even know about what my son was up to! I hope they'll get a little bit more out of this book because there are so many sides to people. This book will show a whole 'nother side—it goes a lot deeper.

Jack: *The Osbournes* shows us as these characters. If you're going to do a reality show, do a reality show. Show everyone's angle. That's what this book should do. I hope that this book could give a true sense of who everyone really is—especially my dad.

Ozzy: I hope to think there's more in-depth truth in the book than the TV show, and if there's one message that gets across, it's love your family, no matter what.

Do me a favor: Don't tell Sharon I smoked pot in this room today. . . .

Ozzy: I don't know whether I should thank the guy who gave me my first drink or kill him.

I was fourteen years old and screwing around outside the pub while my father was inside getting shit-faced. This wasn't the first time I had followed my dad to the local watering hole. It was more like a daily routine, something we had been doing nearly every day for years, since I was a young boy able to keep up on the walk. I would follow him down to the pub, but because of my age I had to sit outside and wait for him to have his fill. I spent hours there each time, listening to him and his friends sing songs and get totally smashed. The drunker they got, the worse the songs and the louder they sang 'em.

I thought of the place, which was an ordinary corner drinking establishment for the working man, as having a magical quality for the effect it had on my dad. He would go there steaming mad after having fought with my mom, called her an asshole, and knocked her around a few times. "Come on, John," he yelled as he left the house, and I would scramble out the door with him, keeping my distance, though, as I was very scared he might hit me the way he did my mom. Then within ten minutes of being in the pub he was singing and having a great time.

What's this fucking beer taste like? I asked myself.

After years waiting and wondering, there finally came that fateful day when a guy I knew leaned out the window and asked how old I was. "Fourteen." A moment later, apparently taking pity on me, he passed a pint out the window. I handed him the equivalent of a quarter. I spit out the first sip. It tasted awful. No way could that be the shit my old man drank. I tried it again, though. And again and again. Pretty soon I had a warm feeling and I forgot how bad the stuff tasted.

That night I drank six pints. One right after the other. I got absolutely one hundred percent fucked-up and woke up the next morning in a park, covered in piss.

"What the fuck did you do that for?" a friend of mine asked the next day as I told him about my first drinking episode.

"It made me feel good," I said.

There was precious little of feeling good in my early life. The fourth of six children (I have three older sisters, Jean, Iris, and Gillian; plus two younger brothers, Paul and Tony) of John and Lillian Osbourne, I was born on December 3, 1948. My mother had me at home, 14 Lodge Road, delivered by a midwife, in Aston, a working-class neighborhood in Birmingham, England. My dad was a factory worker, a toolmaker at the GEC steel plant. He worked nights and wouldn't miss a shift if his life depended on it. My mom worked day shifts, testing horns in the Lucas car factory.

Life was a fucking struggle. I always thought my mom had more money. I wished my dad would stay home more. But my generation, we had a work ethic.

We were working class. I was born from working class. We never had a car. We never went on holiday. I didn't see the ocean until I was fucking fourteen. Though we never went begging, money was scarce, and the living was hard and cramped. The eight of us crammed into a small two-bedroom house, the second floor of which was as big as my son's bedroom now. My parents had one room and the kids had the other one. If we wanted a mattress, all six of us had to cram uncomfortably into one bed and fight for space. Until we had an indoor toilet, we pissed into a bucket at the end of the bed, which stunk when we didn't empty it regularly, and often we didn't.

I was eight or nine when my dad built a bathroom on the back of the house. He and a group of cowboy workers put that thing in as cheaply as possible, and every time it rained the ceiling or a wall caved in. My dad cursed that thing more than he did the bucket it replaced. He spent most of his free time hauling in tar and plaster, struggling to fix that fucking thing once and for all.

Coming out of the bombs, terror, and destruction from World War II, people had a different attitude. Whether or not things worked, we got by without sitting around and complaining about how miserable we had it. Ours was a working-class lot. We ate stew and bread and listened to the radio for entertainment. My parents worked hard, my dad was drinking at the pub nearly every moment from the time he got off on Friday night till Monday night when he had to go back to work. He and my mom fought and occasionally he smacked her around. Parental surpervision was there—and not. I had a lot of respect for my father. If he said something to me and there was that certain tone, you knew you would get a clip around the ear or something.

My father and mother worked damn hard to give us things. Did we wish we had more luxuries? Yeah. Did we moan about what we didn't have? No fucking way. I had a shirt, one pair of pants, one pair of socks, shoes, and a jacket. There was one summer when my mom couldn't afford to get me shoes and I wore my winter galoshes. I was always dirty and smelly, which the kids teased me about unmercifully, and which is why years down the road I spent the first bit of money I earned from music on drugs and strong fucking cologne.

If you're ever in my company now you'll think I bathe in cologne. But no amount can wipe out the odor of a life that stinks. My earliest memories are fear. My first ever emotion was being scared. I've never been comfortable in my own skin. For some reason, I'm a frightened soul. I had strange thoughts as a kid, nightmares that were incredibly disturbing. I heard voices that told me to do terrible things: "Kill your mother." "Hang your brother." "Burn your sister." I was out there, man.

School was a horror story. It was a four- or five-mile walk to Prince Albert Road Juniors, my early school, and I would just wash my hands and face and hit the fucking road. I wouldn't wash my neck, and would have what they call a tide mark. I got caned every day, or they would send me back home either for being late or not washing the dirt from beneath my chin or not doing my homework.

That misery continued at Birchfield Road Second Modern School, where both teachers and classmates called me stupid and much worse for always being behind or not knowing the answer.

There was always talk of me being retarded or weird, and I heard the tauntings and teasing. But I wasn't stupid. Not by any means. I just couldn't do the work. It turns out I was very seriously dyslexic, something that wasn't diagnosed back then, and that disability made it so the lessons others got so easily were too hard for me.

To this day, my biggest dread is having to stand up and read out loud. I'm exactly the way I was as a kid—so fucked-up I get it all wrong.

I suffered a terrible stigma. Tired of being called names and getting beat up, I was around twelve when I eventually started to skip school on a regular basis. It was such a relief not to have that trauma. I cut as often as possible, passed the time hanging out at the snooker hall with my closest friend, Patrick Murphy. He committed suicide a few years ago. I had a few other friends—Tommy Sutton, Robby Vaughn, and Steven Hudson—Steven was a big gentle giant, I was with him all the time at school.

But with Patrick, we were always waggin' it—hooky-playing hoodlums. It was small, kidlike crime, like scrumping, which was stealing apples off people's trees. By our early teens, we graduated to lifting candy, soda, and cigarettes from the little shops.

Patrick was fearless. He had nerves of steel. I, on the other hand, was possibly the worst child criminal ever. I didn't have the temperament. As soon as we started talking about ripping off a store or whatever fucking thing we were going to do, my conscience started talking to me and I got scared of getting caught. I got even more scared afterward when the cops were called. But it's strange what happens to a person in those situations. When the cops chase you, you run, and so I ran as fast as I could run, down alleys and over walls. Unfortunately I wasn't a fast runner. I was also scared of heights.

I was much better at making people laugh. That was my thing. I was a natural clown. I was always getting myself out of trouble by coming up with a funny line. Never a good athlete, I always fucked up when my friends forced me to play soccer. Invariably I ended up ruining the game, and when they got mad at me, I always said, "If you can't kick the ball, kick the person next to you." Those were the kind of stupid, silly things I picked up from TV and movies. I was a huge fan of anything from Hollywood, especially the women. Debbie Reynolds was a hot one for me. Maureen O'Hara—a babe. My all-time favorite was Hayley Mills. She was my sweetheart. I loved her.

The thing about women in those days was they looked like people. They had real bodies. They had some flesh on them. Nowadays the women are matchsticks with enormous boobs and arms and legs. They have no shape. All the movies and TV shows from back then seem better to me than current ones. I loved films like *Giant* and the original *Time Machine* and *Those Magnificent Men in Their Flying Machines* and my favorite film of all time, *Good-bye Mr. Chips.* My favorite TV shows: *Sea Hunt* and *Palladin* and *Bonanza* and *Wagon Train.* I loved *The Rifleman* and *The Lone Ranger.*

As I write this, I'm just realizing all my favorite TV heroes were similar. They were strong men, not afraid of a fucking thing, riding to the rescue of people in trouble, and I fucking loved them. But I was the opposite in every way, shape, and form when I was a kid. One day while Sharon was going through chemotherapy, I was telling a friend that I had always felt scared as a kid, even as an adult, and that for as long as I could remember I'd never been comfortable in my own skin, and he surprised the hell out of me by asking, "So, were you abused as a kid?"

At first I said I didn't want to talk about it, but a few days later we were together again and I brought it up. I said I felt like telling him something I hadn't told anyone else other than Sharon, and within a few minutes both of us were crying. I couldn't believe that I was a total fucking basket case all over again, shaking and full of tears.

But what happened is that suddenly I was reliving a horrendous experience I'd gone through when I was eleven and had been sexually abused. I've never come to terms with the incident. How could I? I've kept it inside all these years. Why it came out is as mysterious to me as why the Osbournes suddenly became famous. I don't know. It took place so long ago, the abuse did. There were actually two guys. One day I was walking home from school, one of those rare days I went, with my sister, and as I passed their homes the bigger of the two guys, Robert, called me over to where his family's laundry was drying on the clothesline. He said someone was ruining his mom's clean whites by putting black marks on the sheets and clothes.

"It wasn't me," I protested while looking helplessly at my sister, who I think was as scared as me.

He said he had to check. I asked how? He said whoever was doing it had a black mark on their willy and was rubbing it off. Then the one guy held me while this dude Robert pulled my pants down and messed with my willy. It was in front of my sister, which fucked me up even more than if they'd done it without her there. They threatened to beat me up if I told anyone. They also said if I didn't keep coming back, they'd kill my mother. The next time they said they'd kill her if I told anyone.

This went on a few times until eventually they grew tired of their sick fucking game and left me alone. If I'd had a gun back then I would have killed both of them. If I came across either of them today I'd want to kill them. That has never happened and it likely won't, though I thought about it for years. Nonetheless, the damage was done. Taking into consideration I was already scared, the abuse further unstabled me.

I retreated further into myself, which was not a pleasant place to be. My mind was full of all these sick fantasies. That's how I got through the days. As for having any relationship, well, it fucked me up. I thought sex was kind of wrong. No, let me clarify. I had so much shame and fear, I didn't know what to do. I couldn't relax. I just wanted to get the job done. I never made love in my life until I met Sharon, who helped me, and continues to help me, deal with the frightened little boy inside me who has never grown up in all these years.

I'm not saying I was antisex. Far from it. I was for anything that let me feel good, from booze to the fleeting sensation of an orgasm. At fourteen, I lost my virginity to a woman. Actually, I didn't lose it. I knew exactly where it went. I had been hired to baby-sit for this woman's two young kids. Her old man was a truck driver on a trip. She had gone out to the pub and when she came back she wrapped her arms around me, attempted a few sloppy kisses, and then she just jumped me.

I didn't complain. At fourteen, I was like, "Holy shit, lady, I want to baby-sit for you every night of the week. Have another kid, please, so I can keep doing this."

That was one more secret I hid from the world. Full of torment, I did what I needed to in order to get by. I smoked. I drank. Eventually I started smoking pot and trying whatever pills were around. As one of my heroes later sang, whatever gets you through the night . . .

Except I had trouble getting even that far. One night I became so despondent, like someone drowning in the ocean, I went outside, took down my mother's clothesline, and fashioned it into a noose. I slipped it over my head, threw the other end over the tall metal gate in back, and jumped off a chair. My dad, on his way to work, came by just as I jumped and he got me down.

"What the fuck is wrong with you?" he said disgustedly.

"I don't know," I said.

I didn't, either. My head was filled with these insanely dark, depressing, muddled thoughts I couldn't explain. I guess I was just hanging around.

"I don't know about you," he said upon sending me inside. "Sometimes I think you're mad."

I couldn't have agreed more.

𝕾𝔥𝔞𝔯𝔬𝔫: As someone who has always turned a blind eye toward price tags, I have purchased my share of designer clothes, diamond jewelry, and fancy furniture—just ask them at Tiffany's, Barneys, Armani, Van Cleef, Asprey, Valentino. Hell, just walk into Beverly Hills and ask where Sharon is, and odds are someone will know. My taste for beautiful things began when I was a little girl decorating my bedroom.

I got it from my father. He had fabulous taste. He thought nothing of spending ten grand on an antique table if he liked it. Not that we always had the money. Just because you like champagne doesn't mean you can afford to drink it. I was around ten years old when my parents moved my brother and me from one of the poorest sections of London to one of the richest, Barclay Square. I was eleven or so when the creditors came and carted everything away.

My life was like that—we were always up and down. One week we had a Rolls-Royce, and then the next week we were back at bus stops, our dining room table was carried out, and the electricity turned off.

That sort of rise and fall in fortune has been part of my life since I was brought into the world at Westminster Hospital, right in the center of London. We lived at the time in an area that was sort of like meat factories. For the last twenty years it's been kind of the worst area ever, with crime and race riots, but when I was brought up there it was great. There were knife throwers on the next block, and the whole street was full of these characters, variety acts, trailers, and costumes. It was like a little artists' community.

I am the oldest of two children raised by parents who had show business in their blood. Early in their marriage, both my mom and dad performed in traditional musical and comedy shows. We did, too: We did pantomimes. We performed at the London Palladium.

We lived entertainment. My dad burned with ambition that wasn't satisfied by his meager earnings on stage. He knew his talent could only take him so far, so he started producing shows for the tens of thousands of troops stationed in Europe after the Second World War, and he did better.

The first five years of our lives—mine and my brother, David's—were spent touring with my parents. They'd leave us in the hotel while they did the show and then come back and get us. Nobody would do it today. You'd get arrested. My brother and I would go up and down in the elevators, break into kitchens, get on the night porter. We had a blast.

Once my dad started producing shows, he was constantly on the road, crisscrossing all of Europe. If there was a buck to be made, he was chasing it, and along the way he was learning the ins and outs of every aspect of putting an act on the road. I spent the first five years of my life going from one military base to another. By the late 1950s and early 1960s, my dad had given up producing for management. Actually, he produced the shows for the acts he managed—Brenda Lee, Chuck Berry, Little Richard, Jerry Lee Lewis. If there was an American who had an album out and came to Europe, my dad managed them. Gene Vincent taught me how to swim. In ten years, my dad had made a huge progression: from being an artist himself to being a producer, an agent, and a successful manager.

All the traveling we did ruined me as far as school was concerned. I couldn't settle down enough to study. Forget math. I never did well. But put me in a store with 25 pecent off and a credit card and I saw numbers fly in front of my eyes. Scratch that. Thinking about it now, I've maxed out an embarrassing number of credit cards. So I guess numbers *aren't* my thing.

They weren't my dad's, either. On the one hand, he was a terrible role model. If he had money, he spent it lavishly. If my brother or I broke something, it wasn't a big deal. He bought something bigger, better. On the other hand, he paid less attention to bills than he did price tags. His business was all cash, and when the flow slowed to a trickle or less, it would all go—the furniture, the cars, everything, right down to the electricity and the telephone.

But there were no tears. Normally children crave stability, but I must've been a rare breed. I didn't panic when he lost it all. I stood beside him and waved good-bye to our favorite belongings as they were wheeled out the front door. I believed my dad when he said we'd not only get it back, we'd get even better stuff. The ups and downs were harder on my mom, whose temperament was best suited for stability. But for me, it was the best education I could've ever had, because it taught me how to enjoy nice things but not to look at them as a source for my happiness.

Whether we had platinum or plastic, I learned to adapt to change. No grumbling. No looking back with regret. You got on and did it.

You either loved my father or hated him. Usually both. Though physically small, he had a larger-than-life personality. He fought for everything, even those things that came easily. That was residual from his background as a Jew from Russia who came to England, where he constantly encountered anti-Semitism. Despite being small, he was the kid who stood his ground, his fists raised and ready to fight rather than run.

He taught that to me, too. When I was nine or ten he bought me a Star of David necklace and matching earrings. The next day my brother and I took a shortcut home from school, and as we walked down an alley we ran into a bunch of kids who saw my necklace and called us dirty Jews. They wanted to beat up my brother, but I spit at them and told them off. Even then I had a mouth. Later that night we told my father what had happened, and he said, "Good. They can eat shit."

Such was a phrase he employed often. He also used Yiddish a lot and was able to speak with his contacts in Germany. That was the music scene back then: London, Liverpool, and Hamburg. In 1960, he was doing a lot of business with the Star Club in Hamburg, which was run by the German mafia. That was my dad's world—that whole hardcore end of the industry.

One day this club owner called and raved about a new band that was driving everyone at the club mad. They were called the Beatles, and he wanted my dad to take them on. My dad was interested until he heard they came from Liverpool. You have to picture my father to understand how he made this decision. He was like Jimmy Cagney in the music business, a cliché in the pin-striped suit, the gold chains, the big cigar. He was living the American Dream in London. He only wanted to deal with the American acts. To him, anyone coming from Liverpool was a loser.

"What is this? Ridiculous haircuts, ridiculous behavior, this isn't what it's about." Biggest mistake of somebody's career. And that guy at Decca Records, Dick Rowe, who passed on them because he thought guitar bands were on their way out? He was my father's best friend! Two *alter kockers*—that's Yiddish for "old shits"—together, right?

Everyone knows what happened next. The lads from Liverpool turned into the Fab Four. The American sound died overnight in Europe. I mean, it just *died*. The Beatles changed the whole music scene—then it was the Mersey Beats, the Dave Clark Fives, all the spin-off bands. The Beatles were household names everywhere but ours. Despite the hits and the pandemonium, my dad decided their music was rubbish. It didn't matter how popular they became, he described every one of those early songs as crap. Not only that, he prohibited anyone in the house, meaning my brother and me, from playing or even mentioning the Beatles.

And when we did, you know what he said? "They can eat shit."

I'm laughing now, but it wasn't funny then. My dad was a big-time screamer and when I heard him yelling, I would go, "Oh shit. What the fuck have I done?" It was extremely rare for me to incur his wrath. Other than liking the Beatles, I didn't give him many reasons to get angry at me. I idolized my dad. Some children inherit the gene for addiction from their parents while others get special skills in science or art or a fondness for cooking or tennis. I got the management gene from my dad. By the time I hit puberty, I knew the basics of contracts, booking dates, and half a dozen ways to get an act from Chicago to Rome.

At fifteen, I dropped out of school to work in my dad's office. I'm not putting the blame on my parents, but education was never a high priority. It was something that you had to do. Once you learned to read and write you can get your ass out of there and go into the world. That is the way I was brought up, with a really strong work ethic, and you work, work, work. I'm glad that I did because I wouldn't have been the person that I am today. Everything I've learned in life about art and whatever is self-taught. I'm quite proud about that.

I can't say being around him at the office showed me a side I didn't see at home, but I heard a lot of new words come from his mouth. If a disagreement arose, and invariably there were several dozen a day, he never said, "Okay, we have a problem. We need to talk this out." No, when my dad got angry he went straight to saying, "Your wife is a fucking whore. She's fucking half the people in your neighborhood. Your kids aren't yours. Your father's gay, and your mother is a bigger whore than your wife." He went straight for the balls with a razor blade. It would always be big-time personal abuse. I simply appreciated the artistry with which he strung together words that scared men double his size and triple his wealth into giving in to his demands.

Eventually my father got his footing back managing groups like the Animals, the Nashville Teens. He basically helped create this famous rock producer Mickey Most, who was just an engineer whom my father gave a break working with Gene Vincent. Mickey then went on to become hugely successful, and my dad went on to work with the Small Faces.

Ozzy: Everyone has a button in them waiting to be pressed. In some people it's a button and in others it's a stick of fucking dynamite. I had both, and the one was pressed by the Beatles and the other was lit by drugs, and when I think back over the history of my life the two of them hit pretty close to each other.

How old was I when I first heard the Beatles? Thirteen, fifteen, whatever. I know that one day I was whistling Neal Sedaka's "Oh Carol" and singing along to songs by Marty Wild and Adam Faith and the Everly Brothers, and then the next day my life changed. I heard the Beatles singing "She Loves You." It's funny to think back on it. I didn't like "Please Please Me" or "From Me to You," but as soon as I heard the opening to "She Loves You," my whole life stopped and I paid attention to something.

From the time I heard John, Paul, George, and Ringo I knew what I wanted to do with my life. I had a lot of shit part-time jobs. I was a paperboy. I delivered food. I delivered coal for three guineas per six-pound bag. After all day of doing that in the snow and sleet my feet would be fucking frozen. It was painful. One time I had the flu, plus a really high fever, and as I laid in bed I suffered a frightening delirium, with all these overwhelming fears, and the only thing that calmed me down was turning on the radio and hearing John or Paul singing in front of those great tunes.

I spent every dime I earned buying posters, magazines, singles, and albums, and then papering the walls with them. I carved out a little corner of my own and if anyone touched my shrine, so much as laid a finger on it or even thought of borrowing a record—well, they didn't dare. I could've opened a fucking Beatles store with the amount I had. God, if I still had that stuff I could sell it and get rich all over again.

I got myself through the toughest moments of my life then by fantasizing about the Beatles, with myself in the starring role. In one, I dreamed my oldest sister married Paul. That was probably the best one, because I could get myself really worked up by imagining him coming over for dinner, ringing the bell, and me answering the door. I pictured him singing a few ditties after dinner. But then I would come to my senses and go, "What the hell? He wouldn't like her anyway."

I also dreamed about joining the Beatles. Who didn't? If you heard one of those songs, you sang along. And if you were a poor, troubled outcast like me and saw those guys from Liverpool in the center of a frenzy wherever they went, with girls going crazy just trying to get a glimpse of them and millions of dollars, you wanted to be just like them. I mean working-class Liverpool and Birmingham— there just wasn't a fuck of a difference to me. Except for talent and looks, I was practically a twin for either John or Paul.

At least I could grow my hair. As for learning guitar, I couldn't do it. I tried a few times, but with my attention deficit disorder I didn't have the patience. So I sang Beatles songs all day long. One time at school some assholes caught me singing "I Want to Hold Your Hand" to myself and they beat the crap out of me for it. Not too long after I left school. Fuck that. I was fifteen, and I decided to be a plumber, which didn't last. I hated the cold. Then I briefly tried construction. Too hard. Harder than any workout. Next I landed at the slaughterhouse—perfect for a guy known as a cutup.

Bad joke, worse job. The place was bleak—long, low cement buildings, cement floors, everything damp and dank, and cows and pigs and sheep everywhere. Those unfortunate enough to be alive knew it wasn't for long, and those already dead were in various stages of being butchered, dissected, and packaged. My first day on the job I was given six thousand sheep stomachs to cut up. I threw up all day long. An old-timer taking pity on me said, "You get used to it."

I never did. I can't remember a day when I didn't puke my guts inside out from the combination of stink and savagery. Though I'm sure I got used to it, I still regret the disgusting things I did there. It's one part of my life I haven't reconciled. Not that it's possible when you got a perverse joy, as I did at the time, from torturing the animals to death. I once bit the head off a pig just to entertain my coworkers. Actually, I did it more than once. Another time I met this girl for a date and put a little gift for her on the table. She unwrapped it and then before vomiting she managed to ask what it was. "It's a cow's eye," I said, laughing. "And even if I can't, it'll see you through the week."

Only two things saw me through that job—a daily shower, which I took right there at the plant after my shift, and drinking. The Midnight City was next door to the slaughterhouse. It was an all-night pub where everyone went. My hair wasn't dry from the shower and I was on my second drink. Like everyone else who spent eight hours a day eviscerating animals, I got shit-faced drunk every day. You had to numb yourself to the guts, the blood, the stench, and the cries from the animals just before they bought it.

At least I could end my suffering. And after two years, I did. I quit. I wanted that glamorous life the Beatles were living, but that fucking job wasn't going to get me there. All I got was frustrated. And drunk. The next few jobs I had were less memorable but just as fucking stupid, including two weeks carrying caskets in a funeral home. Then my mother helped get me a job at the car factory where she worked, testing horns. I spent the entire day with eight other men in a soundproof room putting a screwdriver in horns so they would go off as they came 'round on a conveyor belt.

One day I turned to the man next to me, a guy around my father's age, and I said, "How long have you been here?"

"Eighteen years," he replied.

In a way, it was worse than killing pigs. I thought, Man, people work here until they die. You might as well shoot me now. I left.

The only reason I worked anyway was to pay for all the pills I took. Mostly speed. The occasional Seconal to sleep. The next part of my life is as well known as it is laughable. I did what most unemployed drug-taking alcoholics do. I turned to crime. Only I wasn't any good at it. Obviously I wasn't a criminal. Despite ripping off gas meters and climbing through the window of the old lady who lived next door to us, I didn't have a criminal mind-set. I proved that one night when the cops caught me coming out of a clothing shop carrying about thirty-five dollars' worth of merchandise I'd just burgled.

"Don't you have any gloves?" one of the cops asks.

I was like, "Yeah, I do. I left 'em inside." I went back in and returned with the last bit of evidence they needed.

My father, hoping to teach me a lesson, refused to pay the fine. So I was sentenced to three months in Winson Green Prison, where my education began upon arrival when guards performed a strip search. They made me remove every stitch of clothing I had on as a bunch of prisoners watched like it was a fucking show. The guards looked me up and down while shining bright lamps on me. They shoved something up my ass. Then they hosed me off and dusted me with this powder disinfectant so I wouldn't bring any scabies or crabs into the prison. I'd never felt more humiliated.

The actual jail was worse. In one sense, it was just like you see on TV and movies. I walked in and the prisoners looked me over, some whistling, some calling me names, others just giving me silent looks that said, "Don't fuck with me." I was doing everything I could not to piss myself. What you don't know from watching those prison shows is how fucking bad it smells. At Winson Green, the odor came courtesy of Jay's Fluid, a superstrong cleaning solvent that made every square inch smell like a public toilet. Once that smell got in your nose, it never left.

Though I tried keeping to myself, I had to fight off a few perverts wanting to have sex with me. One fight got me thrown into solitary for a few days. Afterward I went to doing what the rest of the guys did, cleaning my cell, or "peter" as they were called. Nothing else to do. Some of the people in there polished their beds, sinks, and floors so obsessively they could see their fucking faces in them.

After serving six of the twelve weeks of my sentence, I was let out. Any thoughts I had of stealing ever again had been erased. I didn't want to go back to prison. I took home a reminder, too. While biding my time in jail, I'd used black shoe polish to tattoo my name on the knuckles of my left hand. The next time I was around some girls in a park I tried to impress them by letting them watch me use the tricks I'd learned in prison to tattoo happy faces on my knees. My luck: The tattoos stuck, but the girls didn't.

I had to figure out what to do. At eighteen, I didn't want to be living with my parents the rest of my fucking life. Neither did they want me there. One day I bumped into an acquaintance, this guy whose band was looking for a singer, and with visions of the Beatles in my head I volunteered for the job. He told me when rehearsal was and said to bring my equipment. Rather than admit I didn't have any gear, I said okay and promised to see him later. Then I wondered what I was going to do.

Sharon: When people say to me, "Ozzy? Don't you think he's extreme?" I laugh. He's the most normal person I know! *My* family is the extreme.

My father was always on the edgy side of the business, which was reoccurring in the nineties with certain rap managers and labels. You know whom I'm talking about. That's how it was in the sixties. Everything was payola. Everything was "You fuck with me? You don't deliver? You're over!" A real kind of that street mentality. My father was very much that breed. He could get violent and he had a reputation—but all I knew is my dad's side of it and I was never privy to those . . . *situations.*

Once my dad tied a producer to a tree and put a shotgun to his knee. He was going to blow his kneecaps off because he was trying to entice the Faces to leave and sign with him. He came home and laughed, "God, you should have seen this guy shit! I beat the shit out of this guy because he said this, this, and this." But again, that's how it was done—in my family it was nothing shocking. "Oh, did you dad? Okay, pass the peas, could you? More gravy." That's how it was.

You know what? That's very much my take on life. I keep my head down. I don't do anything to anyone, but if you want to fuck with me, I'll fuck with you and I'll win. I am not a violent person, but I can make your life hell. I don't want to, but if you start with me I can be much nastier than you because I learned from the governor!

My job was receptionist, but it was clear from early on my dad wanted me to do lots more than answer his telephone. It was more like keeping the phone connected, the electricity on, and the land-lords from kicking us out. If the job hadn't worked out for me, I could've always signed up as a juggler, because that's what I did.

Take a typical Friday afternoon when we didn't have the cash we needed to pay the wages or the bills. My dad had to con the bank manager, Mr. Kaplan, into fronting the money. So we staged a well-rehearsed charade. I called Mr. Kaplan and pretended to be the overseas operator connecting my father from New York. He was actually in his office waiting for a cue from my brother, who, having removed the tiny box around the phone line, would jiggle the wires with a screwdriver as my dad spoke to give the impression of a bad connection.

"Hello, international operator calling for Mr. Kaplan," I'd say, and then the bank manager would get on. "Mr. Kaplan, I have Mr. Arden calling from New York. Go ahead, please."

"Great news," my dad would say. "I picked up the money. Lots of cash. I'll be in Monday morning. Let the wages go through."

We did that week after week, and Mr. Kaplan fell for it every time. Despite my key role, I was paid slave wages. I got twelve pounds a week, if we had it. The sum was nothing compared to the sweat and thought I put into the business every week. I had ideas, energy, and enthusiasm. Everything except the raise I wanted. My dad and I were so much alike—scrappy, passionate, and stubborn. I didn't have that kind of relationship with my mom, who wasn't really keen on girls. She wasn't the sort of mother that would muddle-coddle and sit there and do makeup with me. She would have gone to bat for my brother, whom she was close to, but the two of us were oil and water. It totally affected the way that I brought up my children, especially my girls.

I was a daddy's girl. I was always closer to him than my mother. If anything was wrong or I was sick, I would always go to my father. Even so, at age sixteen, I quit and vowed to make a living on my own. I tried working in a bar, but got fired for not knowing the different types of alcohol. Then I applied for a waitress job at the original Hard Rock Cafe in London, but I couldn't get through the training as my arm wasn't strong enough to carry a tray heaped with plates and glasses. Frustrated, I went back to work for my dad. It seemed I wasn't cut out for anything else, and I was fine with that.

Or so I convinced myself. In reality, I was too scared to cop to any other possibility. My biggest fear in the world was rejection. My nonrelationship with my mom was one type of rejection. Being at odds with my father was another one. I dealt with the pain of the first and the anxiety of the second by shoveling food in my mouth. Cake, fried food, cheeses, anything and everything. Any time I felt a pang of fear, I ate. Though a big gorge would make me feel better, there was a side effect. I gained weight.

Even after I settled back into the old routine and my dad gave me a bit of a raise, I kept packing on the pounds. I wasn't happy with the way I looked. I wanted to be fashion-model thin, like

Twiggy. I believed all those magazine articles that said I had to look a certain way for guys to like me, and the last thing I wanted to risk was rejection from guys. All my girlfriends were starting to date. Some were going steady. But I did neither. I played it safe (and sad) by making myself the fat girl who was best friends with all the guys so I didn't have to worry that no one wanted to have me as their girlfriend.

Further analysis isn't necessary. Did I have the same sexy dreams as any other teenage girl? Yes. In fact, soul singer Sam Cooke, one of my dad's clients and quite possibly the most gorgeous man I've ever seen in my life, was my first love, though he had no idea about my girlish crush on him. Did I ever date? Yes. But nobody was good enough in my dad's eyes. Everyone was gay and a loser; whoever I brought in, "gay, gay." Did I ever wake up next to someone I didn't know? Yes. Did I suffer from not having the kind of open, loving, communicative relationship I made sure to have with my own daughters? You bet. My first serious relationship was a disaster.

I'll spare his name, except to say he was a guitar player in one of the bands my dad managed. He was a great guy, good-looking and all that, and we're still friends. Yet I ended up pregnant. I was stupid. No, I take that back. I was uninformed. I'd never talked to my mother and when I needed to, when I came to her in tears and confessed that I was pregnant, she was hard and unfeeling. She said, "It's your fault. You did it. Now you have to get yourself over it."

I needed a hug. I needed comfort and reassurance. I needed to talk. Unfortunately, I didn't get any of that. This was my darkest moment. As calm as I sound while recounting the story now, I am shaking on the inside. I'm terrified all over again as well as sad, thinking of all the girls facing similarly desperate situations.

And I am talking desperate. I told my parents on a Friday. On Saturday morning, as I left for the clinic, my father stood in the doorway and said, "Make sure you're home tonight." I checked in by myself and had the procedure, crying the entire time. A couple of hours later, I got myself out of bed and walked home. The nurses were saying, "Oh gosh, you'll hemorrhage, you have to come back." I was like, "No, I have to go home."

I went to bed and wept through the weekend. Neither of my parents asked if I wanted water or tea. Neither asked how I was doing. At one point, my dad said, "Okay, you're an adult now. If you want to fuck around, this is what you get." My mother's way of dealing with it was she wouldn't talk to me or do anything to help me. That was her punishment.

I went to work on Monday and acted as if nothing out of the ordinary had happened over the weekend. It was awful. After you've grown up and had children, I realized the gift of life I could've given to someone else. It's one of the biggest regrets of my life. I never talked about having had an abortion until I mentioned it to my daughters many years later.

They were more sophisticated than I ever was. "Wow, Mom, you fucked up."

Ozzy: Telling my father I wanted to sing in a rock 'n' roll group wasn't odd. He had no reason to give me one of those looks I saw so often when I did say something unusual. Singing was a part of the family. As a youngster, I'd performed in numerous school plays from *Pirates of Penzance* to *HMS Pinafore*. Sometimes after dinner my sisters harmonized beautifully on Everly Brothers stuff like "Dream"—they would do the harmony perfectly. Occasionally I joined in and we put on little shows. My mother also sang around the house. Plus my dad belted out his favorite folk tunes so loud when he was drunk I could hear him coming home on the bus.

No, the strange thing was when I told him I had an opportunity to join a band with my friend Mickey Breeze and it might take off like the Beatles, except that I needed microphones and a PA system, which I couldn't afford, he signed for a loan. I used the three hundred dollars to buy a fifty-watt amp and two microphones and showed up for rehearsal. We named the band The Approach, which we thought was a cool name, and I learned a bunch of covers, like

Otis Redding's "(Sitting on the) Dock of the Bay" and Crosby, Stills & Nash's "For What It's Worth." But we didn't get a gig.

End of band; but not my career. It was easy to find your way into bands in those days. I did. There was the Music Machine. Then there was Rare Breed. Bands lasted several days or weeks, depending on if you made enough money to buy beer and rehearse a few more times. Mostly you didn't. A lot of us backstreet boys changed groups more often than we changed our underwear. A band served two purposes. It gave guys like me a dream to pursue. And it passed the time when otherwise we'd just be hanging out and getting high, though we did that anyway.

In 1968, I hooked up with guitarist Tony Iommi, a guy I knew from school, Geezer Butler, who'd played bass in Rare Breed, and drummer Bill Ward. After seeing an advertisement I'd tacked up in the local music shop, they came to my house, where I tried shocking them into liking me by wearing a bunch of mismatched clothes I'd grabbed from my parents' drawers. Tony had long hair down to his butt. Mine was virtually nonexistent. But I promised to grow it as long as they wanted.

We had a hard, bluesy sound that was purposely different from the peace-and-love hippie music coming from San Francisco and L.A. and London. We called the band Earth, and the music—loud, aggressive, angry—seemed to rise from the red-hot molten core. I described it as slum rock. Tony was basically the leader of the group, though when the definitive history of heavy metal is written credit should go to his mother, a candy shop owner, who bankrolled our earliest days by signing for the band, letting us drive her van to gigs, and packing us sandwiches and coffee.

We rehearsed at the community center in Six Ways, named such for the six roads leading to the town. If we weren't playing, we were getting high on alcohol and pot and listening to Cream, John Mayall, Fleetwood Mac, and Jethro Tull, a group that once took us out on tour as their opening act. Just as Tull had Ian Anderson jumping around as he played his flute like some medieval minstrel on Dexedrine, we needed something to make us stand out from other bands.

One day we noticed the movie theater across the way from where we rehearsed was showing a horror movie. We talked about the popularity of that genre. All of us loved those movies. Tony suggested writing scary music that would sound like those films. Then someone suggested renaming the group Black Sabbath after a Boris Karloff picture. Rumors have since abounded. Were we Satan worshippers? No. Did we sacrifice animals? No. Did we drink blood or any shit like that? No. But I did say, "Let's scare the whole fucking planet with music," and we set out to do just that.

We played loud and looked strange with our long hair, ragged clothes, and oversize crucifixes that my dad fashioned out of tarnished sheet metal. At our first gig as Black Sabbath, we stunk—literally. The club's manager came up to us afterward and said all of us had to bathe before he'd book us again. But he wanted us back. At another show, I poured a can of purple paint over my head and sang as it dripped down my face and torso. Our reputation wasn't based solely on music. Gigs at pubs and clubs usually ended in bloody fights with the audience. I've never seen anyone tougher than Tony, who could take someone's best shot without flinching and deck a guy twice his size.

One thing about Sabbath: If anybody threatened us, we all went. We moved as one. My thing was to move in a different direction, though. While Tony, Geezer, and Bill punched their way through the melee, I went through the crowd and picked through ladies' purses, taking their money. That extra dough let us survive.

In late 1969, things took off when we let local promoter Jim Simpson be our manager. He was a lovely man who put bands on tour at all the universities. He booked us into the Star Club, famous as the Hamburg club where the Beatles broke through. We turned in our best, loudest, and rudest performances yet. On the way back from Germany, Jim had us stop at Regent Sound in London to make our first album. It was quick and dirty. Though we spent a mere three days and less than a thousand dollars making it, we thought it was a fucking masterpiece.

The real test came when I played it for my parents. My father put it on the radiogram, the old polished box that had over the years provided the family with their musical entertainment. But when they heard the church bells and rainstorm in the opening song, "Black Sabbath," I could feel the tension in my father from the way he traded worried looks with my mother. They listened to the whole album, and when it finished, my dad said, "Son, are you sure you're just drinking the occasional beer?"

III

Reflections

————— ✺ —————

Q: So, do you guys eat bats?
A: Yeah, all the time. You should come over—we're
   having a bat barbecue this weekend.

—AIMEE OSBOURNE, *ROLLING STONE*, 2002

Kelly: What was I like as a child? You mean other than the fact I was probably crying before I came out?

Children are a reflection of their parents. I'm a real combination of both. I have my mother's sense of humor—very sharp and sarcastic. I also have my dad's bad habits, like the way he eats terrible things and the way both of us put our foot in our mouth by saying outrageous things that get us attention.

Aimee: I'm a strange combination of both of them. I have my dad's emotional complexity and his quiet, observant side, and I also have my mom's powerful mouth and some of her drive. She's got a drive to succeed like no one I've ever met. But I have some of that, too. I have a vision and want things done my way.

But I prefer calmness, which is in contrast to the world we were raised in. I'm sure that had a profound effect on me.

Jack: We are like an action-packed family. There's always something going on. There's always some drama. It's never like, "Oh honey, I'm home!" Our house is like a fucking party house. I guess I'm kind of mellow—very passive. I like to think I'm the only sane one, actually.

Aimee: I always knew I wasn't the same as other kids. I was the emotional sponge. Whereas my brother and sister were happy little kids, I absorbed everything for everyone. Jack was the typical boy—he hated that he didn't have a younger brother. He had two older sisters. Kelly was a mixture of Veruca Salt and Baby Jane, always dramatic, always telling stories. She was the pretty one, she had blonde hair, she was a girly girl. I had short hair, I was kind of the quiet one, I was kind of the outcast.

Kelly: I don't think I'm like anyone else. My sister and brother care what other people think of them—I don't. If I wake up in the morning and don't feel like taking a shower, I don't. If I don't feel like getting dressed, I won't. I don't care. I was always the scruffy one. I always wanted to stay in my pajamas, which pissed off my mom.

I didn't get along very well with Aimee because she was very, very bossy. And I was never a girly girl and she was. I didn't want to play dolls or put on makeup and play mommy and daddy the way she constantly did. I usually ended up in Jack's room in the middle of the night, after I peed. Or I crawled into bed with Mom.

Sharon: Kelly was the little devil in the house, and she just clicked with Jack. That was it, they were a team. For the longest time, they used to tell everyone they were twins—they both had that white-blond curly hair and they were a team, and such drama queens. I mean, my kids are all drama queens.

It was like when Kelly and Jack were little they told us a man just passed inside the house, but you couldn't get into our house. There were big gates. There was no way. So we go, "Did he have a black hat on?" Yes. "Did he have a black mask?" Yes. "And did he have a stick, with a big bag on the back saying SWAG?" Yes. "Did he have a black-and-white shirt on?" Yes, that's the one. Uh-huh, that was the one.

Ozzy: You know, the kids are fourth-generation entertainers through my wife's side of the family. Her father was a singer. Her grandfather was a dancer. Her mother was a chorus girl. Even her great-grandfather was in show business.

Aimee: My mom is a very passionate person. She loves to laugh. She loves to make people laugh. She loves to shop. She loves to eat. She loves to travel. She's a very caring person. She loves her dogs. She is very over the top, whereas my dad is more of a simple person. All he really needs is a couch or a bed and a TV and a phone. My dad would rather take a walk in the park, read a book, see a movie. Have coffee.

My dad, I think, didn't come from much. He had a very hard kind of working-class, English upbringing. I think there were a lot of children to feed and very little money. I think he definitely suffered.

I also think he did come from a lot of love.

IV

Sabbath Bloody Sabbath

In the industrial side of Cream country lie unskilled laborers like Black Sabbath, which was hyped as a rockin' ritual celebration of the Satanic mass or some such claptrap . . . well, they're not *that* bad.

—LESTER BANGS, *ROLLING STONE*, 1970

Sharon: One look at Black Sabbath, with their long hair, dirty clothing, and huge crosses, and you'd know they weren't going to be anybody's darlings.

There are always performers who for whatever reason—looks, music, fashion—get the coolest people at their shows. You get guys like Beck or the Wallflowers and other bands the critics like. They get showbiz people going to their shows. It's a Who's Who in the audience: Brad Pitt, Winona Ryder, you know.

Not at a Black Sabbath show. Even back in 1969 when I first saw them, Sabbath was never like that, so guys who ran record companies in those days weren't interested. They went to hip shows. They didn't like the talk of witchcraft. But it didn't matter. They were the people's band, and Ozzy was a hero to the working class. Their first album came out in February 1970, and a month later they were in the Top 10 in England and they'd charted in America. I remember hearing about them, checking out the album, and sometime later asking a record company executive visiting my dad what he thought about Sabbath.

He said, "I've never heard of them. Who's Black Sabbath?"

I'd see Sabbath at the Marquee in London. Making an impression was not a problem for these guys. I'd never heard anything like them, and I gathered neither had most of those at the club that night because everyone kept looking at each other, going, "What's this?" They were loud and their sound was heavy—louder and heavier than any of the hippie-type music back then. They sang about death and destruction and graveyards and the devil. I didn't know how to answer. All I knew is they gave me goose bumps.

Ozzy: Led Zeppelin's drummer, John Bonham, once took me to a restaurant and ordered twenty-four bottles of champagne. That much made even a heavy-duty alcoholic like myself ask what was going on. "We're going to have a race," he said with a straight face.

"We'll see who can drink the most." Of course, that was when Zeppelin ruled the world and John was paving the road for his fellow rock 'n' roll crazies like me. But back in the early days when we first started hanging out, he had much saner moments. At that time, the biggest thing a British band could do was tour the States. When it was our turn to go soon after Black Sabbath's first album came out, John was the first to congratulate me. "It's very cool," he said. "But I could give you some advice if you want it."

"Sure," I said. "What should I know?"

"Before you go, make sure your dick is rested and you got plenty of penicillin," he said with a knowing grin.

He was right on all accounts. We flew over on a 707 and sat in the very back of the economy section. I was so naïve at the time that at one point I looked at my watch, saw we'd been in the air five hours, and wondered nervously how the fucking plane could stay in the air that long without refueling. To me, America was a mythic place full of danger. Whatever I knew about it came from TV and movies, and so I expected to see gangsters and cowboys and Lucille Ball.

We may have gone into culture shock as soon as we landed at New York's John F. Kennedy Airport, but we survived. It was October 1970. It had been cold and miserable when we'd left England, but the weather in New York was so warm we thought we had gone to the tropics. We were picked up in limousines, the biggest cars we'd ever seen, and driven to the Lowe's Hotel, where everyone from the doormen to the concierge to the people checking us in gave us a look that said, "What are you doing here?" Rock 'n' roll was not as widely accepted as it is today.

Nor had it ever been as loud as we played it. We actually blew out our PA system during sound check the first time we played New York at some small club called Ongono's, not realizing that the European electrical current was different than the States'. The next time in New York we progressed to the Fillmore East, but Rod Stewart's band fucked us about, so we couldn't even get a sound check. So credit for one of the heaviest of the heavy metal concerts ever given has to go to them. We got pissed off and cranked it to like fifteen when we got onstage—as loud as it could fucking go. We played really well and got a standing ovation from the audience.

The difference between then and now is you would never get Rod Stewart and Black Sabbath on the same bill today. But in those days it was more open, more of a variety industry. I remember we played for Canned Heat in Florida, we did gigs with Lynyrd Skynyrd, the Eagles, the Allman Brothers, we even opened up one time for fucking James Taylor.

One thing about Sabbath: There was no holding us back. We were a great fucking band.

Another thing about Sabbath: We were great at fucking; and as Bonham promised, much to our surprise and enjoyment, there was plenty of that to be done in the States. Backstreet boys like us didn't know shit about groupies. In England, you'd meet a chick, take her to a movie, and buy her a drink. Three weeks later, if you were lucky, you'd get your hand on her left tit. After another three weeks, you might bang her. It took time. Not in America, though. The fun started as soon as we got off the plane.

I'm not kidding. I checked into the Lowe's Hotel about nine o'clock at night. By 9:15, there was a knock at the door. I figured it was one of the guys forgetting something. But it was a girl. She had a great body and a face to protect it—not that I noticed anything after I heard her say she wanted to ball me. "Ball me?" I said. "Do you mean you want to play ball?"

"No, let me show you what I mean," she said and then for the next few hours she fucked my brains out. Under normal circumstances I'd never been magical with the women, and so I usually got drunk and fell down before I did anything, so if the chick wanted sex she had to do it. But these circumstances were far from normal. I hadn't even had a drink yet.

I wasn't the only fortunate one in the band. Later the next day I knocked on the door to our adjoining room to tell Tony what had happened and walked in while he was fucking his own chick. As hard as we performed onstage, we played even harder off it. There was one city where the groupies showed up all night long. I'd finish with one and another would knock on the door. One after another, like a crazy train. We'd screw, get high, then the chick would leave, and soon there'd be a knock at the door and it was another one wanting the same thing.

It was the spoils of war, man. In every city, I had a bag of dope, a gram of coke, a bottle of Jack, and as many chicks as I could bang. It was a holiday from heaven. But while in New York I discovered something that, if it wasn't better than drugs, booze, and chicks, was just as good: pizza. I ate my first slice at some dive in Lower Manhattan, and I swear to God, just like coke or booze, I couldn't get enough.

I also learned, as I would many times over the years, you pay a price for obsessive indulgence. Too much pizza was the least of my worries. Though we were still pre-AIDS, there was that old bugaboo the clap. I remember going to a doctor's office slightly embarrassed; well, enough so that I said I had a pain in my lower back that needed examination. The doctor came in and asked if I happened to be with that bunch of other guys. Then he opened the adjoining door, and I saw the whole band with their pants down and a nurse holding a handful of syringes.

That wasn't the only thing happening while our pants were down. I am only learning now to what extent we were fucking shystered by our managers. But we were there for the taking, we were so fucking innocent. Four kids from Aston Burney, who hadn't had anything more than a one-pound note.

Sharon: They were what we called "prime pickings."

Sabbath's second album, *Paranoid*, was selling even better than their first, they were recording their third, *Master of Reality*, without a decent deal, and tickets to their shows went quickly. Best of all for someone like us, their manager was in way over his head.

If they were like every other new band, the boys were blowing all their money on drugs, cars, and women. Or they were being cheated out of everything due them. Either way, they were probably not seeing much of the cash being generated by their success. They wouldn't know what was due them because they wouldn't know the questions to ask, but you could bet they'd want more.

And they'd listen to whoever came to them and said, "You're being ripped off. You should be ten times as rich. And I can help."

Enter my dad, who made an appointment with them after seeing them with me at the Marquee. Having been part of the music scene for a while, they knew of Don Arden's reputation, and as I recall they were as frightened as they were curious. I was the receptionist when they came into the office, and my first impression of the group was not a good one. They frightened me. Seriously. And I was a hard one to jolt.

But I was used to dealing with the Everly Brothers, that sweet-smelling baby of mine Sam Cooke, Brenda Lee, Little Richard, and Jerry Lee Lewis. Even though they could behave like the most insane of an asylum's lunatics, they always looked sharp, always like a million bucks. Sabbath, by comparison, looked like vagrants. As I recall, Ozzy had on a dirty pajama shirt, jeans, and sandals. An old water faucet on a fat chain dangled around his neck. That passed for jewelry.

When my father was ready for them, I ushered the group into his office and said to take seats. Then I watched them sit on the floor. Why? They wanted to be different, intimidating, beyond any normal conventions. Many years later I asked Ozzy about it and he said they were scared to death of my father. He was, anyway.

As for being the first meeting between Ozzy and myself, it was the first time we crossed paths and were introduced because little else happened except for the mental notes we made about each other. You know how you see someone and go, "Hmmmm, that's interesting." Ozzy and I did that. I thought he was cute. I found out later that my stylish clothes made an impression on him. And he thought I was smart, classy, outgoing, fun, and impressive. I mentioned having seen the band perform and getting goose bumps.

Years later, he'd say the attraction was instant. Something was there.

I also knew Ozzy was involved with Thelma Mayfair, a girl in Birmingham who was about to become his wife. I actually paid more attention to Tony Iommi, who was the group's unofficial leader. He took charge, and since this was a business meeting, we were drawn to him more than the others. Tony and I hit it off, too. Over time that turned into a close friendship. Ultimately it would lead Ozzy and me to each other. But at that time we were all business.

Only we didn't get the business. Unbeknownst to my father and me, two guys from the office, Wilf Pine and Patrick Meehan, took the band out to dinner later that night and then the next week handed in their resignations. They were going to manage Sabbath, they explained. We'd been stabbed in the back. My father went ballistic. He wanted to kill Wilf and Patrick, who had started out as Gene Vincent's driver and worked his way up through the organization. Just as he'd done with the Beatles, my father banned any mention of Black Sabbath around him.

The band's growing fame made that impossible. My brother remained friendly with Patrick, who was very sociable and gave lots of parties where we'd see the band. At one New Year's party, Ozzy and I chatted. This time the sparks were more evident, but Ozzy, in all his insecurity, worried that I was out of his league. I told him that was nonsense, although there was another more real factor preventing us from getting together. "What's that?" I remember he asked.

"Aren't you getting married?" I said.

"Oh yeah," he said. "I am."

Ozzy: When I first got a taste of money, I bought shoes and Brut cologne. I remember buying a Rolls-Royce, driving down to Lodge Road, and taking my mom for a drive. But something was missing from the picture I had in mind of a life as a success. I fixed that soon after I met Thelma, a pretty, dark-haired twenty-two-year-old who was working the cloakroom at a club. Married before, she had a five-year-old son, Elliot. We lived together in her apartment, and things between us quickly got serious. I proposed because I thought I was being like Paul McCartney, whose wife Linda had a child from another man.

Not that our relationship was anything like theirs. We married in the Birmingham Register's office in 1971. I spent twenty thousand dollars on a three-acre farmhouse in Staffordshire. Later I added more land down the road, including a wine bar situated on the edge of the property. In 1972, Thelma got pregnant and gave me what was at that time the scare of my life when we were in a coffee shop out in the countryside and she asked if I heard "that clicking sound." No, I hadn't. But I looked down, saw she was sitting in a puddle of water, and thought, Oh fuck, she's going to have that kid right here.

We hurried into my brand-new Triumph convertible, which I could barely drive, and we lurched the forty miles to Queen Elizabeth Hospital, where Thelma gave birth to our daughter. It was five minutes past eleven on January the twentieth, 1971 and I was a dad. I remember seeing a bright star out the window and saying, "I'm going to call her Jessica Starshine." When I became a father, from that moment on I could not remember what it was like before I had children.

Three years later, while I was on the road, Thelma gave birth to our second child, Louis. I suffered for not knowing how to be a father to those kids. They've never wanted for money, but that's the least of it. Jess has never forgiven me for being a fuck-up. While she's made me a grandpa at age fifty-four, we've barely spoken as adults, and that's been terribly hard on us. Louis has been easier and, I suppose, more forgiving, and he's close to Aimee, Kelly, and Jack.

Of course, guilt was not anything I worried about during my first marriage. Even calling it a marriage was a stretch. We were amicable, but not intimate and sharing. I was a rock star, and I thought rock stars got to make their own rules. So I did. I screwed

Thelma's friends, had sex with groupies, and disappeared for stretches whenever I binged. No one could tell me otherwise. Our fourth album was another success; there was money, drugs, and women, including my wife's friends, who pressed their tits against me and said, "Will you fuck me?"

I was an utterly heartless bastard. I was this big fucking commodity, a rock star, and that gives me a license to be a fucking asshole, as well. Being an asshole—I mean, it comes with the turf, man. In my defense, though, few people could resist the sinful temptations of rock stardom.

My father was never a great one for giving advice, but he once said, "Remember, son—a standing dick has got no conscience." And I had no willpower. Of course, the road is no place to cultivate willpower. Between 1970 and 1976, we toured practically nonstop, which meant my life was a series of taking drugs, banging groupies, doing shows, taking drugs, arguing with the guys in the band, taking more drugs, and taking still more drugs.

Life on the road ain't that good or grand as people fucking think. Once you get over the initial thing of late nights, chicks, and parties, it wears thin. The schedule is always the same. You get up in the morning feeling like shit, go to the venue, do sound check, get wasted, do the show, get wasted, have sex, and get wasted again. I watched way too many highway signs pass by my bleary eyes. The first five hundred times it's not bad. But soon you're going, "Fuck, it's Jell-O again."

On the other hand, a guy's got to eat. If drugs count, I had at least three and often more well-balanced meals a day consisting of a combination of grass, speed, vodka, quaaludes, and acid. Though I tried heroin twice, I got too violently ill to like it. Thank God for blessings like that. If I'd had a taste for heroin, I'm sure I'd have died long ago. Cocaine was always my favorite. Leslie West of Mountain gave me my first blast of coke, and soon the entire band was having coke shipped by the box. We had dealers on tour with us.

I never worried about the dangers of being around such large quantities of illegal substances until I went into this one dealer's hotel room and looked into the suitcase where he kept the coke. This guy traveled with a suitcase filled with kilo bags of pharmaceutical cocaine—that's 2.2 pounds a bag, each one a different strain—and I saw a big fucking gun on top and I about shit my fucking pants.

Not that fear ever got in the way of getting high. His coke was a brown-colored paste, not white, and it gave me a rush so hard and fast I thought I was going to drop dead. That kind of experience should have been enough to make me quit on the spot, but when the dealer asked if I was okay I said, "Let me have another line." Don't get me wrong. I knew I was playing Russian roulette by consuming the quantities of drugs that I put into my body. The amount of alcohol could be staggering. Some nights I downed three or four bottles of vodka. Other nights it was Hennessey. None of it made me feel good. But I couldn't stop myself.

That job fell to others. On those rare times when I came home, my poor wife begged me to taper off the drugs and alcohol. Though I enjoyed puttering in the vegetable garden and playing with the kids, I got bored quickly. That's when I turned into my unpredictable, explosive evil twin. One time Thelma asked me to feed the chickens. Muttering to myself, I grabbed my shotgun, went outside, and shot every single bird. Another time I shot the wife's kitties. That episode caused her to take me to the hospital for a couple days of cooling-off time.

Stronger measures were needed. One time I was having dinner at a Japanese restaurant in Memphis, Tennessee, drinking sake out of a soup bowl, snorting coke, sipping cognac on the side, and getting as wasted as possible without an anesthesiologist being involved. Then I wanted to go back to the hotel. Somewhere between the restaurant and the hotel I got tired and laid down. It happened to be in the middle of the freeway. Then I had to take a piss. I got up and felt my way along the side of the road until I came to a parked car. My good fortune, I thought. It was something sturdy to lean against. But it was a police car. And through my tired, bloodshot eyes I saw a policewoman, who, smiling perversely, drawled, "When you finish shaking that thing, your ass is going to jail."

Sharon: Once I peed on one of our clients' clothes.

My dad assigned me to do the day-to-day for Linsey de Paul, a vampy singer-songwriter popular in the seventies. She thought I was a reverential little yes-girl to follow her orders without question. Wrong!

We were in the Seychelles Islands, the last stop of a brief road trip, and I was fed up with her finicky ways. Paranoid about gaining weight, she pecked at her food like a bird. She didn't drink, either. Aside from doing her show, she stayed in her hotel room and didn't want to have any fun. Neither did she want me to. But when we got to the islands I couldn't take it any longer. After dinner, I left Linsey at her room and went to the bar, where I met a bunch of people and had the fun I needed. I crept back to the room we shared late at night.

While I tried to be as quiet as possible, I was drunk. Naturally I stumbled on one of her shoes and woke Linsey, who sat up in the pitch dark and chewed me out. I could feel the pressure building. As soon as she put her head back down, I opened her suitcase, squatted over it, and relieved myself.

The seventies were huge, huge golden years for my father and the family. He kept rebuilding himself. He had a group called the Move that became the Electric Light Orchestra and through them was able to get his own label, which was hugely successful, with offices in London and L.A. I moved to L.A. to help run Jet Records and loved it!

Ozzy wasn't the only big-time abuser in the mid-1970s. The whole decade was one nonstop party. The thing was, when you live in it, you don't think there's anything wrong with it. When you see all the excess eating, drinking, and drug taking—or people on the floor, drunk and throwing up—it's just normal behavior. I used to buck around with drink, but I was a terrible drinker. Terrible. I really couldn't conduct myself well under the influence. I used to mess around with quaaludes in my day.

But there were still times when there'd be no money because my dad would have money, and *boom!*—invest it right back in another band. The fortune he'd made on band A he'd put in band B and maybe band B wouldn't make it, so we'd be broke again, until band C came along where we could make money.

I may not have done kilos of cocaine, but I put some serious numbers on my credit cards. Though I never stole money, as my father would later accuse, I did take advantage of the family's money. I had accounts all up and down Rodeo Drive, the most expensive stretch of stores in Beverly Hills. I had the same relationship with Giorgio's as Ozzy did with his coke dealer. Nothing was too much. That was also true at Brown's in London. And Tiffany's in New York. I spent millions.

And when I was broke I sold the stuff. The clothes, the jewelry, the paintings, and the cars. They all went. No big deal. But that was the attitude I got from growing up in a household where money came and went like the London sunshine. I might not have been mature enough to articulate it, but deep down I always knew the things that mattered most in life weren't for sale.

If they were I would've bought them. But for all my sass, savvy, and style was the sadness of not having a relationship. Throughout the go-go party time of the 1970s, I wondered if I would find a guy who'd love me and in turn give me the courage I needed to share the deep emotions I hid beneath all my weight. I needed to let someone in so I could let myself out. For a time in 1976, I wondered if Tony Iommi was that person. Mutual acquaintances drew us together, and we had a tight friendship going as Sabbath climbed the rock 'n' roll mountain.

Ozzy has always thought Tony and I had something more. Over all these years he has never come out and asked. He says it's none of his business. In a way, it's cute. Ozzy's shy, insecure, and very jealous. The truth? I was never *with* Tony. I wanted it to be more, but I wasn't stamped from the rock 'n' roll mold that turned him on—tall, skinny, and blonde.

Nonetheless we were good pals, and in 1976 Black Sabbath had a show in Long Beach, California, which wasn't too far from my encampment in Beverly Hills, a semipermanent office my father had set up to avoid the astronomical taxes in England. I went to the arena that night and watched Tony tune his guitar in the band's dressing room. Just when I was about to faint from boredom, I turned around to leave and saw Ozzy, who began talking to me. Obviously I knew him, both from brief hellos over the years and of course, his reputation as the original heavy metal headbanger. He was the wildest of the wild men. And yet he was funny, sweet, and attentive. He made a good impression.

A year later we met up again, this time in Amsterdam, at a small hotel that had been turned into a posh bed-and-breakfast. I was up early, struggling with my cases as I was hurrying to catch a plane to New York, and because it was a bed-and-breakfast there were no porters or bellmen to help me down the narrow stairs and into a taxi. Then suddenly I glanced up and there was Ozzy, who, because he can never sleep, was up at 6:00 A.M., looking for someone to talk to.

"Do you want to have breakfast?" he asked. "What are you doing?"

Once again, I could tell by the look in Ozzy's eye that he was sweet. This time I also felt a bit of a connection between us. He did, too. Maybe it was both of us wondering at the same time why chance had us bumping into each other in all corners of the world. London, Long Beach, Amsterdam. Unfortunately I had a plane to catch, and I said, "I have a plane to catch, but I wish I could stay and talk to you."

I truly did wish it, and I saw in Ozzy's eyes the look of a little boy who also wanted something he couldn't have.

Ozzy: There have been times when I've gone into a museum, wandered around looking at the artwork, and then a week or a month later I think about a particular painting. I don't know why it pops into my head, but it does. The picture has touched something so deep inside me that I don't even understand what it is, but I know something about it intrigues me enough that I need to keep seeing it.

That's the effect Sharon had on me. She was a nice, gorgeous, stylish woman with a head for business, which none of us had. In the mid-1970s, Black Sabbath was experiencing a difficult time financially. We were a fine example of how it used to be a million dollars to the executives, one dollar to the band. We fired our managers, Pine and Meehan, and signed with Sharon's father, Don. With his muscle and know-how, we felt we might be able to fix the problems that were tearing the band apart.

Don moved us to California for tax purposes and then whipped off a greatest hits album to fulfill our contract so he could renegotiate with the record company. He wanted us to tour as much as possible, too. Everything was about cash flow. But Sabbath's problems went beyond money. We were tired from near constant touring, making one record after another, and we were confused and extremely bitter for not having as much money to show for our effort as everyone else. Then there were the drugs. When mixed with our egos, they were lethal to the group's health.

As usual, I was my own worst enemy. In 1977 my dad died after suffering far too long from cancer of the esophagus, and the loss sent me spiraling into darkness of such frightening depth I couldn't climb out. He passed on January 20, the same day as my daughter Jessica's birthday. I couldn't handle the pain he'd gone through right up until the moment he died in my arms. I was drunk at his funeral.

From the pit of my depression, I quit Sabbath. The guys ignored it, knowing that I was going through something bad. I had to be hospitalized several times. The treatment only helped so much, though. I have always felt uncomfortable in my own skin. My drinking and drug taking made me feel more like I could live in myself.

But after my dad was gone no amount of medication, legal or otherwise, helped.

My absence from Sabbath was brief. They needed me, and I thought I needed them. So in early 1978 I returned and recorded *Never Say Die*, the eighth album the group had made in eight years. The tour that followed was a glimmer of Sabbath's glory days. Tony and I were constantly at each other's throats. The others, falling under his influence, turned against me, as well.

That fall the band was holed up in L.A. and set to make another album. Creatively, we couldn't have been more at odds, Tony and me. The first four Sabbath albums were a fucking blast to make. After that was all fighting. The disagreements turned serious on the previous record, and they got worse as we talked about what to do on this next one. I felt like Tony was going soft on the band, relying on weird sounds and production tricks, while I wanted to go harder and heavier onto the next thing, whatever that was.

Here's the difference: He was listening to bands that had listened to us, and I was still listening to the clatter in my head.

It was a recipe for disaster.

Sharon: Nothing was ever simple with Sabbath. In fall 1978, everyone in the band but Ozzy came to L.A. to write the next album. They knew they wouldn't get anything done if they worked at home in England, though with all the dealers and groupies they collected the same could be said about Los Angeles. But the setup was exquisite. I found them a palatial mansion in Bel Air, put in furniture, and transformed the garage into a recording studio with soundproofing and state-of-the-art equipment.

Ozzy was a no-show on account of visa problems. He stayed at home with his wife and children, where he should have enjoyed a restful break from the grind. Not Ozzy. Instead, he obsessed over the work being done without him, the band's direction, and how he was going to contribute when he joined his mates. On a good day, Ozzy is an insecure, questioning soul, but those weren't good days, and he was extremely paranoid. And rightfully so. At the time, Tony,

Bill, and Geezer were all very anti-Ozzy, blaming his drug use and unreliability for the friction they were having off the stage. Poor Ozzy drove himself crazy wondering what they were doing and saying behind his back. He knew the fight he had ahead of him.

Meanwhile, I was in L.A. fielding complaints from the anti-Ozzy faction. They were always going, "Ozzy's this and Ozzy's that and Ozzy's always out of it." Well, so were they! This kind of fighting and getting on one another's nerves occurs in every band that sticks around long enough. Even if they don't stick around, they end up jealous of one another and divided into various camps. Sabbath was everyone versus Ozzy.

Just days before Ozzy came to town, Tony came up to me and asked what I thought would happen if they got rid of Ozzy. I said I knew a singer named Ronnie James Dio. Tony thought he was a guitar player. "No, he's a singer," I assured him. I knew Ronnie's wife at the time. "Okay," Tony said. "Let's bring him in."

Then Ozzy finally arrived. Not only had Tony and the guys been writing for a few months, they'd secretly started working with a new singer. Ozzy didn't stand a chance. Not that he didn't try. He took the few tracks they had and got some melodies together and started working on lyrics. They hated everything he did. But he could've been working on a masterpiece and they would've called it shit.

One day I had a knock on my door and it was Bill Ward, who was out of his mind and holding a cassette tape. "Listen to this," he said. As the tape, a rough of Ozzy roughing out lyrics to a riff, played on my stereo, Bill walked around and ranted, "It's shit! It's shit! Shit, shit, shit!" Then he ran to the bathroom and threw up. I said, "Look, go lay down in the bedroom because you're out of it."

Twenty minutes later Ozzy shows up holding a tape, the same one, it turned out. "I put this vocal line on and nobody likes it," he explained. "What am I going to do?" As we were listening to the tape, Bill wandered back into the room. He was stark naked, stinking of vomit, and oblivious to Ozzy. "This song's shit!" he started in again. "Shit, shit, shit, total shit!"

Then Bill saw Ozzy, and Ozzy stepped toward Bill, and suddenly there was a whole very tense scene in my living room. I said good-bye to Bill, whom I didn't need to see naked. Then I calmed down Ozzy, who was the next to go. In those days it was chaos and pandemonium every minute of the day and night, and I could see the seams coming undone.

Ozzy: We had more doctors coming to the house in Bel Air than show up at a hospital, and none of us was sick. All of them were bringing drugs, and the best supplier of all was a nefarious fucking creature named Dr. Max. Everybody in certain circles knew of Dr. Max. He didn't even start work until after midnight.

One time he called at 4:00 A.M. and said my caps were ready. That was code for my Dexies and Seconals. Sharon was aghast that he was bringing them over at that ungodly hour. Worse than the hour was his wife. Dr. Max was about sixty-seven years old, and his wife at the time was twenty, though she looked seventeen. Sharon couldn't believe it. "She's younger than his sperm," I said. Which was lucky. That night Dr. Max was so loaded that he tripped in the kitchen and his wife had to carry him out.

Dr. Max loved coming to the band's house. And why not? It was like *Caligula*, but more decadent. Everyone was drunk, screwing, getting blow jobs from groupies running around half or often fully naked. Another time he showed up unannounced at 1:00 A.M., looking for me with some urgency. At the time I owned a couple of those little whippet dogs, those really skinny, fast things, and I was playing with them when he walked into the room wearing a plaid golf cap and an evil glint in his eye.

"I've got some really good pharmaceutical coke, if you want to try it," he said.

Silly question. The two of us went into the bathroom so we wouldn't have to share and snorted an obscene amount. I think we were in there for hours. At some point, I fixated on his plaid hat and convinced myself he was a dog racer from England who knew something about whippets. When we finally exited the bathroom my dogs were waiting in the room, and I said to Dr. Max, "Do you race them?"

"Race them?" he asked, puzzled. "Race who?"

"The dogs," I said.

"Ozzy, why on earth would I race dogs?" he replied. "I'm an old man. I just want to screw young girls."

The all-nighters there were constant. The debauchery was non-stop. It was a den of sin that never closed. And yet one day the party stopped. Everyone disappeared and the place was perfectly, unusually quiet. It was as if a death had happened. Little did I know one was about to—my own. If I'd listened to the vibes I would've heard the silence through the empty mansion and been more prepared for the moment when Bill Ward walked into my room. But I didn't hear a thing. It was afternoon, and he was the one in the band with whom I was closest, which is why he was the one elected to break the news. "I've got to talk to you," he said. Before I could ask what he wanted to talk about, he said, "You're fired."

The words ricocheted through my brain like a stray bullet. Sabbath without Ozzy? Me without Sabbath? I didn't see it coming. Neither did I have any clear explanations. There were probably a thousand reasons for me getting dismissed, drugs being one—granted a big one—of them. Predictably, I was sad. It was the end of an era, of history, of a major part of my life. Yet I also felt a strange, unexpected relief. Which wasn't to say I was happy about the situation. No, far from it. I was as blue as a corpse as I packed my things and prepared to move out on my own.

Bandless and too much of a burden to go home to my wife and children, my next stop was Le Parc Hotel, where I checked into a minisuite that became my new home for weeks. If anyone had asked for my new address, I would've said, "It's Do Not Disturb," a reference to the sign that hung on my door at all hours. If dealers wouldn't bring supplies in, I went out, but that was the only reason I ventured into the world. My room filled up with pizza boxes, half-eaten pizzas, bottles of beer, vodka, wine, and whiskey, and baggies of cocaine. I mean, bags that once held coke. I did every speck.

Women came and went like the booze and the cocaine. I got so far out of my head on cocaine so many times that I developed telepathic powers. I would sit on the sofa and start a fire in the gas fireplace just by thinking it on. One night I was with this chick, the two of us getting high while my fingers went here and there, and then I said, "Watch this." Without moving, I thought the fire on. It was *poof!* A flame.

She jumped like a freaked-out cat in a cartoon and ran out half-dressed.

"Fucking Satan!" she screamed.

Those days were when anything and nothing was possible. I was running through the money I had and then I planned on going back to Staffordshire to tend bar at the pub on the edge of my property. I told Sharon my idea later. She said, "What could be worse for you than owning a wine bar? Why don't you just buy a loaded shotgun?"

Sabbath would send someone over to my room at Le Parc with a release or a statement about a planned reincarnation of the band, and I'd say, "Go kiss my ball sack with your mother's lips." I remember another lawyer coming in and telling me I couldn't form another band and use the name Sabbath in any way. "For instance, you can't call yourself Son of Sabbath," he said. "Kiss my ball sack with your mother's lips."

One morning I was in the hotel lobby getting coffee when I ran into Mark Nauseef, the drummer for Gary Moore's band, who were also managed by Sharon and her father. On his way out of town, he handed me an envelope and asked me to give it to Sharon when I next saw her. It was five hundred dollars of leftover expense money. "I'll call her and say you have it."

I didn't have it for long. Soon it had been spent on booze and coke. If I had a big TV, a few beers, and some cocaine, everything was good with me. It was the next day, actually, when I heard a knock at the door and opened up. Sharon barged in like a fucking thunderclap. "What the fuck is that stench in here?"

I was like, "Whaaa . . ."

"Don't you ever open a fucking window in here?"

She made her way through the room like an unstoppable force of fucking nature, kicking pizza boxes, tossing a few beer bottles in the corner, opening the shades and the sliding doors. Then Sharon said, "You motherfucker. You spent my fucking money on fucking drugs, you asshole." Then she stopped.

Sharon: For me, it was his eyes. I just looked into Ozzy's eyes and saw the vulnerability of a little boy who was lost. Not only that, I poked around that bunker, that garbage pit that was passing for a hotel room, and found a whole bunch of half-written letters to his wife, as well as a few in which he'd gotten only as far as "Dearest Darling," and they made such a huge impression on me. He was a puppy scratching at the walls.

Yes, I saw a guy with problems, but I also saw someone with a lot in his favor.

Ozzy: Sharon had my attention. When she starts in with a plan, it's pointless to do anything but listen and agree. She wasn't dead set against letting me quit and go back to England and drink myself into an early grave. After hearing the nonsense I envisioned for myself, she laid out the basic plan we've followed ever since: Her father was going to continue to manage Sabbath, while she would sign and undertake management of my career.

It sounded good except for one thing. What career of mine was she talking about? In my own mind, I was finished and not just going into retirement but permanent hibernation. Not according to Sharon, though. After I explained to her that I didn't see any other options, she went ballistic. If she believed in me, she didn't see a reason why I wouldn't believe in myself, and then she said, "If I see you on this side of the stage, I'll kick your fucking ass."

I'm sure she meant it, too. I hung my head and asked, "Are you going to help me? What do I do?"

Sharon: Ozzy let me convince him to at least try. The guys in Sabbath resented my interest in him. They thought we should've dropped him and taken a more serious interest in revitalizing the group. But my dad was dealing with them—he knew how to handle disgruntled rockers like them—and I was dealing with Ozzy. And my brother loved Ozzy, and Ozzy loved my brother, so it wasn't a problem.

I got off to a good start when Sabbath flew back to England and left me alone with Ozzy in L.A. for a few months. Step one in my reclamation project: sobering Ozzy up. The job was hard. It required nonstop vigilance and confidence building. Not that it was easy spending that kind of time with Ozzy, but take away the cravings and the lies and the groupies and the paranoia and the drugs, and I genuinely liked him. I saw that he was a lovely, warm, funny, caring person.

Did I worry about his addiction? Not in those days. Hey, we were in rock 'n' roll and everyone was fucked-up. It was an occupational by-product. But Ozzy is a natural entertainer. He has the gift. He is a blue-collar hero. Success never changed him. Though he spent a hundred dollars on a gram of coke, he never got over the shock of having the hundred dollars to spend. Or a thousand dollars. The telephone repairman stopped him. So did the guy delivering the water. They loved him. Everyone did.

The sad irony of his life?

The only one who didn't love Ozzy was Ozzy.

Step two in my plan: surround Ozzy with people who would love and support him. That meant putting together a band that would be *his* band.

V

Resurrection

———— ⟿ ————

Black Sabbath died the day I walked out . . . this is a
new band I have now, and it's fresh, and we're working very hard. Forget all this Rolls-Royce/limousine
garbage. The only thing to do is just get on the bus
like anybody else, have fun, and be real. It's back to
the basics again.

—OZZY OSBOURNE TO *MELODY MAKER*,
SEPTEMBER 1980

Ozzy: "I want you to start looking for players."

Sharon had no idea I hadn't done that sort of thing since putting the advert in the window of the music store in Birmingham that led me to Tony, Geezer, and Bill. She was determined. "We're going to put a band together."

Downtime was over. Sharon was on the phone for days, calling musicians and managers to let them know I was still in business. Slaughter's bassist, Dana Strum, was first on the list of players trying out. He was a good guy, but his biggest contribution was telling me that I had to meet this incredible guitar player, a young guy named Randy Rhoads. Dana went on and on about him like he was the second coming of Jesus. "If he's so incredible, you have to tell me so I don't miss him," I said.

I'd never auditioned anyone for anything in my entire life. Sharon was good at it, though. While I hid in the shadows, nervous and too shy to comment, she checked people off a list with businesslike efficiency. "Thanks, we'll call you," she said. Or she went, "Next." She could be cold. And colder, as on those occasions when I remember her just snapping, "Unplug his instrument and get his ass out of here. He's a fucking cokehead." But both of us were excited about Randy. Dana's enthusiasm intrigued us. Nobody raved about anyone else's playing. "Try to stay relatively sane tonight when you see him," Dana said. "You'll thank me."

At least I thanked him. Unfortunately, but not surprisingly, I showed up drunk the night Randy auditioned. It was after 1:00 A.M., and Randy came into the Hollywood recording studio we rented with his guitar and a small practice amp. He joked around and told everyone about the show he'd played in earlier that night with his band, Quiet Riot, filling the studio with a good energy. As he finished setting up, I kind of passed out, or at least my head dropped and hit the mixing console. Randy giggled. "I feel guilty," he said. "Are you sure you want me to play tonight?"

I was more than sure. Despite my condition, I was intrigued from the moment I laid eyes on Randy. He looked like someone created by David Bowie, a girly kind of man. Randy was small and beautiful, with long hair and a deep voice, and when we shined a spotlight on him standing in the center of a small stage he literally caused both Sharon and me to gasp. Maybe both of us fell in love with him at that instant. Love at fucking first sight and all that. Whatever it was, he had something special and we sensed it before he played a single note.

"What do you want me to play?" he asked.

"Play any shit," I said. "Play anything."

He started to riff a little, and then he stopped.

"I have a solo," he said. "Want to hear that?"

I nodded and he lit into this thing that was like Fourth of July fireworks. I didn't need to hear any more. Neither did Sharon.

"I don't know who the fuck you are, man," I said, "but if you're willing to write with me, I'm willing to write with you."

Randy smiled. He thanked me and said something about thinking I was crazy.

"A lot of other people think I'm mad," I said. "But it's a good mad." Then I said something else. "Will you please do me a favor?"

"What's up?" he asked.

"Just so I know I'm not having a fucking dream right now, will you come around tomorrow when I'm straight?"

"Yeah, sure," he said with a laugh.

I was sober the next night when he came around and played. Drunk or straight, it didn't matter, Randy was phenomenal. "Fucking hell, man," I said after he finished another breathtaking performance. The two of us talked later in the night, and later Sharon came in and the three of us talked. Then it was just me and Sharon, and both of us had similar opinions. Randy was a one-in-a-million player *and* person. "This guy is too good for the Earth," I told Sharon. "Sometimes you meet people who are in phases of reincarnation that make them too good for this place. They're at the end. Randy strikes me as one of those guys."

She knew what I meant.

"He's such a good human being," I said. "I don't think he'll make it to be an old man."

I was just blathering nonsense. I don't believe in reincarnation. With all that I've witnessed on this planet, I hope it's not true. I don't want to come back. Nevertheless, between the two of us, Randy was a much better bet to end up gumming his sheets in an old-age home. Then Sharon took me and Gary Moore and his wife away for the weekend to San Francisco, where the two of us talked about Randy. That conversation moved on to her dreams and my fears for what we were trying to create. Over many drinks, both of us revealed so much of ourselves. When I got back to my room I was thoroughly shit-faced and in love with Sharon.

In fact, I tried to find her. In my fucked-up state, I spent hours wandering around the hotel, going from floor to floor in search of her room. All the doors looked the same and I ended up back in my room, alone, frustrated, and wanting Sharon more than I'd wanted any woman in my life. Why didn't I pick up the phone and call her? I didn't think of it. I was fucked-up.

Sharon pulled everything together. A band was put together and she moved all of us to London, where we began writing and recording my first album. Very quickly she and Randy and I became a team. She likened us to the Three Musketeers. We worked our asses off, and, though it sounds corny and weird, the three of us began a love affair that has lasted to this day. It was us against the world.

𝕾𝖍𝖆𝖗𝖔𝖓: We were a team. We worked hard all the time. All of our energy in our own way was poured into launching Ozzy. I saw the whole thing, and people I told thought I was stark raving mad for believing Ozzy could be a star. None of the record executives in London took me seriously when I told them of my plans for Ozzy. "He's over," they said. "Sharon, he's a joke."

Not that they were entirely wrong. Everyone had taken from

him, and what they hadn't taken he'd pissed away. But I saw a guy who'd been to hell and was coming back. Day after day I saw his potential. Ozzy was a good person. He had feelings that were extremely deep. He was fun. He worked hard. He clicked with Randy, who was brilliant. The more I committed to the challenge, the more I was drawn to the person.

I knew how Ozzy felt about me. For months we did everything we could to ignore the passion building between us. Or at least I did. Not one who's able to conceal his emotions, Ozzy made it clear on many occasions in and out of the studio exactly what he wanted to do with me. But I'd always say, "No, Ozzy, you're married."

Rejection wasn't easy for him. He'd pout and sulk and worry that "I don't have a chance with you, do I?"

"You're married, for chrissakes," I'd tell him.

"No, it's because you're dripping in diamonds and mink coats and I'm a fucking hippie and all fucked-up. Why would you like me?"

"Fuck you," I'd say. "You're just feeling sorry for yourself."

Poetry it wasn't. But our chemistry was undeniable as we built this dream, and with each day that passed it was harder to deny it.

Ozzy: I went back to England, but it wasn't the same as when I'd left. Instead of moving back in with my wife and children, I got an apartment in Kensington. I said it was to be closer to rehearsals, but in my heart I knew there was another reason. It was Randy who kept me company, moving into my apartment, where we collaborated like two long-lost brothers. The first song we wrote together was "I Need Your Love," a ballad clearly born from my longing for Sharon.

I've always gone through the same routine when writing songs. I try to find the melody, then I walk around humming it over and over until words come to mind. I was doing exactly that in the apartment when Randy came in and asked if that was by the Beatles or one of my own. I said it was one of my own, and soon he sat down and played the music. One thing: He changed the key, which unblocked me, and the words suddenly flowed out of my mouth. The other songs came equally fast. Randy never wrote two songs on an album in the same key, so all of them were different.

The two of us couldn't have been more different. He probably saw more of London than I had in my life. His passion for collecting toy trains took him all over town. He practiced guitar from the time he finished brushing his teeth in the morning until he went to bed at night, while I didn't do shit. And he was a neat freak, while I was a mess. One afternoon I passed out on the sofa after I'd been drinking Guinness and smoking my own magic potion since 6:00 A.M, and when I opened my eyes I heard Randy finishing up a classical guitar lesson as an older woman tidying up the place reached for the half-finished beer bottle in front of me.

"I don't know who the hell you are," I said, "but that's mine."

"Sorry," said the lady, who then took a few steps toward Randy and asked, "So, when am I going to meet Ozzy?"

Randy laughed.

"Ma, that's him there," he said. "You just tried to take his beer."

Randy and I cracked up.

"Screw the two of you," she said.

In any band, the fun begins when the band begins—when all the money comes, that's when all the backstabbing and sleazy shit goes around. You're lucky if you get to experience that fun period once. For me, Black Sabbath and Randy Rhoads were quite possibly the two biggest leaps forward in my life.

𝕾𝖍𝖆𝖗𝖔𝖓: It was the summer of 1980, we were finishing *Blizzard of Ozz*, and we were paying for everything: the travel, the studios, Ozzy's and Randy's hotel bills. We sent *Blizzard* out to the record companies as a finished master, ready to press and go.

Ozzy was signed with Sabbath to Warners Bros., so if any of them did side projects, they had to take them to them first. We got a letter back from Warner Bros. chief Mo Ostin saying the record wasn't what they expected, but good luck. So they let Ozzy go. Then I sent it to EMI and Rupert Perry—now *Sir* Rupert Perry— who sent back a polite letter saying that he didn't think that it was something that the public would be interested in at the time—that it didn't fit any particular musical genre. Basically saying it sucked and to kiss off. Yes, I was upset, but you know, we all do that. I mean, look at my dad with the Beatles. I don't hold that against anyone.

As much as I was doing for Ozzy, he helped lead me into new territory. As we worked on *Blizzard*, he began telling me about himself. Not that I didn't know about him. But this wasn't the court jester Ozzy. Nor the life of the party Ozzy. No, this time he revealed the real person, John Michael Osbourne from Birmingham. He told me about his boyhood and family, his marriage and children, and his fears, his failures, guilt, and shame.

He was probably the most truthful, vulnerable, childlike, and loving person I'd met. His honesty was as disarming as it was painful. And it caused a completely unexpected response in me. I found myself willing to risk the pain and fear of rejection by sharing the feelings I hid beneath layers of fat. I wanted him to love me, and he did.

But Ozzy was married and every time we got close to crossing the line, his wife appeared. They weren't together frequently, but she seemed to appear on the scene at crucial times. Whenever I was in their presence, I was like, "Oh shit, I'm out of here."

And when I didn't leave it was ugly. The first show Ozzy played as a solo act was in Glasgow, Scotland, in September 1980. It was a small club, and I'd booked Ozzy under a fake name. Thelma was at the soundboard, as was I. As Ozzy came out for his encore after tearing up the place, I cheered like everyone else in the packed club, "Come on, Ozzy!" But when I pumped my fist in the air, she pushed my hand down and said, "What are you doing? What are you so fucking happy about?"

There was never a first kiss. It was a first rape—we did it to each other.

We'd just finished the last night of technical rehearsals before starting live performances, and I'd given him a lift to the hotel in Shepparton where all of us had rooms. He asked me to come up for a drink. He didn't want to say good night yet. Neither did I. I let him walk me up to my room and come inside, where we had a drink. Several drinks. I ran a bath and went into the bathroom. Ozzy followed. And that was it. We climbed into this bath together, then had furious sex for the rest of the night.

We couldn't get enough of each other. Our hunger couldn't be satisfied no matter how much sex we had. At one point Ozzy's wife went to my father and told him to find someone else to work with Ozzy, but that didn't happen. For a little while we led her to believe I had finished with Ozzy and hooked up with Randy, but that act was impossible to keep up over the long haul.

Then we were just like, "Why try?" But Thelma fought back, as I suppose I would have done, too. Her weapon? Guilt. She made him feel terrible, as if Ozzy didn't already feel bad enough about falling in love with another woman when he had a family with Thelma. He carried the world on his shoulders and often complained out loud, "I didn't intend to fall in love with someone else."

"It's okay," I tried soothing him. "It happened. We'll figure it out. Or it will figure itself out."

Ozzy's album had gone Top 10 in England, his comeback was the buzz, and all the things we'd planned were working, except our personal life, and that took its toll. Ozzy was continually fucked-up, and I continued to drink, too. In fact, months earlier, before leaving L.A., I'd been arrested for drunk driving. My friend Britt Ekland bailed me out of the drunk tank. I couldn't remember a thing and swore I'd quit. But I didn't. The repression and strain of having an affair kept me on the bottle all the while we were working on Ozzy's album.

My low point came as we toured the U.K. in low-budget vans and cars instead of private planes and luxury buses as had been routine with Sabbath. Ozzy and I were a couple of wild animals. We drank and fought and ransacked our way through hotels. Ozzy compared us to Vikings on a shore leave. Randy was so amused as we got kicked out of one hotel after another. As always, he said, "You people are insane."

We were. At the last hotel they got pissed off at us not because Ozzy and I got in a row and threw plates and glasses at each other, as was our practice. No, the hotel management lost their patience when I shot a BB gun out the window. Of course, I was plastered. Then I woke up the next morning and felt like death. "I swear I will never, ever do this again," I told Ozzy, and I haven't.

In fact, after that I decided to get myself together as a woman. Love was giving me self-respect. As was success. I lost a huge amount of weight, about eighty pounds, by not eating anything, just consuming this powdered diet drink from the University of Boston. That was four months of not eating any fried foods or cakes, my favorites. I was like an addict going cold turkey. But it worked, as most diets did, temporarily.

I wanted my relationship with Ozzy to be permanent. We knew we had to sort out our relationship once and for all. "This is ridiculous," Ozzy said as we prepared to go to L.A. "I'm going to leave her." That's what I wanted to hear. I bought our plane tickets and made plans while Ozzy arranged to go home to Staffordshire, tell Thelma and his children that he was leaving, and then meet me in London. "I can't wait for this to be over, Sharon," he said on the phone. "I love you."

But the next morning Ozzy called and said he couldn't go through with it. I literally fell apart. I ached through my body and got incredibly sick. What could I do? Nothing. I wasn't in a position to fight or give ultimatums. I couldn't make him get in the car and drive to London. Only Ozzy could do that. Soon he was phoning me, in tears, and explaining that as desperately as he wanted to leave, he felt terrible about leaving Jessica and Louis.

Ozzy: Under the best circumstances I'm the worst at making decisions, but it was the worst of circumstances when I was trying to leave Thelma. I got scared. Normally Sharon kicked me in the ass to get me going. But not this time. I was on my own. And I chickened out. I felt like a failure. I worried about what would happen to my children after I left. That's what kept me from joining Sharon.

Thelma and I had booked a holiday to the Caribbean many months earlier. With sadness permeating every cell in my body, I broke the bad news to Sharon. "I'm going to take them," I said.

𝕾𝔥𝔞𝔯𝔬𝔫: Thelma knew what she was doing every step of the way. She was one jump ahead of us. Ozzy was so tortured by inner conflict that I ended up feeling bad for him. He phoned me every day from the hotel bar. Three times the first day. Five times the second day. He was distraught. "I miss you, baby," he said. "I can't survive without you. I love you more than life itself. You've got to get me out of here."

"My darling," I said. "I can't help you this time."

"I want to get on the next plane," he said.

Finally I said, "No, you've got to stay and get yourself sorted. Something will happen and you'll be able to figure it out."

And something did. On the plane back to London, Thelma told Ozzy she wanted a divorce. Not only were the papers ready, she had him served the next day.

Ozzy's emotions covered the spectrum from jubilation to despair. After telling his wife that she could have everything, as he should have, he moved in with me in the guest cottage I had on the back of my father's property. Between the two of us, we didn't have much of a pot to piss in. It didn't matter. We were together.

But if Ozzy and I were to get our life together—I mean, really do more than just get Ozzy's career off the ground and screw each other between meetings and concerts—I needed to straighten out my own life, too. To me, that meant independence from my father. I couldn't be his lackey and devote my all to Ozzy. My father was spending most of his time in L.A., leaving the day-to-day business of management, as well as running the Jet Records label, to my brother and me. For years, I had signed for nearly everything related to his life, from his house to his work. As evidence of his slippery character, he didn't exist on paper, or if he did it bore no relation to his real life as a music industry mogul.

I no longer wanted to worry whether my father was going to make the week's wages or pick up the phone every fifteen minutes with him giving me another task. Ozzy gave me the support I needed. I spent several weeks dropping hints to my father and brother. But just when I had worked up my nerve to give notice to my father, fate intervened when my brother's wife gave birth very prematurely to their first child. The baby girl weighed less than two pounds and needed heart surgery. My brother had to take time off, and suddenly I had my father asking if I could help the family through the crisis.

How could I say no?

Unfortunately the business was a mess. None of us had paid much attention to it, least of all me while I was occupied with Ozzy. We had forty employees with cars and expense accounts. We owned an office building. And as had been the case since I started working for my father at age fifteen, we were out of money. The business existed on vapors. "You've got to get rid of people," I told my father. "Let's go through the artists and see who's essential, get rid of what we don't need, and get things in order."

He replied as he always did: "You do it." So I oversaw a major overhaul, which was tremendously stressful as it sent my father into an angry tailspin because he couldn't conceive of himself as the head of anything but a large organization. He yelled at me constantly. And when he wasn't yelling, I was dealing with Ozzy's divorce. And when I wasn't calming him down, I was worrying about breaking Ozzy's album in the U.S. And when not doing that I was eating and putting weight back on.

Finally our turn came. In March 1981, Ozzy and I flew to L.A. to drum up support in the U.S. It hadn't been easy. After being turned down by every one of the labels we approached, we signed for a paltry sum of $65,000 with my father's label, Jet, which was distributed in the States by Epic. Though *Blizzard of Ozz* was a huge hit in England, it was, I thought, underperforming in the U.S. I thought if the public relations and promotion people met Ozzy in person, they would like him more, get excited, and do a better job taking it to radio and stores.

So I scheduled a meeting at Epic and thought about how we could go about making a good impression.

VI

Imaging

———————— ⟿ ————————

Perhaps the simplest way to dispose of heavy metal demons is to explain what they represent. Bill Wickersham heard his eight-year-old daughter singing Ozzy Osbourne lyrics that she had picked up from other kids at school. "I took her to the record store and showed her his album covers," he recalls. "I said to her, 'This is Ozzy Osbourne. This is what he is about. Do you want that?'"

—TIPPER GORE, *RAISING PG KIDS IN AN X-RATED SOCIETY*

Sharon: Ozzy says it will be on his gravestone: "He who bit the heads off birds and bats here lies."

We're talking about something that happened twenty-four years ago and somebody who's a Grammy winner, who's sold zillions of records, who has paved the way for other artists—it's just amazing. But, what are you going to do? We can't change that first thought that comes into somebody's head. So why fight it? It will never change.

Ozzy: Whatever people thought of me, Sharon sought to update. She dyed my hair blond and made over my wardrobe, but the pièce de résistance in her scheme was this meeting at the record company, which was my idea of hell. Before leaving home I began drinking cognac straight from the bottle, and by the time we arrived at the record company in Century City I had nearly finished it. That's when Sharon handed me the doves. Three of them.

"What the fuck?" I said. "Live fucking doves?"

"They symbolize peace and they're beautiful," said Sharon, who then explained she wanted me to put them in my coat pocket and let them go a few minutes after the meeting began. I listened to her. As we entered the conference room, my single "Crazy Train" was blasting from speakers. I stood in the doorway for a moment or two, taking in the twenty or so people looking at me, and then I went into performer mode. I sat down on the knee of a young woman who turned out to be head of publicity and in a grand gesture let two of the birds loose.

Agitated, the doves flew around the room, banged into windows, and buzzed all the record people around the table, freaking them out. Thanks to the cognac, I was in a state, too. When one of the birds landed on my knee I automatically picked it up, put it in my mouth, and bit its head off. Someone snapped a picture. Half of those in the room ran out sickened by what I had done and the sight of blood dripping out of my mouth. The rest were pushed over the edge by the headless carcass of the bird flapping across the polished top of the conference table.

On our way out, I realized the third dove was still in my pocket. I don't know why, but I reached in, bit off its head, and threw the bloody mess at the receptionist.

Amid the shrieks and screams a legend was born. Though the stunt had backfired, it turned out to be the kind of attention-getter Sharon and I could only have imagined in our wildest dreams.

Sharon: Our phones rang off the hook. Requests for interviews poured in as the picture of Ozzy with blood dripping out of his mouth made its way into the press. Reporters had questions. Were we banned from the building? Yes. Was it true Ozzy was getting thrown off the label? No. Did we sacrifice small animals often? Never. In fact, we usually ate pizza. In virtually every corner of the world where kids talked about rock 'n' roll, they knew Ozzy had done something so gross they had to buy his album, and they did. *Blizzard of Ozz* was among the hottest albums of that summer.

As was his U.S. tour. Ozzy was never a darling of the critics, but his shows sold out in hours. The kids came in droves, but it wasn't only to listen. Ozzy's tour always involved audience participation. At one point in the concert he gave a signal and the front section was showered with a bloody mix of butcher shop leftovers. That was their cue to throw anything from rubber bats and snakes to actual beef hearts and livers, pigs' heads, and steaks onstage. Ozzy not only didn't mind, he encouraged it. He had as much fun whipping a strand of intestines over his head as his fans did watching it. Like a horror movie, it was innocent and harmless fun.

Up till a point. In October 1981, Ozzy released his second solo album, *Diary of a Madman,* and after the first of the year we went out on another tour. On the January 20 date in Des Moines, Iowa, Ozzy cemented his reputation as rock's unrivaled real-life madman when he bit the head off a live bat. It was completely unintentional. He thought it was one of the rubber animals that pelted the stage every night. But I saw its wings move. After he spit out the head, the bat flapped on the side of the stage where he threw it. Then I saw the blood and thought, Oh my God, what has he done?

Ozzy: News reports didn't get out until the following day. By then I had already visited the hospital emergency room. We filled out various forms and then a doctor asked questions. Did I intend to eat the bat? No. Did I still have the bat? No, I'd bit its fucking head off and then continued with the show. Do I know where it came from? No.

As he explained it, bats aren't necessarily rabid, but according to the public health guidelines the incident had to be reported to the police and the Department of Animal Something or Other, and I also needed to have preventative treatment. That meant a series of shots over several weeks, starting immediately. I pulled down my pants and stared at Sharon while he stuck me in the butt. I screamed. The pain was incredible. It felt like he'd injected a golf ball up my ass.

Though I tried to back out of the rest of the shots, my life depended on taking the entire series, and thanks to Sharon, who left with a packet of syringes loaded with serum and instructions, I was able to go on with the tour. About a month later I finished with a clean bill of health.

My reputation was another thing. Animal rights groups were outraged. Picketers stood outside my concerts. Representatives from the Humane Society spoke out against me. A large donation to the American Society for the Prevention of Cruelty to Animals didn't stop the criticism that followed me from city to city, including an editorial in Omaha warning I was a danger to the city's mental health.

While the publicity benefited ticket sales, it was bad for me personally. "With all the hounding, someone should start a society for the prevention of cruelty to me," I said during one interview. Though it sounded brash and belligerent, I was tormented by the attention and the labeling of me as a killer. I didn't want to be thought of as a fucking bloodthirsty circus geek and wished it would go away. I already felt uncomfortable in my own skin. Better to eat the wife's cooking, as I joked.

Not that I was able to laugh it off. Far from it. The only way I knew how to escape such pain and shame of myself was to drink, and I binged quite heavily after that. Drugs. Booze. Anything that got me out of my own head. Of course, management frowned upon such out-of-control behavior, but we were working it nonstop. At that point, Sharon and I had slept literally three years in a bus promoting those first two albums. I'd visit like ten retail stores a day and I'd do as many radio stations—getting as much coverage as we could get.

Sharon got on my ass and we fought all the time. She issued orders to keep me away from drugs and booze, but then I'd wander around towns and find whatever I needed. Not only was I desperate, I was resourceful.

After we arrived in San Antonio, she tried a new tactic: locking me in the hotel room and hiding all my clothes. But that proved as effective as restraining a Doberman with a piece of string. As soon as I heard the devil whisper to me, I slipped into one of Sharon's dresses and left the hotel for a night of drunken debauchery. As I've said before, everything bad that's happened to me in my life is a direct result of alcohol, and this time was no exception. I got fucked-up, found some whore and had sex, and drank myself through the shame afterward. But instead of wandering back to the hotel and getting reamed by Sharon, I stayed out and partied until nine o'clock the next morning when I had a photo shoot set up with a photographer from the local paper.

No one has to tell me to remember the Alamo. I showed up at the Texas landmark wearing my wife's dress and holding a bottle of cognac. Despite the photographer's reservations, I convinced him to go ahead with the shoot. As he changed rolls in his camera, I needed to take a leak. I relieved myself against an old wall, as I'm sure countless dedicated, patriotic, and drunken soldiers had done a hundred years earlier when they were shooting at attacking Mexican fighters. By February 1982, though, the times had clearly changed. A guard caught me in midstream and said something along the lines of, "What are you doing, you disrespectful faggot?"

Soon the cops arrived. Upon my arrest, one of the cops provided a clear explanation of my crime. "Son," he said, "when you piss on the Alamo, you piss on the state of Texas." After a night in jail, I was banned from playing San Antonio ever again. Though it was rescinded in 1992, no one would ever have imagined that in another ten years I would be trading jokes with the president of the United States, a former Texas governor!

But if you live long enough or through enough shit, you learn one thing is true: All sins can be forgiven.

𝕾𝔥𝔞𝔯𝔬𝔫: Was I thrilled by Ozzy's behavior? No. But from the first time I chose not to walk out on him when he got drunk, stayed out all night, and came home stinking of the street, our relationship took on a dynamic that's impossible to understand unless you've lived it, too. We were devotees of dysfunction. Ours was the classic relationship. I tried to control Ozzy, and he tried to survive without changing. In between were lots of terribly abusive fights and over-the-top apologies that paid the monthly mortgages for umpteen florists and jewelers around the world. Bottom line—we didn't want to lose each other.

But when I talk about the early days of our love affair I have to be honest. It wasn't just me and Ozzy. Randy was a vital part of the tale. He was the softer, kinder, more understanding peacemaker. Or put it this way. Our friend was the sunshine between the thunderstorms. When Ozzy and I weren't speaking to each other we turned to Randy, and when we were on loving terms he was there, too.

Was that different than most couples? Was it ever. During a stop in Phoenix, Randy got terribly sick and found out he had to have all four of his wisdom teeth pulled. The surgery left him in agonizing pain. Ozzy and I nursed him through the night by putting him in the middle of our bed and sleeping on either side of him. Quite honestly, it wasn't the first or the last time the three of us slept together. On the road we often ended up in the back of the tour bus together, watching TV at three in the morning and dozing off without thinking anything of it. Other times it just felt good to be together.

Not that we were having sex with one another. There was one time I was with Randy, and Ozzy knows and has never wanted to discuss it. That's his way of dealing with it, which means the details will remain with me until I'm gone. But don't read any dissatisfaction into it. Ozzy knows the onetime occurrence was loving, not lustful. And you know what? He was just as in love with Randy as I was. He still tears up when talking about Randy. So do I.

Anyone present at the time understands the bond. Consider: Ozzy and I talked all the time about getting married when his first wife signed the last of the papers making it legal, and then we would wonder about what would become of Randy. It was the weirdest relationship we have ever had, and yet it wasn't weird at all. Thinking about it, he was the true wizard of Ozz. He gave Ozzy confidence. He gave me compassion and understanding. In a way, he kept us together through the roughest waters.

And then the unthinkable happened.

Ozzy: I didn't want to think about the day I wouldn't look to the side of the stage and see Randy Rhoads next to me, but that's exactly what he had in mind. It was late at night, probably around two or three in the morning, and the two of us were in the back of the tour bus, heading to Orlando, Florida, from Knoxville, Tennessee. The two of us had been drinking and talking, the conversation darting like passing road signs from the show we'd finished to the show we were scheduled to play with Foreigner and UFO to how both of us had gotten to this spot.

Aside from Sharon, Randy was the only person I dared share real feelings about my growing up and the trouble I had coping with life, and that night I remember going over a familiar theme about how I didn't feel I was born as much as I was shot into this world, struggling to find my way. "I'm like a stray bullet," I said. Randy looked up at me without breaking the tune he was playing on guitar and nodded in a way that said, "Keep going. You'll get there."

But then he broke the news that he might not be with me. Dark, handsome, and just twenty-five years old, Randy could have done anything. After talking about falling in love with music and starting Quiet Riot when he was just seventeen, he told me that he felt as if he'd experienced all there was in the rock star thing. "When we're done I want to go to UCLA and get a degree in classical music," he said.

I knew he wasn't a be-all and end-all rock star. Randy was into his instrument and that could take him any direction he wanted. But I said, "Take some advice from a guy who's been around the block. Before going off to UCLA to become the next Beethoven or Bach, wait until you save a few sheckles. Soon you'll have enough to buy your own entire school."

Around four or five we went to bed and a while later the bus driver, Andrew Aycock, stopped the bus near the Flying Baron Estates, a private development about three miles outside Leesburg, Florida, where Aycock lived and kept a Beachcraft Bonanza airplane. A bit later that morning Aycock showed off his piloting skills by taking our tour manager, Jack Duncan, and keyboardist Don Airey for a ride. Then he convinced Randy and our seamstress, Rachel Youngblood, who was also Sharon's best friend, to take a ride with him. Though both were scared of flying, they agreed to go up.

At 10:30, tragedy occurred. I don't know the exact details, but Aycock was buzzing the tour bus and the mansion. There's lots of speculation what was going on. Some accounts have maintained he hadn't slept all night and had done coke. Others had him fighting with his ex-wife. I don't know and don't care because it no longer matters. The fact is, after circling above the private airfield fairly low he came in for the third time, then mysteriously dipped below the tree level, clipped the tour bus, and slammed into the side of the mansion where several people in our entourage had spent the night.

As soon as I heard the explosion I jumped out of bed and ran outside. Not till later did I notice several windows of the bus had been shattered. All I saw were flames devouring the big house. It looked like a bomb had struck it. People were freaking out. I heard someone say a plane had crashed. I ran into the main house, where I thought people might need help getting out, and I was immediately met by an old man who told me to get the hell out of his house. I yelled that his house was on fire. It turned out he was deaf. But I got him out anyway.

The crash destroyed the upper bedrooms and the garage. None of the three on board survived the crash. Aycock's body was found outside the garage. Randy and Rachel were discovered atop the burned-out cars inside. I went into shock. All of us did. We watched the firemen and told the cops what we knew, and then all of us went into seclusion at a nearby inn. Except for calls to Randy's and Rachel's families, Sharon and I locked ourselves in the bedroom of that inn till we flew back to L.A. and attended Randy's funeral, where I pulled myself together enough to help carry his coffin.

It was the least I could do, and I didn't plan to do much more afterward. I wanted to retire. "Fuck the bright lights," I told Sharon, who would have none of my talk about giving up. You couldn't have illustrated the two of us better than the way we dealt with the devastation of losing our best friend. I wanted to drink myself into the grave next to him, and Sharon wanted to get back to work. Three weeks later she started auditioning new guitar players. Not to replace Randy. We couldn't replace him.

It's like this: I experienced Jimi Hendrix, I experienced Eric Clapton, I experienced Jimmy Page, I experienced Eddie Van Halen and . . . I experienced Randy Rhoads. There are certain people that are fucking timeless, man.

No, we simply had to carry on. The core of our lives was me looking at her looking at me, and I didn't want to lose that. In a way, we've never lost Randy completely. We continue to play his music, and every year on March 19, the day of the plane crash, Sharon and I light a candle for our friend, and cry.

Aimee (age 3), Kelly (age 2), and Ozzy
in England

Aimee in Hawaii

Ozzy and Kelly (age 1) (1985)

Ozzy and Jack (age 1) (1985)

Sharon, Kelly, and Jack at Kelly's
second birthday, Hampstead, England
(1986)

Ozzy and Jack at Donnington Park,
England (August 16, 1986)

Ozzy and Jack

Family photo

Ozzy, Aimee, and Kelly in Hawaii

Aimee, Kelly,
and Jack

Ozzy and Jack

Ozzy, Sharon, and Jack skiing in Switzerland at Christmas.

Ozzy and Jack camping in England

Aimee, Jack, and Kelly (1989)

Jack with his teddy bear, "Baby"

Ozzy and Kelly in Antigua (1995)

Ozzy and Jack getting ready for battle

Ozzy, Sharon, and Kelly in the South of France (1992)

Kelly at Disneyland

Aimee's fifteenth birthday at Ozzfest 1998

Ozzy in Beverly Hills (1997)

Ozzy and Kelly at Ozzfest (1998)

Aimee and Kelly—Piper's Corner (England) school photo

Ozzy's fiftieth birthday party (1998)

Kelly, Aimee, and Jack at Christmas (1998)

Family photo—Beverly Hills (1997)

Ozzy and his dogs

Family photo—
Beverly Hills (2000)

Ozzy in Bora Bora (or as Ozzy calls it, "boring boring")

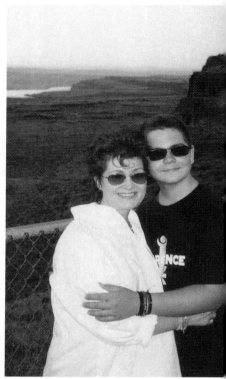

Sharon and Jack at Ozzfest '99—Th[...] Gorge in Washington

Ozzy in South Korea (February 2002)

Aimee

Ozzy and his dog Sonny during
Christmas at home in England (2000)

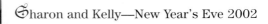

Sharon and Kelly—New Year's Eve 2002

Ozzy and Paul McCartney at *The Howard Stern Show* (2002)

Kelly and Elijah Wood (2001)

Jack and Kelly (2002)

Ozzy and Queen
Elizabeth at the
Queen's Jubilee,
Buckingham Palace
(2002)

Ozzy and Sharon—Ozzfest 2000

VII

Even on
the Bad Days

— ⌇ —

Q: Are you afraid of your wife?

A: God, isn't every man? Sharon gives me tough
   love and she's also given me some tremendous
   bollockings when I needed it. . . .

—OZZY OSBOURNE, Q MAGAZINE, OCTOBER 1998

Sharon: Everyone expected Ozzy to have one of those big-titted, blonde, plastic surgery–enhanced MTV video sluts. Instead he fell in love with a short, fat, hairy half Jew.

Ozzy: I honestly don't think God ever made two other people more perfect for each other.

Jack: I came up with a reason why Mom and Dad's marriage has gone so long—it's because they work together. I think that's what makes marriages last. When your spouse is so directly involved in your life as you are in their's, that's what makes things work out.

Aimee: It is kind of strange, because in a way they balance each other out, and in some ways, one is obviously the controlling one—who that person is is obvious to everyone.

Sharon: It's really, really hard balancing the roles of wife and manager. You just have to check yourself constantly. Three summers ago, Ozzy was in Dallas with Sabbath and about to go onstage, and was really, really stoned out of his mind. But we had thirty thousand people in there and I'm like going, "Okay, what do I do?" As his wife, just for his pride, I was thinking he should not go out there. But as a businessperson I knew if he didn't go on, there would be a riot.

I let him go onstage, and it was probably one of the worst shows he's ever, ever done.

Aimee: It's so hard, because my parents are both so eccentric and weird. My mother has never given him a chance to get to know himself and to find out what he really wants to do. She's always had him working.

Sharon: It's very, very tough to find that fine line. I can remember when Ozzy was asked to present at the Grammys. And work-wise, I wanted Ozzy to do it—any artist that appears at the Grammys sells more records the next week. I'd be, "You have to do it. You have to do it. It's what's best for your career." But emotionally, he'd be, "I cannot do it, it's not what I do. I fall to pieces doing shit like this."

"You have to, you have to, you have to."

Then I look back and go, "How could I ever put him in that position?" He never did do it, but I know that ambitious side, the side that wants to win. It's very hard to do.

Kelly: The secret to their marriage? I think it's true love. I've no idea for sure, but if it weren't for my mother, my father would be dead right now. She says that that's not true, but it is.

Sharon: If you wanted something traditional and something predictable, you wouldn't marry Ozzy. Do you know what I'm saying? I married Ozzy for Ozzy and you take the good with the bad.

Ozzy: If you stop telling your wife "I love you," she ain't going to know that you love her. Every day I've made a point of saying it. Even on the fucking bad days. Even when I'm angry I still love her. If I didn't love her I wouldn't get fucking angry.

Sharon: So why did we get married? Not because of love. That was already understood and agreed upon.

Nor did we do it because I was waiting for a proposal. Ozzy asked me to marry him the way some men ask what's for dinner. It was that often. And there were that many engagement rings, too. Wherever we were he managed to buy a ring (usually after coming back drunk) and give it to me, pledging his eternal love. But then we'd get into a fight, and I'd throw the pricey diamond out the window.

Part two of that story is this: We got married because I tired of tramping through hedges and gardens outside hotel windows. It was so much easier to say yes. However, that's not exactly right, either. Here's the truth: We got married because Ozzy's first wife finally signed the papers, making it legal, and as soon as that happened we couldn't wait to exchange I do's.

It was late June 1982, and we were preparing to leave L.A. for a show in Hawaii and then a brief tour in Japan when the good news arrived. While Ozzy and I had always imagined a blowout in London that would be our way of signaling triumph to everyone who ever doubted what we could be on- and offstage, I reconsidered the plan and organized a smaller, more intimate wedding in Maui. I just wanted to do it, damn the pageantry and pomp of being rock 'n' roll's version of Di and Charles.

I bought a wedding dress in about fifteen minutes and flew to Hawaii. After two shows in Honolulu, Ozzy and I and the band went to Maui. The actual ceremony was on July 4, my idea, so Ozzy could remember it. My parents flew in, as did Ozzy's mother, and one of his sisters also attended. Our drummer, Tony Aldridge, was the best man. I had one more idea: a morning wedding. That would ensure Ozzy was sober.

But he didn't stay that way for long. Although our vows were traditional, nothing else was. The wedding cake had seven bottles of Hennessey in it. Everyone thought the multitiered cake was inedible except for my new husband, who washed it down with a bunch of drinks with little umbrellas in them. After taking over for the musicians we hired and banging out a chorus of Beatles songs with his bandmates, Ozzy did one of his disappearing acts that was so familiar to me when he drank. I found the honeymoon suite on my own.

Early the next morning I was awakened by a knock on the door. It was the hotel's security. That worried me until he pointed to a body lying on its side a few feet down the hall and asked if that was my husband. The flowered shirt looked familiar. So did the hair. And the posture. But I still took a look. Yes, he was definitely mine.

"We were just married," I said, smiling.

The security man helped get Ozzy up and drag him onto the bed, and then I kicked Ozzy's ass.

Ozzy thought he was marrying into a family that was tight with each other, like a unit, and with money. He didn't realize it was all just a front, that there wasn't any real money there. And that the family was about to have a serious separation.

He soon found out, though.

Ozzy: I would have found out after we returned from Japan. We'd worked nonstop for two years, gone through my divorce, and suffered the death of our best friend. We also had deals to negotiate and songs to write and record. We needed time off to our fucking selves. But then we came back and found out Sharon's father had committed me to more U.S. tour dates and promised Epic I would deliver a live album. He was getting big, fat paychecks. We got shit.

"This is Sabbath getting ripped off all over again," said Sharon, who went berserk in our suite at the Sunset Marquis. "I'm not going to let it happen again."

Sharon: Henceforth it was war. And I knew my father was acting in retaliation. On my wedding night four weeks earlier I had told him I wanted out of all of his companies. Enough was enough. He was going into Ozzy's accounts and taking 100 percent of this and that or charging us for all his trips and expenses. By the end of the month, his accounting showed we were owed nothing while he was lighting his cigars with hundred-dollar bills that rightfully belonged to Ozzy and me. It was wrong.

Seeking to straighten things out once and for all, we flew back to London for five days in hell. My dad started things off by taking Ozzy to lunch and telling him I was an untrustworthy thief. Then he offered to get our marriage annulled. If not for the fact that he was his father-in-law, Ozzy would've beaten the crap out of him. Instead he walked home by himself, stopping for something to drink every few blocks.

The next day Ozzy and I were returning from lunch when one of my mother's very large Great Pyrenees dogs attacked me. While I was down one of her Dobermans jumped on me, too. Dazed and bleeding, I was rushed to the hospital, where later that day I was informed a blood test showed I was pregnant. I was stunned. Not in my wildest dreams had I allowed myself to imagine raising a family of my own. I'd been bred to work, not to breed. A personal life had never been emphasized.

But Ozzy and I were going to be parents. Suddenly it seemed even more imperative for us to break free of my father. This wasn't battle mode, it was survival. Ozzy and I returned to L.A. and put all of our belongings in the guest house behind my father's where we lived into storage. As we figured out where to go and what to do, I got wind that my father's accountant was heading to New York to pick up a huge check of pipeline money from Ozzy's album. That was basically the last straw.

"This has to stop right now," I complained to CBS Records president Dick Asher as I made an appointment to see him in New York the next morning. Then I made reservations for us at the Plaza Hotel and we caught the red-eye to New York. The plane landed at 6:00 A.M., we arrived at the record company at 7:00, and Asher walked in at 9:00. "My father's stealing all our money and we want to leave the label," I explained. Asher didn't want that to happen, and so the meeting turned out favorably for us. I arranged for our account to be frozen and negotiated a deal of our own.

Once my dad found out, the shit hit the fan. He reiterated that I was a thief and said it was my fault bands weren't paid. As the coup de grâce, he threatened to put me in an insane asylum. How'd that make me feel? That was my dad being my dad. That's what you did in his world. He went straight for my jugular. He was losing this big cash cow with Ozzy, and he would do whatever he could do to maintain that. In those days, my dad couldn't have understood what I wanted or what Ozzy wanted or what we needed or what was right. He couldn't have understood that.

He followed the name-calling with lawsuits. And it was downright devastating when, amid the stress of fighting with him and touring with Ozzy, as he'd obligated us, I suffered a miscarriage in a hotel room somewhere I can't even remember because of all the other crap going on.

That was it for me. As if the miscarriage wasn't enough, Ozzy was buckling under. One night he disappeared and came back the next day with his head shaved. I feared something terrible was going to happen to him—an accident, a suicide attempt, an overdose, God knows what. As he would often say, the air was filled with bad vibes. Knowing the enmity had to stop, I negotiated a settlement with my dad. We agreed to pay him $1.5 million and record the live album he wanted, though when we recorded it in September 1982 at the Ritz in New York, Ozzy sang only Black Sabbath songs. I felt bad for Ozzy's fans, but I wasn't going to give my father anything of value.

Neither could I give him any more of myself. I knew the stakes once I froze him out of our account. There was no going back. The thought that we could have any relationship was ridiculous, and we didn't speak again for twenty years, not until November 2001. Actually, that's not true. A few years earlier I spotted him in Beverly Hills while driving with Aimee.

I spotted my father standing in front of Nat 'n Al's delicatessen. Before I knew what was happening, I whipped a U-turn, pulled up, and started screaming at him through the car window. He was stunned. The people with him took a step back. Other people looked frightened.

"Mom, why are you yelling at Tony Curtis?" asked Aimee. "And why is Tony Curtis giving you the finger?"

I tried to calm down, but I couldn't. A moment later, I whipped another U-turn and had another go at him.

That was how Aimee, Kelly, and Jack learned their grandfather was still alive. Fortunately things would improve, but the years of silence were horrible. I lost track of how many nights I woke up in physical pain because I didn't talk to my family. I ached. It's like when I see Muslim women on television wailing from the loss of a family member. I know what it is to wail.

Yet I couldn't have done it any differently and survived.

As I see it, I lost a family when I married Ozzy, but I gained a husband and the thing I wanted most of all—a life of my own.

Ozzy: During the time off I wanted to be closer to my children Jessica and Louis, so we bought a house in Staffordshire, out in the country.

Sharon: It was a big compromise that he made in his life, because we were literally a few miles from his children. The house was in a valley—a little thatched cottage right out of an English storybook. It was darling, it had charm. Before the furniture arrived, Ozzy insisted on lighting a fire in the fireplace—we smelled smoke and before we knew it the fire brigade was there. You can't do that with a thatched roof! We nearly burned down the house.

It was a tiny, tiny cottage and I tried to make it very grand. So I had this grand staircase carved and built, but it took up the whole cottage! All it was was a staircase, and this tiny little room with a fireplace. Then I was trying to bring in all these bathroom suites from Harrods and it just looked ridiculous. Nothing fit, there was no room—it was just like that old TV show *Green Acres*! Ozzy was outside digging, saying, "Let's grow our own potatoes and tomatoes," and I'm like, "Oh no, Ozzy—just buy them!"

I'd been so used to living in cities. I wasn't used to driving ten minutes to a little store, passing all these fucking farmers' wives on the way down. Did you ever see the movie *Babe*? Remember the farmer's wife—big lady with dirty old boots? That's what everybody looked like. You know, big red, rosy cheeks.

After Aimee was born, we moved back to London, and that was a huge thing for me. I could breathe again. You know, I didn't like the smell of cow shit.

VIII

Crazy Babies

━━━━━ ✑ ━━━━━

Every time Ozzy and I look at each other, I'm pregnant. . . .

—SHARON OSBOURNE TO *ROLLING STONE*, 1985

Ozzy: Who said the third time's the charm? I disagreed after Sharon suffered her third miscarriage in as many tries. The first one was when we were fighting with her father. Then she lost babies two more times. The last time it happened we were traveling someplace where the trees were changing colors, and she wept till her eyes matched the red of the leaves outside our hotel window. Her sadness was countered by the frustration I endured trying to remain close to my kids, who were growing up with their mother polluting them with who-knows-what kind of stories about me.

If seeing me with children from another woman was like putting salt in her wounds, Sharon never showed it. We supported each other in everything. Just as I helped her through the miscarriages, she encouraged me to have regular contact with my kids. Not that it was easy. My situation would be familiar to almost any divorced dad. You try to stay in touch with the children, but you feel guilty it's not more frequent, and when the ex asks for more money you send it without griping too much.

Sharon griped in private, but it wasn't a big deal. I had a soft spot for the children, who'd been like toys when they were little. As they grew I tried changing my approach. One time I began calling my son Bombins, and I floated the idea of changing Jessica's name to Burt Reynolds. He was a big star and she was named after the brightest star in the sky, I reasoned. Of course, that didn't fly.

Few people knowing me only from the press accounts that painted me as the pack leader in a world of sickies and devil wor-shippers would have guessed the soft place I reserved for family and children. But Sharon knew, and she knew I was serious when I encouraged her to try getting pregnant again. My view of the uni-verse has always been that good is balanced by bad and bad is bal-anced by good. We'd had so much terrible shit happen to us lately that I knew there had to be a pot of gold someplace with our name on it. Better than a pot of fucking gold was a baby of our own.

At my urging, Sharon underwent various tests and learned a

minor medical problem of the female variety was the reason she couldn't hold a baby after three months. Her doctor corrected the problem by implanting a cervical stitch. Not long after we got a chance to see if the operation worked.

Actually, little children were the last thing on my mind the day we found out. It was early morning in late 1982 when I woke up dazed and sick in Germany and needing very badly to relieve myself from the previous night's poisons. But Sharon already occupied the bathroom. She was throwing up.

"What the fuck, babe?" I said.

She admitted this was the third time that week she'd gotten up to hug the crapper. I went straight to the pharmacy, bought a pregnancy test, and brought it back to the room. But the directions were written in German. The two of us spent a good deal of time looking at the pictures and wondering what color it was supposed to turn after she peed in it. We went through ten kits before I held one up like a trophy and declared, "Congrat-u-fucking-lations, babe! We're going to be a family."

𝕾𝔥𝔞𝔯𝔬𝔫: I loved feeling a life growing in me, and unlike previous pregnancies this one kept growing. Still, my obstetrician ordered me to bed for the last four months, which was difficult because Ozzy spent part of that time touring and part working on his third solo LP, *Bark at the Moon*. Hardest of all was being stranded in Staffordshire, this quaint town where I didn't know a single person and hated the afternoons when the smell of the fields wafted through the windows.

On September 2, 1983, Ozzy and I welcomed the arrival of our first child, our precious baby girl, Aimee. Ozzy had barely made it back to the hospital in time for the delivery, after dashing out while I was in labor. I figured my husband had gone to the nearest pub to calm his nerves, but then he slipped a gorgeous diamond ring on my finger moments before I was wheeled into the birthing room. I think I smiled through the whole thing.

Ozzy had his queasy moments. But later he told the disbelieving press that he'd been at my side the entire time, which was true. Also true: When my doctor asked if I needed more painkillers, Ozzy had said, "Fuck her, give them to me."

From then on, our lives were spent juggling family and career. In December, *Bark at the Moon* was released. The next month was a double whammy: I got pregnant again, and Ozzy left on a world tour with Mötley Crüe as his opening act, a combination that was so toxic I'm still amazed any of them survived. Don't get me wrong. Ozzy and I absolutely love those guys, especially Tommy Lee and Nikki Sixx. But from the moment they got together at the start of the tour in Portland, Maine, they were lethal.

Ozzy: I will say if you ever wanted to see a bunch of lunatics, you should've been on that tour. It was absolutely fucking bedlam. A bedlam of fucking. They had contests to see who could fuck the most chicks. They traveled with their own lingerie supply. Drugs and strippers every night.

Every day—every *fucking* day—there was something major happening. We were doing the craziest shit you can imagine. Fighting every day, fucking brawling . . . food fights, drugs—cocaine, heroin, the full nine yards, man.

Before shows Nikki got his band together in the dressing room and had them watch while he pulled down his leather pants and wiped his ass. If any crap showed up on the toilet paper he said it meant they would have a good show. Vince of all people would say, "Why don't you work a little harder and get it all the first time?"

I shit all over Tommy's bathroom in Nashville, helped Vince wreck a car in Memphis, and got completely fucked-up on Bourbon Street in New Orleans.

Mardi Gras was happening, and so it was like we showed up for the world's biggest cocktail party. As we passed one place, we saw a girl's legs sticking out the window. Tommy climbed up and pulled her out the fucking window. Probably fucked her. He fucked everything else. We ended up in this bar where Tommy and Nikki rode a mechanical bull while egging Mick Mars to try. Mick was always looking like he was depressed, but they were still going, "Dude, don't be a pussy. Try it." Finally he gave in, but what they didn't tell him is that while they'd done it the thing had been set on low. When Mick got on they shoveled in all the money needed to get it to the max. The poor guy was on for a second before he went flying straight over the fucking bar and landed in a pile of bottles. I nearly shit my pants from laughing. Every day something fucking crazy happened. We're lucky to be alive.

𝕾𝕳𝖆𝖗𝖔𝖓: One night while Ozzy was in Italy with the Crüe I got the full dose of his Dr. Jekyll and Mr. Hyde act when I rolled over in bed, picked up the phone, and heard him say he wanted a divorce. Alone in Staffordshire and several months pregnant, I responded the only way that made sense. "Fuck you," I said. "Just shut up and go back to bed."

Though the *Bark at the Moon* tour was a massive worldwide success, I was thrilled when it ended. I wanted my husband back and our life together. We had one infant and another on the way. My pregnancies were too iffy to manage entirely by myself. After getting past the crucial third month, though, I had tons of energy. And I needed every drop once I went into labor, which lasted eighteen horrendous hours, while through it all Ozzy whispered in my ear as persuasively as possible, "Please, Sharon, if you could make it a boy, please do."

As controlling as I could be, I still had limits. Ozzy apparently didn't. He was in the pub across from the hospital on the afternoon of October 28, 1984, when the big moment finally came. He'd been there on and off all day to deal with my pain. Yet he was by my side again when Kelly was brought out. "It's a girl," said the doctor, who was watching with me as Ozzy took the swaddled newborn from the nurse and, apparently no longer concerned about a boy, beamed, "I love her."

And because I loved Ozzy I told him the day after we brought Kelly home that we were moving to Palm Springs, California, and he was going into the Betty Ford Center. There was no way he would survive if he kept up the habits that had made him such a mess on the tour with the Crüe. Neither was I sure I could survive. But we had two children, which made things different. Knowing Ozzy had never heard of the Betty Ford Center, I explained it was a "place where they teach you how to drink like a gentleman." His face lit up. I could almost see him think, Behold the golf course!

Ozzy: As I recall, I was duped by my wife. Sharon said her family had a place in the desert where they taught people to drink properly. It was like a clinic, she explained, which made me immediately think of well-bred men in evening suits and ties learning about the fine art of martinis and aged cognac. While I was gone Sharon was going to buy a new home in London, where I would join them after coming out of my new finishing school like Douglas Fairbanks, debonair and suave. So I said, "That'll do, mate."

When I arrived at the Betty Ford Center, I told the first person I saw I was dying for a drink and asked for directions to the bar. She said, "Boy, are you in the right place." That was it for levity. They went through my belongings and confiscated my cologne and aftershave, then sent me to Eisenhower Memorial Hospital for three days of detox and drying out. Because they give you pills to help you get through withdrawal, I didn't think it was too bad.

But the next nine weeks were sheer misery. When I transferred into the rehab, even I knew this was different. There were strict rules, starting with breakfast in the morning, group meetings, followed by lunch, more meetings, dinner, and more talking. The twelve steps of AA were taught and followed. Having honed survival skills since boyhood, I adapted quickly. I also used my know-how as a professional entertainer to charm people into letting me get by with the minimum amount of work.

The majority of the others struck me as more interested in banging each other. In a way, it was like the Crüe tour except I was a spectator. Not that I was the master of self-restraint, but I wasn't dumb enough to get involved with people who'd been shoving needles into themselves. My biggest problems at the Ford Center were with my roommates. The first guy, coming off a habit of fifty fucking Valiums a day, snored like Grizzly fucking Adams. I sat up at night threatening to beat him up if he didn't stop. He would roll over and groan, "Go ahead." Eventually I got another roommate. Not only was this guy a fucking mortician battling with depression, which he'd handled by drinking vodka and gin all day, he snored worse than the first motherfucker.

"I'm wondering if I can ever get over it," he once said to me.

"I doubt it," I said.

"Why do you think?" he asked.

"Look at the fucking job you got," I answered. "Wheeling bodies in and out of rooms. Telling people their loved one is dead. What a fucking blast that is."

Finally I got my own private room. Between sleep and sobriety, I felt much better by the end of the program. I looked it, too, tan and thinner. Sharon was delighted and hopeful that getting more involved with emotions I'd been out of touch with since childhood would help me to control my addiction. Deep down, I was, too.

My life felt better. Sharon had moved the kids to a nearby rental house and various times I slipped out of the Ford Center and we made love the way we did when we first hooked up, with renewed thirst and passion. I couldn't wait to get out and work again. Neither of us could. We had a new home in Hampstead, a four-story Edwardian mansion, and the future looked as bright as ever.

My final obligation at the Ford Center was the graduation ceremony, a meeting in which patients and counselors offer encouragement, and during it nearly all the counselors complimented my effort and said they thought I was going to make it. Then one little old lady patient stepped forward and said, "You have no chance on the face of this earth of every staying sober. You're young. You're wealthy. You're famous. And you've conned everyone here but me. Good luck."

"Thank you, ma'am," I said politely.

"I want to tell you one more thing," she said. "After you leave here, you'll never be able to drink or take drugs the same way. Remember me saying that."

That was a curse. For the longest fucking time I saw her face whenever I picked up a drink or took a snort of coke. She fucked up my head so badly. But not that badly. Some two hours after leaving the Betty Ford Center I was at the hotel bar, ordering a vodka, and by midafternoon I was drunk. I couldn't help myself. Yet Sharon was so disappointed. She tried very bravely to accept me and my addiction, but with two kids it wasn't the life she'd pictured.

Not that she'd talk about it with me. But a few weeks later the two of us were flying to the Rock in Rio festival in Rio de Janeiro, Brazil, and I was as drunk as ever. And I remember waking up on the plane as she stuck me with a fork and with tears falling down her cheek said, "You fucking asshole."

Sharon: Some women get a reputation for being loose, others are said to be nice, and others are admired for their style and intelligence. I was regarded within the music industry as something of a viper. When I started managing Ozzy, I was constantly put down by male record executives. More than one echoed the sentiments of former Sony chief Walter Yetnikoff, who once said, "Sharon, go home to your husband, lose weight, and have some babies. This isn't a business for you."

Only what those chauvinist pigs didn't realize is that my upbringing prevented me from being intimidated. I didn't cry. Even before I took on Ozzy, I'd seen and been through too much to let someone threatening to destroy me mean anything. By the mid-1980s, I'd added clients, including Lita Ford and the London Quireboys, proving I could not be run out of the business. No, I was born into it, or, as the Crüe's Nikki Sixx once said, I was "a homely, rotund little British woman whose very name sets lips trembling and knees knocking."

The only person able to destroy me was me. For the first time ever that loomed as a viable option in those early days of 1985 when Ozzy was out of control again. When he went on a jag with coke and booze, he was up every second of the day and night, talking nonstop, or worse, moaning in agony. Between Ozzy's career, his addiction, and the two babies, I didn't have a second to myself. This one time on the road I screamed, "Ozzy, if you don't give me a second of downtime I'm going to die."

That was my bottom. Unable to stand any more, I started bashing my head against the bedroom wall in our tour bus. I didn't know what else to do. Then one of the road managers came in and said, "Sharon, you've got to stop it." He made me look in the mirror at the bruises appearing on the side of my head. "Take one of these," he advised, putting a bottle of pills on my nightstand. "It'll calm you down."

I took one and then a few minutes later I said, "What the hell," and I swallowed the rest of the bottle. The next thing I knew I was waking up in the hospital. Ozzy, overwhelmed by guilt, was apologetic. Holding flowers and a necklace, he took me back to the Sunset Marquis. Under his doting, attentive eye, I recovered. I knew he was frightened of losing me, and I loved him. So we started again. When you're in a relationship with someone who's that far into their addiction, you have a lot of times when you swear to start afresh.

I channeled much of my energy into motherhood. I got pregnant again and gave birth to Jack on November 8, 1985. If it's possible to enjoy childbirth, I did with him. His was the most comfortable of all three births. This time, Ozzy was anticipating another little girl. The shock of finding out he had the little boy he'd wanted caused him to faint. After he hit the floor, a dozen airplane-size cognac bottles rolled out of his jacket pockets. The doctor, who knew us, said, "Cheers, Ozzy."

Ozzy: I'll tell you something, man, I was there for the birth of Jessica, Aimee, and Kelly. I didn't make Louis, I didn't make Jack. But fuck away. So many guys are fucking weird, man. They will have sex and make love to their wives. They'll make the baby and then go, "I can't see all that shit." You are 50 percent of the fucking deal, son. It's the fucking least you can do, you know. So I made sure, as bad as it was, I was there for as many births as I could.

𝕾𝖍𝖆𝖗𝖔𝖓: I have to say that it was great having Ozzy there. Every mother goes through it, when you think you're holding the baby too tight, and you don't want to hurt them, and you're really, really cautious when you first have them. Ozzy was an old hand at it; he was used to holding babies. After I fed them, he would burp them, and put them on his shoulder.

If I'd had my way, Jack wouldn't have been my last pregnancy. Both Ozzy and I wanted more children. For a long time, we tried to increase the size of our family, but complications prevented any more celebrations. While I was pregnant with Jack, Ozzy's first wife talked him into getting a vasectomy. I think she worried he was going to lose interest in Jessica and Louis, which I couldn't imagine, but putting myself in Thelma's position, if he did stop visiting the money he sent might dry up, too. So I think she convinced him he had plenty of children.

IX

The Cradle Will Rock

Bam bam bam-bam, Buh-bam bam bam-bam—
I wanna be sedated!

—THE RAMONES, 1978

Aimee: I remember my dad used to play Michael Jackson's *Thriller* for us and a lot of the Beatles' music—kiddie music wasn't really a big part of our childhood.

Sharon: My kids weren't raised on Big Bird. They were raised on adult music and they found what they connected with at such early ages. Aimee liked Boy George at the age of one. She was dancing around and holding up the record. "Oh, I love this!" She was weaned on Slade, Boy George, and the Beatles because that's what was around. Jack became a big Simply Red fan. He loved them from two years of age.

The kids loved everything from the Backstreet Boys to Kylie Minogue when she first came out to the musical *Annie*. They must have listened to *Annie* twenty times a day, every day—I used to think, If I have to hear "Tomorrow" one more time, I'll go crazy!

We were constantly taking them to the theater. It's very important. I know with myself, some of my great memories as a kid were going to the theater with my parents and seeing different musicals and whatever.

I was raised with music in my house constantly and that's what I wanted to bring to my kids: to educate them not just in their dad's music, to respect and understand what their dad does, but also other genres because I didn't want them to be blindfolded musically.

Kelly: When we were kids my dad had his studio in there and there was, like, a music room and it had this jukebox. It had singles by the Beatles, the Kinks, Michael Jackson, David Bowie, T-Rex. I liked pushing the buttons. So the first music I heard was anything that was in there. I remember my favorite song was the Ramones' "I Wanna Be Sedated." I didn't know what that meant and I used to sing it. Every time, my mom, she'd be like, "Don't sing that song. You don't even know what it means!"

Jack: That old jukebox never actually worked. I mean, it worked for a while, but I was real young. I probably never put two and two together that you actually had to put a coin in to get it to work.

Ozzy: "I think they used to watch MTV more so than [listen to] the jukebox because MTV was a new thing at that time. You know that Paul Young song, "Everytime You Go Away," with the lyrics, "Everytime you go away you take a piece of me with you"? My kids used to think he was singing something else. They would ask, "Why's he saying, 'You take a piece of *meat* with you'?" It was so sweet.

Jack: What I do remember is that I used to listen to a Muppets cassette all the time, with Dad and Miss Piggy. They did "Born to Be Wild." That was pretty awesome. I was pretty stoked for that. "Yeah! My dad's on the Muppets! You guys can fuck off!"

X

Ozzmestic

———— ⚬ ————

Manhattan therapist Sheenah Hankin said the family's tendency to turn any conflict into a shouting match might make the children "yellers and screamers" as adults—something that could hurt their relationships and careers. . . .

"They can suck my freshly lipo-ed ass, because no, we're not perfect . . . if they want to grow up to be yellers and screamers, so what?"

—SHARON OSBOURNE, RESPONDING TO THE EXPERTS ON
ABC NEWS SHOW *20/20*, MAY 10, 2002

Sharon: Nothing about my upbringing was normal. I think I suffered some kind of culture shock the first time I went to a friend's house for dinner and realized her entire family sat at the table and talked to one another rather than scream at people on the telephone, as was the practice at my house.

I was in my teens before I knew there were normal people in the world. My parents worked obsessively and associated with celebrities. I wanted to raise my kids in the real world.

My children didn't get traditional family meals, but they attended a normal village school in Buckinghamshire and did their lessons at home.

Okay, so they came home to an enormous mansion on the historical register—Beale House was its name. There was no denying that their dad was a rock star who made a good living and their mom, meaning me, worked hard in a business that necessitated leaving the cooking and cleaning to a staff. Still, I think anyone coming over sensed the hominess of our lives then. You always smelled something delicious in the kitchen. We had pets and toys everywhere. And the children played in the yard. It was what I had envisioned.

Jack: We had a great yard. I loved running around. My parents built an incredible tree house in the backyard. I was very happy there. Life was simpler. Dad took me for walks in the forest. Mom took us into London. I was going to grow up to be a pirate. Or a fireman.

Kelly: In England we lived in a big old house. It was stunning—my brother and I were always running out in the yard. I don't think I stopped for a second!

I shared a bedroom with my sister—it was pink and beautiful. I was the bed wetter so my bed was near the toilet and Aimee's was near the window. My favorite thing about the bedroom was there was a tiny, tiny dressing room that was supposed to be a closet of my mom's, and she put two little dressing tables in there that were for me and my sister. And I remember I had my "me me" doll—when you pressed its stomach, it sang this song—"me me." I wouldn't go to bed without it.

Jack: I would set things on fire, and I wouldn't get a toy unless I could bring it into the bathtub with me. Every toy went in the bathtub.

Sharon: Jack was always the one in the middle that was friends with everyone. And so he would sometimes share a bedroom with Aimee, sometimes he'd share it with Kelly. But as they got older, Kelly and Jack kind of became a team.

Jack: I miss big houses.

Kelly: Jack and I went our own way and climbed trees, built forts, and played Ghostbusters.

Sometimes Jack was like our toy—Aimee and I used to dress him up in my mom's mod clothes from the sixties. We'd put him in long wigs, dresses, and white leather boots. When he was dressed up like that we called him "Tallulah"—he loved it!

Jack: They would pin me down and put makeup on. I didn't like it. It was like I was a toy.

Aimee: Jack was like a little toy to us. On Christmas Eve when I was three I wandered into Jack's bedroom and lifted him out of his crib, got him dressed, and dragged him down the stairs by his little pudgy arm as if he were one of my dolls. It was late at night, and I got him halfway down when my mother heard the *thump thump thump* and rushed out to see what was going on. She quickly took her little baby away.

I loved living in that house. It was a five-hundred-year-old estate in the English countryside that my dad purchased while my mom was in L.A. He'd taken me with him, and I can remember holding my breath in awe as we toured the property, acre after acre of forest and pasture with reindeer and goats. Living there was a real-life fairy tale. Life was as close to normal as we ever got. Those were the years when my mom got it all right.

Sharon: Aimee was always my serious child, a miniature adult at age five. She kept her bedroom immaculate.

She was always so together in contrast to Kelly, who was always in the middle of chaos. She never cared about her appearance. She pooped in her pants or pissed herself and kept right on going.

And Jack was always the friendly one, easygoing.

They were good, cute, loving kids who, though sheltered as much as possible, were exposed to the strange, disorderly, hectic world of rock 'n' roll. By 1986, they were old enough to be aware of the lifestyle. Ozzy kept strange hours because he was recording his *Ultimate Sin* album. Then he went on tour. I traveled back and forth to L.A. as if it was a commute to London. The kids knew how to dial a telephone before they could count to ten.

Kelly: I would call my mom seventeen times a day. I hated being on my own.

Sharon: But we tried to keep things stable. I was strict about rules, like cleanup and bedtime and manners. Ozzy has his own sense of right and wrong. There was the time he told Aimee and Kelly to pick up their clothes. First, they asked why he didn't pick up his own clothes. "That's my point," he explained. "If you don't pick up your stuff off the floor, I have no place to put my own."

Kelly: We had rules just like all other kids. We weren't allowed to use the phone past a certain time. We weren't allowed to watch TV past a certain hour. We had to clear our plates after meals and put them in the dishwasher. Oh, and here was the big thing with my mom. When we were really little, we couldn't say the word "shit." That was like the dirtiest word in the world.

Aimee: I never understood why I couldn't go with them. I remember we had lots of nannies. I used to have so much fun with them because they were young girls.

Jack: I can remember always crying when dad left or mom left, saying, "I don't want to be left with the fucking nanny. . . ."

Kelly: Actually the dirtiest word in the world was "good-bye." We seemed to say it all the time. My mom went to L.A. for business the way my friends' mothers went to the grocery store, or else she was meeting up with my father, who toured regularly in the mid-eighties. I only had to see the suitcases come out and I started to cry. I'd hang on my dad's leg until someone pried me off as he walked to the car that was picking him up, and I made my mom promise to call every hour.

During the *Ultimate Sin* and *No Rest for the Wicked* tours in the mid-1980s we tried more desperate measures to keep our parents from going away. The three of us, ranging in age from five to two, secretly removed the clothes from my mother's large steamer trunk and climbed inside. Then little Jack stuck his tiny hand out and brought the lid down, and we said, "Now you have to take us."

Sharon: Nothing in my life has been as heart-wrenching as when my kids cried because I had to go on the road. Kelly cried the loudest, but Aimee had it the hardest. As the oldest, she saw the most. She was also so sensitive. I can still hear her saying, "Mommy, please stay home. I'll be good."

Aimee: My mother would catch me staring at her and ask, "Why are you so angry? What's wrong with you?" I buried things so deep where I didn't even know. I would say, "Nothing, Mommy," but tears would be falling. I wasn't old enough to explain those emotions.

But they had to work, and their work took them away from home. It was like, "Fend for yourself, kids—take care of yourself." I didn't think that was right.

Sharon: It was terrible, terrible. You need to be together in order to make a marriage work. You know, you can't let your husband go out on the road for four months, and just say, "See you! I'll be here when you get back." Well, he ain't coming back!

It's not that you have to be around a person to make sure that they love you, it's just things happen, and when you spend a lot of time apart, it can really damage your relationship. Both sides get lonely. You know, a week, or two, or three, that's fine. But four months apart—we could have never kept a family together. So we decided to take the children. . . .

Kelly: I grew up on the road—I think a lot of people forget that and don't realize that I spent the first year of my life on a tour bus.

Jack: Aimee is the one with the most road experience. She toured for like the first four years of her life!

Aimee: Those times when we went on tour were the best. I got treated very well—I was pretty much the princess. If we were on the road, we had a regular dinnertime. We went to sound check, ran around empty arenas, stood behind the drums or at the side of the stage, watching Dad. It was fun to see all the different bands that would work with my dad.

Kelly: I always had the best time. I had my bunk and my toys set up in the bus, and I remember the English tour buses had an upstairs and a downstairs, with two lounges upstairs. In the front lounge, where the windows are where you can see the road, there was a couch on either side that could turn into cots. That's where me and my brother used to sleep.

My mom always wanted me to put on a fancy dress before each

show. There was one time I gave in because, actually, I didn't have a choice. We were going to a reception for radio people beforehand, and so my mom put me into a pink party dress with lots of frills and ribbons. As she carried me in, some guy said, "It's disgusting how women can take their little girls to a show like this." My mom went fucking nuts—ripped the guy a new asshole!

Jack: Let's see—I have little flashes of things. They all kind of melt together because I was touring since I was like a month old. I remember going fishing with Dad at a show in Minneapolis. I think the most memorable tour was the one with Ugly Kid Joe because Whitfield Crane, their singer, is still one of my best friends. I remember at the last gig, Dad had the rigging guys go up and drop eggs and flour on them while they were playing. We were sitting there laughing. I probably threw something at them from the wings, but I was like five, so I don't think it did any damage.

Kelly: It's so weird because I only remember certain things about certain shows when I was young. I was still very much restricted to my dad's dressing room and catering and production office. I remember when we were onstage, Randy Castillo, Dad's drummer, would always hand off a drumstick and me and my brother would just sit there hitting the drums and singing along.

I remember I was in Japan on my fifth or sixth birthday and my dad took me onstage with him. I was terrified because I'd never seen so many people. They were just looking at me and I was like, "Ahhh!" All of these people are here to see my dad—and all of them sang along. It was like some secret society I didn't get. I thought every dad did what my dad did.

Aimee: I remember that, but it wasn't really a reality for me, more like a childish game. No school, no rules, and no bedtime, and all the kids, the crew, the band, the traveling, being with both our parents. And it was kind of bizarre for a little child to be on a stage and have all these thousands of people screaming, where we could see my dad at his best.

Sharon: I wanted them to see their father onstage; I wanted them to see the adulation from the crowd; I wanted them to see how great their father was—because that's where he really shined, and also that's what was providing us with the means to live the way we were living. I wanted them to fully understand. I mean, they got to meet some incredible people, great experiences. But at the same time, too, they were taken away from a lot of the madness that went on on the road.

Aimee: We cheered till we were hoarse. Late at night we'd crawl into bed with my parents in the back of the bus and watch movies. For the most part it was tame. My mother kept us away from the drugs, the groupies, and the craziness, and if my father seemed bent on getting out of control, she whisked us back home.

Jack: For all his outrageous antics, there was a side of my dad no one got to see. The home Ozzy. He changed our diapers, took us for walks, played games with us, and chased us through the gardens. The so-called Prince of Darkness would pretend to fall asleep while we were watching TV and when we got involved in the show he'd scream "boo" and scare the shit out of us, which made us all laugh. He was big on bedtime stories, too, but his dyslexia would get to him and so he'd make up the story, which was as entertaining as the book.

Sharon: In 1986, we were still establishing Ozzy as a solo artist and ourselves as a family. Then out of nowhere the parents of Joe McCollum, a nineteen-year-old in Florida who killed himself, filed a lawsuit against Ozzy and the record company. They claimed his music had forced this poor kid to put a gun to his head. Yes, Ozzy has a song called "Suicide Solution," but read the lyrics—it's against suicide.

I was really, really angry. When you read the foundation of their suit against Ozzy, it was so ridiculous and ludicrous that I couldn't even believe that a lawyer would take on the case. This child was doing badly at school, he was very depressed, he would stay in his room and lock himself away from people day after day, and you know, he shot himself with his dad's gun. What is his dad doing with a gun, anyway? And just because Ozzy's record was on his tape deck. You know, there was also a bottle of Coca-Cola in his room, too. How do we know it wasn't the Coke?

In those days we weren't sophisticated about that sort of American-style lawsuit. I'm not trying to say that we're naïve little farm people, but we really weren't aware that such a lawsuit was even possible, and what could happen and could not happen.

Jack: I was only a year old at the time, but I heard about this first lawsuit a few years later when there were another two for the same reasons. Kids killing themselves and they'd happen to have my dad's music near them. I hate the thought of my dad being attacked for his music. People can argue whether or not they like it, but screw those who think listening to an album could make someone kill themselves.

Dad was always controversial, like the first bad boy in rock, because everyone, you know, was banning him from towns and shit like that. I think it's cool in a way, because in a way he was the first Eminem, or the first Marilyn Manson in rock anyway. Everyone kind of forgets that.

Ozzy: The lawsuits? That all came with the territory. I told the papers back then that: People are blaming artists when they should take a good look in the bloody mirror. If I don't want my kids to listen to a certain form of music, or read a certain form of book, or watch a certain form of pornographic video, I damn well make sure they don't.

I know I've offended a lot of people, but kill anyone? I think I've made a lot of people's lives worth living.

Sharon: I don't think it's likely to happen today because it was tried so many times and I think it is a product of the time, and I think that people have gotten more educated to the fact that you have to look within your home, instead of trying to find someone else to blame.

But the lawsuits dragged on and some didn't even come to trial, but we had to deal with them. It was a financial drain—it cost Ozzy damage to his career because a lot of stores refused to stock his music and a lot of radio stations took him off the air.

It was a greater emotional cost—it caused such stress to Ozzy. In 1990, I remember, we were all in New York and Cardinal O'Connor did a sermon one Sunday about how bad Ozzy was, how his music was "help to the devil" and people like him should be stopped. It made the front page of the Monday paper in New York, and our dumb-ass nanny read it out loud to the children.

Jack: . . . the nanny bitches.

Kelly: For the most part, the nannies my mother hired were responsible, good women intent on doing a decent job. Then they met up with us. Not that we were bad or misbehaved. No, as kids, we were generally good. As the offspring of Ozzy Osbourne, though, we knew how to create mayhem. It was in our blood. Consequently, the typical nanny lasted a few months before handing in her resignation, refusing to stay even after offers of pay increases and more vacation time. As they left, all had a look in their eyes that said, "Get me away from those kids."

And perhaps they had reason. Energetic pranksters, we put plastic wrap on the toilet seats and reminded them to leave space in the fridge for Daddy's bat heads. But some nannies seemed to hate not just us but kids in general so much I wondered why they became nannies in the first place. One stands out. I was six years old at the time, and she sat down at the table with us after dinner and began eating a candy bar. I loved sweets more than life itself.

"Could I please have some chocolate?" I asked, salivating as I stared at her candy bar.

She looked around the kitchen as if thinking of the amount to charge me, and then she said, "Only if you wash the dishes for me."

No problem. I washed the dishes and gave her an expectant look that said, "Okay, I finished. Pay me."

"Not yet," she said. "First I want you to lick the floor."

Since I was little, I didn't realize this nanny was into humiliation. How she must've hated us. What neither of us knew is that my mother was watching the entire exchange through a crack in the kitchen door, and when she heard what the nanny asked me to do, she came in and booted the nanny out of the house. Then, of course, I got my chocolate.

Sharon: Nannies were the plague of my life. You think you know somebody. You look at their résumés. You check their references. You make the best decision you can. Then something happens and you realize you've had a psychopath on the loose in your house. People are such bullshitters.

One woman had me ready to give her a lifetime deal. During the interview, she said she was a pediatric nurse, and she impressed me as nice, loving, and capable. She wasn't married, she didn't have children. She was perfect.

"Why aren't you nursing anymore?" I asked.

"I can't take it, being around sick children," she said. "My heart breaks. It's just gotten to me once too often. But I love babies. I love children."

"What do you do for your own time and enjoyment?" I asked.

"I love to go to the library and read," she said. "Books are food for the mind. I also love to crochet."

She was with us for a few months without incident. Then the holidays arrived. On Christmas Eve she says to me, "I need to go early today to catch up on some shopping." I'm like, "Fine. Lovely. I'm home with the kids all day. Whatever." About three hours later, I get a call from her. She's in tears. "Mrs. Osbourne, I've just had an abortion. Will you pick me up from the clinic?"

I was stunned. It turned out she had a husband and a lover and had told about two dozen other lies. Our Mary Poppins was in reality a pathological liar. I said, "I'm so sorry, but you'll have to fend for yourself. You've lied to me and my children." Then I gathered everything from her room and threw them onto the street and never looked back. I still remember her record player shattering as it hit the pavement.

Aimee: Nannies or not, our home life was colored by the complicated relationship between my father's struggle with his addiction to alcohol and drugs and my mother's efforts to control him. At times, I think of Kelly, Jack, and myself as bystanders in a hostage situation. Consider: Once when I was around five years old and we were living temporarily in the south of France for tax purposes, my father took us children for a walk through Cannes.

We went straight to Van Cleef & Arpels, which meant one thing: Something had happened between him and my mother and he needed to apologize. But within a few minutes of being in the store my dad, drunk at the time, stumbled and crashed into several display cases. He came home with pearls and diamonds for my mother and a new watch for himself. The store got over it. I don't know if we did.

We weren't as easily bought. Like a lot of children of celebrities whom I've met, I was wary, anxious, not trusting, and angry. I never knew why. But I can look back and blame the lifestyle. The pace is different, as is the attention from the public, the scrutiny from the press, and the anxiety that permeates daily life, which is something that's not discussed. But those whispers are real. Is there work? Are tickets selling? Is the agent working hard? Is the talent real? Can you write songs? Can you do the job? Do you want to be away from home for the next six months?

Plus, my dad carried around private demons that made him an unpredictable powder keg ready to explode. It tainted everything in our lives. None of us knew what kind of mood he'd wake up in or if he even went to bed at all. He fought with my mother all the time, real screaming fits that sometimes involved throwing pots and pans and vases. We walked on eggshells, not understanding what set him off. At five, I got a hold of some of my mother's pictures and looked through them. When I asked about the individuals in the pictures, he explained they were her parents, and my grandparents, but calmly said they were no longer living.

Then one day I came across several photos of my dad, showing him doing coke with bandmates while they were on the road. I don't know if it was seeing the white powder everyone was sitting around or simply that he looked so different—so blurry-eyed, crazy, and unlike my dad—but I asked my mom what he was doing in those pictures. In her straightforward, honest manner, she said something like, "Daddy does this and that. I don't always approve, and he isn't allowed to do it here."

I didn't understand much of what was going on, but to my mother's credit she was always up front. She provided the information we needed to know and not more.

Of course, I have no idea if she knew the answers herself. Ultimately what happens is that no one talks about anything. You spend a lot of time regrouping.

Sharon: Ozzy was like a broken record. When he was on tour, he wanted off, swearing he'd never go on the road again. But when he was home, he couldn't wait to get back out. He suffered from ants in his pants. There was never any telling which Ozzy I would wake up to. The sweet, sensitive, vulnerable romantic who liked to get up early, make coffee, and surprise me with breakfast and flowers from the garden or the tormented soul who couldn't say no to drugs and alcohol when he got bored.

I tolerated his drinking up to a point, but I always warned that if I ever caught him with drugs at home I'd call the cops. I didn't. But plenty of times I did kick him out the front door and tell him not to come back until he had finished snorting every bit of cocaine he had. Just keep it away from the kids.

Idle time was the kiss of death for Ozzy. Those empty hours allowed the demons to visit him, and he went for the liquor and coke to quiet them. One morning I woke up and found him in bed after he'd been out drinking for a couple of days, and I saw he had a large blue gargoyle tattooed on his chest. "Jesus," I said as I clobbered him on the shoulder, "now I have to look at two ugly creatures every day." He didn't like the way I tried to find entertainment. Somehow I managed to take him to a screening of the movie *Terms of Endearment*, but at the moment when Debra Winger dies of cancer he shattered the mood in the theater by saying, "I feel like fucking committing suicide. Take me to the bar!"

Such small differences were rare. Our fights, which always involved Ozzy getting drunk or fucked-up, were incredible blow-outs. One time we were in the south of France, and we had this huge fight. I had these pots made for Aimee, really thick ceramic pots surrounding me. And I picked one up with the soup still inside it, and threw it at Ozzy. He got this huge gash on his head. He sat there with blood pouring down his face—pouring.

Oh, I hurt him as much as he hurt me.

When we were on tour a few months after getting married, I threw a bag of coke out the window and Ozzy struck me. I hit him back just as hard. When we moved to Staffordshire, we had a party that ended with Ozzy and me going at it till I punched my hand through a glass window and needed stitches.

I was like, "You wanna fight? I'll fight you."

In 1988, I threw a big party for Christmas, a time of year that was always a fucking nightmare in our house. Either Ozzy would miss his children from his first marriage and feel guilty for not being with them, or he would be struggling not to drink. Or he would get fucked-up. But this one year he was on tour, and so I said to the kids, "We're going to throw the biggest, bestest party you've seen in your lives."

And that is exactly what I did. I had a Las Vegas–style band playing schmaltzy eighties tunes. I had carolers. Great food. We had a blast. And I didn't tell Ozzy.

But he heard about it from someone and called from New York. He was insane with anger. "What do you care?" I said. "You're on tour and you hate fucking Christmas. I'm doing this for me and the children." Not that he heard a word I said. Or that it mattered if he did. A few days later I took the kids to visit him. He was drunk when we got there, so I had the kids taken away, and then once we were alone Ozzy beat me. I tried to fight back, but he was so much stronger and out of control. It was the worst yet, and I ended up running to another room for my own protection.

XI

Am I Going Insane?

———————⌇———————

Ozzy Osbourne landed in a British rehab center for
alcoholism treatment after being arrested for threatening to kill his wife. The metal madman was arrested
at his home hear London on September 2nd and was
later released on the condition he immediately go into
detox.

—*Rolling Stone*, October 19, 1989

Aimee: I felt like I was a parent to my parents. When I was younger, I used to get up very early in the morning and clean the whole house so Mom would wake up in a good mood. You know, as a kid, you wake up Saturday morning, and you want to go out and do things, but I couldn't—she wouldn't wake up until one in the afternoon.

Children know when their mom isn't happy. My mom was suffering from depression. She had these three kids, a husband who was out of control, a career. She was a lost soul. And so that definitely took its toll.

Sharon: Just fucking do it, I'd say to myself as he walked in. Get it over with so I can go to sleep.

I got to the point where I lay in bed, listening for Ozzy to come home and preparing myself for the beating I thought was inevitable.

Why did I stay? I wasn't used to being verbally or physically abused, but I was used to being around people who behaved like Ozzy. I've never known anything else.

I was like every other woman who stays in an abusive relationship. I got in a bad place. My self-esteem vanished. I thought I deserved this sort of treatment, that it was okay and the way this marriage worked.

Aimee: I would watch and I would hear the fights and the ugliness that would go on. It would be so strange, because one day Dad would be so amazing and loving and the next day he could be so mean to my mom.

Sharon: Ozzy kept a nightmarish schedule, staying up all night and taking catnaps during the day. Those lasted an hour or so, and then he'd get up and drink more and do more drugs until he collapsed again. Fortunately he had his own part of the house, guest quarters that were separated from the main house by a courtyard. He spent hours there, sometimes stretches that lasted for a day or two. His road manager, Tony, or I would pop over to check on him and make sure he was alive.

Not surprisingly I gained all my weight back and more. Weighing around 170 to 180 pounds, I needed that girth to protect myself from being battered. It was like insulation from the cruelty and punishment. As for the children, I was fiercely protective of them. I did everything I could to shield them from the abuse, but it was impossible to hide everything. One time Kelly was with me in front of the house while Ozzy and I screamed at each other. Much to my horror, she saw him lash out at me.

Kelly: I'm very protective of my mom. I don't like anyone touching her, and when he hit my mom, I'd never seen him so drunk or fucked-up. I jumped on his back and was punching him and screaming, "Don't ever touch her!" He just picked me up with one hand off and threw me off. Then, me and my mom locked ourselves in the bathroom and a couple of minutes later, I think he realized what had happened. He was crying in the corner.

Sharon: At times like those I would take the kids into London for a couple days, explaining that Mommy needed to shop and wanted them to come along for the fun. We'd check into a hotel and I'd call home to check on Ozzy's state. I always thought about leaving for good, but I couldn't ever bring myself to go through with it. Aside from the mess it would create, I got scared. I didn't have any family. It wasn't like I could hide out with the children at my parents' house. I couldn't ask my mother to take the kids for the weekend while I went to a spa to get myself together.

One day I got a call from a girlfriend who'd been at an AA meeting in Chicago where Ozzy got up and shared. At first I was heartened to hear that he was trying to stay sober by attending Twelve Step meetings while on tour. But then she recounted how Ozzy had told the group I was having an affair behind his back and the fear of losing me to another man was making him drink.

Apparently Ozzy got a lot of sympathy and support for that bullshit story, and when I got him on the phone, I said, "What the fuck are you doing? I mean, I wish I were having an affair. I wish I liked somebody else." But I knew the truth. Ozzy made up those stories to justify his own misbehavior. When he got loaded, he fucked around. It happened all the time. He tried to turn the tables to assuage his own guilt.

In 1983, Ozzy had been transformed to look like a werewolf for the album cover of *Bark at the Moon*. Six years later, he didn't need any makeup or special effects; by the end of summer 1989 he had become a real-life monster. "I've got to get some help," cried Ozzy in a rare moment of sanity from the road. "I don't want to tour anymore. It's killing me, and I don't want to die in the back of a bus."

Or from an overdose, I thought. But I kept that to myself. As I did so many other similar concerns. Ozzy was in a bad place physically and mentally as he wrapped up a summer of touring by participating with Bon Jovi, Mötley Crüe, and others at the Moscow Peace Festival. It was more like the vodka festival. There someone told him that I was having an affair with one of the guys in the London Quireboys. The story was utterly untrue, but it nonetheless sent my husband on a downward spiral for several days. He was in terrible shape when he arrived home.

The timing couldn't have been worse. Arriving via private plane, he came home on a whole concoction of drugs that prevented him from relating to any of us, especially the children, who were so happy to see him. Then his two kids from his first marriage, Jessica and Louis, came for the weekend, and Ozzy had a big row with his daughter, which ended with both of them running to their rooms. Aimee has described the house as a powder keg waiting to explode. Well, that lit the fuse. The tension was more frightening than a tornado warning; I could see the funnel cloud bearing down.

While he fell into his nocturnal routine and stayed isolated in his private space, I planned a party for Aimee's sixth birthday. The bad vibes built for days. Our fights were just terrible, very loud and physical. Both of us were angry, and yet there was no communication at all. On the Saturday afternoon of Aimee's party, he downed an entire bottle of vodka. There was more, too. I just don't know what else he consumed. Whatever it was, he went completely insane. I told people I didn't want him around. Something about Ozzy scared me in a way I'd never been previously. You live with someone long enough you know their pattern of behavior, and I just knew that something bad was going to happen.

He came down on like the fifth night of this roll and just said, "*We've* decided that *we're* going to kill you." And I'm like, "Okay. Is he sane?" He used "we." So I said, "I'm sorry." And he was calm, but yet there were shutters over his eyes. It wasn't Ozzy. Ozzy wasn't there. It was the drugs talking—the combination of drugs and drink. He was in a terrible state. And he just lunged at me, you know. Knocked me to the ground. Was on top of me, his hands around my neck, strangling me.

Fortunately I'd already pushed the hidden panic button that summoned the police. But between that time and their arrival, I had to fight for my life. As I struggled to get away one thought filled my head. My babies. My babies. What's going to happen to my babies?

I managed to break free. I rolled under the heavy wood kitchen table. Once I had my breath, I locked myself in the bathroom till I heard the sirens pulling up in front of the house. Only two or three minutes had elapsed. Not much time, but enough to know the police had to take Ozzy away. It wasn't easy. An indication of the extent to which Ozzy was out of his mind, he struggled with the cops, forcing them to lay him out on the floor as they cuffed his hands behind his back. I sat down in a chair and cried.

Aimee: I remember waking up and looking outside and seeing my dad in his underwear being handcuffed. It was very understandable considering how observant and smart I was at that age. I knew why he was arrested. I knew everything that was going on.

Kelly: Here's what I remember: My daddy had done something bad that he didn't mean to do, and that my mom was mad at him for it. When they were taking him away, I remember the back door had this plastic guard screwed on so the dogs wouldn't scratch away the paint, and I was holding on to that on my tippy-toes, leaning over to see what was going on and crying because I saw my mom crying. I couldn't understand where my dad was going and what had happened. Me and Jack, we just sat there and we didn't know what was going on. Then suddenly someone took us away and put us in our room and sat with us until we fell asleep.

Jack: I can remember sitting on the landing looking through the banister, and just looking down and seeing police cars take Dad out. I was just kind of like, "What's going on?" You know? I was so young at the time, probably around two or three, so it was more curiosity than fear or sadness.

It never really kind of struck me as anything big until recently, like the past five years. It's like, "Fuck—you know, he tried to kill my mom!"

Sharon: The kids didn't see it, thank God. They slept through the whole thing. The police coming, him going. They didn't know till breakfast that Dad was gone. So they, thank God, they didn't see that. Jack says he saw the policeman, this, that, and the other. I honestly don't think they did.

Ozzy: I woke up in jail feeling like crap and not sure of why I was there. I didn't remember anything that had happened. Shaking and sick, I asked the guard if he knew the charges. When I heard him say "attempted murder" of my wife, my asshole went into the banger.

"Could you read that again?" I asked.

I went into shock. Nothing could sound worse than hearing I'd tried to kill the woman I depended on for every breath I took.

He turned to a page on a clipboard and read, "John Michael Osbourne, you are hereby charged with attempted murder of your wife, Sharon Rachel Osbourne."

I couldn't believe it.

"I don't understand what you're saying," I muttered. "Attempted murder?"

The word "murder" freaked me out. I couldn't believe it.

I spent the weekend in that cell, where I swear to fucking God I would've gone insane, but the cops on guard duty were looking for a chance to put me down, so when they told me to shut up I listened. I couldn't have felt sicker. Without anything to drink, smoke, or swallow, I went through two days of painful withdrawal that made every part of my body ache. Sweat poured off me. The only thing scarier was the prison itself. The jail reminded me of pictures I'd seen of medieval dungeons. The whole place stunk like rotting shit, which at first I thought was a symptom of my withdrawal. But no, it turned out the other inmates hated the place so much they wiped their shit on the walls. I showered in a kind of indoor yard that had shit on the walls. No matter how much I scrubbed, I felt dirty and foul.

When I walked into court I saw Sharon across the room. As soon as our eyes met, I started to cry. Though we couldn't speak, I hoped she saw how sorry I was. I pled not guilty by reason of temporary insanity, but my ass was saved when Sharon told the judge she didn't want to press charges. At her suggestion, I was sentenced to three months of rehab at Huntercombe Manor, a drug and alcohol treatment facility in Buckinghamshire. I wasn't allowed any contact with Sharon or the children, unless it was authorized by the rehab's doctors and agreed to by my wife. And can you imagine the publicity? I was on the front page every fucking day: "Mad Rock Star Attempts to Kill Wife."

Aimee: I remember the next day I went to school, and my mom picking me up and he still wasn't home. He had gone into this rehab.

Ozzy: Sharon started coming to visit about a month into my stay, and a few weeks later she brought the kids, who broke my fucking heart when they said, "'Bye, Daddy. Get better soon."

As for treatment, I survived. The hardest part was avoiding all the women who wanted to have sex with me. They swarm over newcomers, flaunting their shit. But I knew one thing about chicks in rehab. They're incubators for viruses. Uninterested in temptation, I was like a dutiful kindergartener who followed directions and adapted to the daily structure of exercise, therapy, and regular meals. Sober for longer than any time in years, I felt better physically and tried not to think about the life I was missing beyond the manor's manicured hedges. I had to behave or else the judge at the end of three months could send me back to jail, and no fucking way did I want to take that path.

Sharon: Without Ozzy around, there was an immediate sense of relief at home. It was like I could suddenly breathe. Every day I relaxed a little bit more.

I needed about three weeks before I could see clearly again. When the clouds parted, my initial thought was to file for divorce. I had papers drawn up and took meetings with my attorney. Then as the weeks passed I reconsidered. I talked daily, sometimes hourly, to all of our friends, everyone with the patience to listen to my rants, and eventually I rediscovered my objectivity. Like Ozzy, I was confused, frightened, and sad. I also missed him. I missed us together.

If he hadn't been forced to stay in rehab, though, I don't know that we would have made it. The fact that we didn't see each other daily was surprisingly beneficial. We got reacquainted slowly. It was a forced decompression. Counselors nurtured us into communicating clearly and calmly. If we didn't solve our problems, we at least talked about them in a place where both of us were sober. Perhaps most important, Ozzy got to hear how he was destroying my self-esteem and scaring the children. It got to the point where I was counting the days until Ozzy would be able to come home.

While Ozzy was away, I made myself stronger by working out and dieting. I lost fifty pounds, at least, and felt better about myself.

It's amazing how good a woman can feel when she isn't cowering in bed at night waiting to be hit.

When Ozzy finally came home, I laid down some new ground rules.

"I'll take you back," I said. "I want you back. But if you ever lay a finger on me again I'll call the cops, press charges, and you'll go to jail."

Since then, there have been times when we've argued, I've seen the look in his eye and the way he has stood, and said, "Don't even think of coming near me." I've even reached for the phone and he's gone, "All right. All right, Sharon." But he's never hit me again. Nor have I struck him.

Kelly: Suddenly he was home again. We were always just excited that he was coming home—from the road, later when he would go to rehab and be away—we knew where he was, we knew why he was there, and it was like we couldn't wait to see him, you know?

I never wanted my dad to stay away.

Aimee: I remember being angry at him.

Jack: It was so far in the past I can't remember him coming home. And it's too late for me to be mad—for that.

The only thing that ever really got me pissed off at Dad was just his using. I shouldn't talk now, the pot calling the kettle black. But I knew when he drank a lot. When he was drinking and using opiates he would just get angry. At the flip of a switch he'd be your best friend, and then tell you to go fuck yourself. Not with the kids, it was more with Mom. He'd just get angry real easy with her.

Ozzy: I used to be a wife beater. I'm not proud of it, but I will own up to the fact. I think it's wrong. I don't fucking know why she stayed. . . .

People do all sorts of fucked-up shit when they drink. My father used to beat my mom and she cried—she fucking cried. One time when I was about fifteen my father came home and hit my mom downstairs. I heard the smacks and then the cries. I couldn't take it any longer. I ran downstairs and hit my father. Then I broke down myself. I felt such shame and disgust, felt sorry for myself—for all of us.

I love Sharon more than life itself. And I love my children. I haven't always been the greatest guy. I used to do crazy fucking things. The way I felt when I hit Sharon is the same way I feel right now thinking about it. I hate myself. . . .

XII

Sins of the Father

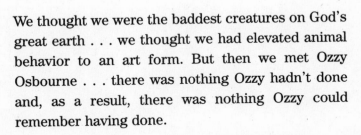

We thought we were the baddest creatures on God's great earth . . . we thought we had elevated animal behavior to an art form. But then we met Ozzy Osbourne . . . there was nothing Ozzy hadn't done and, as a result, there was nothing Ozzy could remember having done.

—NIKKI SIXX OF MÖTLEY CRÜE, *THE DIRT*

Jack: He's not the sort of dad who throws the ball around in the backyard and helps with the homework. Of course, I'm not that kind of kid, either. Most of the time he's mellow and sits around watching TV. But I remember when I was around eleven my mom kicking him out of their room. He came wandering into my room, sort of half-fried. He asked if he could crash—I said it didn't bother me.

Kelly: That's one thing that my mom never hid from us. She always explained it to us, that Daddy's just being crazy. When he got to a certain point, she'd always take us away from it. But I think out of all of us, my sister took it the hardest.

Aimee: I knew something wasn't right in the family. I knew that my dad was a substance abuser. And it began to really affect me. I was very embarrassed because my dad—to normal nine-to-five people—he was a freak. I was ashamed and embarrassed and I was miserable.

This is one of my most vivid memories, during the *No More Tears* time. I remember our nanny at the time said, "Aimee, your dad keeps asking me for beer, what do I do?" And I said, "Don't give it to him." I brought it in to him myself, and sat down right next to him by the fire. He was wasted. This is. I said, "Daddy, why are you doing this to us? Please don't do this." He looked at me and said, "Fuck you. I work hard, I get bread for this family, I have the right to do whatever the fuck I like, get away from me." I remember knowing that this was not how daddies are meant to speak to their little girls. I just remember him being so hard, and I felt it was my fault for some weird reason.

Ozzy: No. I don't remember the children asking me to stop drinking. I'm not just saying that. I just don't remember.

145

Kelly: Aimee will either blame herself or act like a victim. Instead of admitting that he has an addiction, which doesn't mean he doesn't love us. Addiction is a very hard thing for a person to deal with. He has a world war going on in his head. The only reason he fights his addiction every day is because of his love for us and because he knows that it hurts us.

If you have a drug-addict father who doesn't give a fuck about you, then cut yourself off from that person. But if you know deep down that your father really loves you, then you've just got to be there and understand.

Aimee: It was to the point where at any given situation, I was about to explode. My mother began sending me to therapists, but none ever seemed to ask the right questions. It was always "why are you angry?" never "how do you feel?"

I love my mother, but she is in so much denial till this day. How she copes with it is by working, making money: going out there until she gets what she wants and still keeps things going. And my father hurt everyone so much and himself most of all. I saw this talented, funny man wither away from someone who could hold a conversation to where he can hardly hold it together. He's done it to himself.

Sharon: The drugs and drinking—Aimee has seen so much. I try and explain it to her: There is no one hundred percent functional family. Every family has problems. I think that she is beginning to understand that we're probably the only married couple of all her friends, because all her friends come from divorce, divorce, divorce.

Jack: Did I like having my dad get fucked-up all the time? No. But I can see how drugs and stuff have helped him get by. He's fragile and he deals with a lot of fears. He thinks his addiction is a curse, and I know he struggles with it in every pore of his body. I know he loves me. I have no doubt he loves all of us. I think his battle is about loving himself.

XIII

Snowblind

That's the most dangerous shit. It's devil's dandruff,
you know. . . .

—OZZY OSBOURNE

Aimee: My father, just out of rehab, demanded a change of scenery. The stately home in Buckinghamshire that had enchanted him several years earlier was full of bad vibes. We needed to get away.

We moved to Los Angeles, where most of my mother's business was based. My mom explained living there would mean less traveling and more time together. It was a difficult adjustment. None of us were happy about leaving Buckinghamshire. I was particularly heartbroken to leave. Kelly, Jack, and I hated our new schools in the Pacific Palisades. The teachers treated us like freaks, and the kids mocked us.

Jack: It was weird—Christmas was my favorite holiday, and there was no Christmas vibe here. I was used to cold weather, going everywhere and seeing Christmas lights and Father Christmas and shit like that. I was so used to like it is in England, and here when you walk down the street it's so politically correct—you see Santa Claus, a menorah, reindeer, a dreidel, you know.

Sharon: I know, I know. Stability, the structure thing—that's what kids want and need in their lives, and here we were picking them all up and taking them to a totally new place. I know all of that, but I think that it gave them a great education in life. My kids from age eight could find their way around L.A., New York, and London. I think it gave them a certain sense of independence, too.

Aimee: Meanwhile, my parents continued with the late nights, phone calls, recording sessions, and travel. My mother worked as hard as ever. My father toured with his old mate from Sabbath— bassist Geezer Butler—put out a live album, and then spent the end of 1990 writing *No More Tears*.

There were no more tears, at least for a while. For almost a year. But despite my dad's best effort to exercise and stay sober, he couldn't do it. He often said music sounded better to him if he had a little vodka or a few hits of pot, and the urge overpowered him. He's the cliché addict. One is too many and a thousand is never enough.

Ozzy: It was early 1991, we had finished the *No More Tears* album, and so me and a few mates went to Las Vegas for a weekend of celebration.

By the time I got to Burbank Airport, though, I was already out of my mind from doing the entire ounce of coke I'd bought for the weekend. I'd literally inhaled it in the back of the limo. After checking in, I hit the bar with snot and shit hanging from my nose, tweaking madly, shaking, barely able to say anything coherent. Nonetheless, I managed to drop a fifty-dollar bill on the bar and ask for a whole bottle of vodka. That was all before the fucking plane took off.

Once in Vegas, I flew even higher. Friday and Saturday were spent snorting coke, drinking, and fucking around. I can't recall much of anything I did there. It was a blur. By Sunday night, I felt like shit. Absolutely fucking dreadful. For forty-eight hours, people had been giving me cocaine. I couldn't take a breath without half a gram going up my nose. I did not get near a bed the whole weekend.

By seven Sunday morning, I was at the blackjack table, drinking and feeling sick from too much blow. Suddenly I got a bad vibe.

"If I don't get out of here I'm going to jump out the window," I said to one of my friends at the table. "I can't fucking take it anymore."

"What do you want to do, Ozzy?" he asked.

Without saying anything, I got up from the table, walked in front of the hotel, and took a large plastic bag of coke from my pocket and threw it in the bushes. Fucking powder went everywhere, like a paint bomb. The bag, with some coke left inside, snagged on one of the bushes. I stared at it for about fifteen minutes, debating whether or not to climb in and snort what was left.

I didn't. I got into a cab and went to the airport.

Along the way, I found other little bags of coke in my pockets and tossed them out the window, too.

By the time I got to the airport, I'd probably junked five thousand dollars' worth of coke. I went straight to the gate.

It was 9:00 A.M. My plane wasn't scheduled to depart until 4:30. For the next seven and a half hours, I sat there, going through withdrawal, sweating, throwing up, pissing, and twitching from a two-and-a-half-day coke binge. I wanted someone to walk by and shoot me.

I had no idea a plane took off for L.A. every thirty minutes, and so was still sitting in my chair at 4:00 P.M. when my bandmates checked in at the gate. Shocked to find me hours after I'd said good-bye, they realized I was fucked-up and made sure I got back safely. After a fifteen-hour nap, I informed Sharon that I was finished with coke. "I finally understand what I couldn't get in rehab," I told her. "It's like a rocket goes up, but when it runs out of fuel it comes down. The higher you get, the harder you fall."

Not only was I done with cocaine, it looked for a time as if *everything* might be over. The bad news started in November 1991 when I came down wrong on my foot after a scissor kick during a show at the Aragon Ballroom in Chicago. It turned out the foot was broken. An infection set in, forcing me to cancel the rest of my tour. Sometime after resuming the tour the following year, Sharon noticed I was walking abnormally. According to what she later told me, I dragged my leg and onstage I didn't jump or kick the way I always had. She worried herself sick.

As for me, I was blissfully unaware of any change.

Why didn't she tell me? She knew I would obsess, worry, and most likely self-medicate myself into an even more serious condition. But then one day before a sound check at some show I noticed the trouble. My leg wasn't responding; it was like dead weight. Worried I might've had a stroke, I found Sharon and said, "Jesus, what's the matter with me? My leg isn't working right."

Sharon: "MS?" I asked.

My biggest fear was of finding Ozzy dead of an overdose. Never in my wildest imagination did I think he'd fall apart limb by limb. Trying not to panic, I canceled several shows and started visiting doctors. After several different specialists, we ended up with a New York neurologist who did a spinal tap and brain scans. There were a million different possibilities, he said. But then he called with a diagnosis that scared the crap out of me. Ozzy had MS.

"Multiple sclerosis."

I had to apologize for my ignorance and ask him to explain MS. I knew it was bad, but I had no idea of the specifics, that it's a degenerative neurological disease resulting from scarring and inflammation of the tissue that covers nerve fibers in the brain and spinal cord. Hearing that, I knew one thing: I wasn't going to tell Ozzy. Not yet anyway. When he asked the doctor's thoughts, I said, "He thinks you're tired and you have abused yourself with drugs and drinking to the point where you body is beginning to disintegrate on you."

Even that distressed Ozzy, who agreed to make the remaining dates of his tour his final ones ever. Instead of the *No More Tears* tour, we called it the *No More Tours* tour. Ozzy took it easier and made it through those dates. There was one show where he needed a painkiller, and the doctor administering the shot hit a nerve, which made it so Ozzy couldn't move either leg. We wheeled him onto the stage and he clung to the microphone, knowing if he let go he would fall. But the crowd thought Ozzy was being crazy, messed-up Ozzy. Every time he changed his grip and slipped, they cheered wildly. "Yeahhhhhhhhhhhhhhh!"

I was a mess. I attended support groups at UCLA, using an alias so word wouldn't leak to the press. I just wanted to get Ozzy through the tour and back home. That's where I planned to break the news. At the end of the tour I told Ozzy, who took it surprisingly well, though much later he confessed he'd faked much of the pain so his supply of morphine shots and pills wouldn't run out.

"You fucker," I'd say.

"I'm a drug addict," he'd answer.

The day after I told Ozzy I met with Sony Records president Tommy Mottola, a longtime friend, and I confessed everything. I broke down. I realized I'd kept too much inside for too long and I needed help.

"Have you met with anyone else and gotten a second opinion?" he asked.

"No, I haven't," I said.

"I know a world-renowned specialist in Boston, and I will get you in," he said.

A few days later Ozzy and I met with the specialist. After hearing about Ozzy's history of addiction ("It's quite amazing you're alive, forget worrying about MS," he said), he put him through tests. Ozzy stood on one leg, then the other. He hopped up and down. And he twirled around five times to see if that made him dizzy.

Finally the doctor stopped the exam and gave us his diagnosis.

"Ozzy doesn't have MS," he said. "He's drunk. Get out of my office. Let me treat sick people."

That crisis led to Ozzy going back into rehab. Whether he returned to Betty Ford or tried Hazelton, Promises, or Steps, the results were always the same. Ozzy sobered up briefly and then fell off the wagon. One time I came home from New York, and Ozzy, having binged while I was away, quit cold turkey and went into an alcoholic seizure. He was lucky not to have died.

He has wanted treatment to work. But he's never been able to get past the third of the twelve steps in Alcoholics Anonymous. He doesn't want to face it, and so he keeps it all inside.

Ozzy: It was November 1992 and I was tired. My albums had all gone gold and platinum, my shows sold out, and I had my health. I had reunited with Black Sabbath at the end of the tour we called the *No More Tours* tour in Costa Mesa, California. We had played a few songs together at 1985's Live Aid, but that had ended with Sharon's father sending us a court order to stop us from reuniting! Right there backstage she got the writ. And that wasn't really Black Sabbath. I'm not putting Michael Bordin down, who was playing drums, but we always say that Black Sabbath consists of Billy Ward, Tony Iommi, Geezer Butler, and Ozzy Osbourne. End of story.

Costa Mesa was more like old times, with me, Tony, Geezer, and Bill all playing together. The bad shit was behind us, and there was no doubt the four lads from Aston could still crank out the heaviest fucking metal on the planet.

I had earned a rest. I slowed down for a while and tried the stay-at-home dad thing. Ozzy has retired, we told the press. That proved to be a disaster. I was tripped up by boredom. I began boozing again. One drink led to morning beers and vodka and then . . .

Trouble. I went on one of my binges, which resulted in a fucking nightmare of a trip through the gutters and rot of human behavior. In other words, I was not faithful to my wife. I felt so degraded in the aftermath, the girl having gotten the better of me, and so I punished myself with more fucking alcohol.

I finally dragged my ass home and went to bed. I woke up knowing I was in Sharon's doghouse. Over the years, I'd learned it was pointless to hide anything from Sharon, and so I told her everything, which made her angrier. But I had to pay that price. I also, she insisted, had to get an AIDS test.

"Fuck," I said. "That never fucking crossed my mind. The fucking double bubble of AIDS."

She was fucking right, and it scared me. She took me to the doctor's and watched him draw the blood. I shook like a baby. For the next few days, I obsessed about the results. Then I received the phone call, which confirmed all my worst fears. The test had come back positive.

"Fuck," I cried. "Please God, no!"

Sharon was as shattered as I was by the news, but thank God my wife can be a stubborn bitch when it comes to news that upsets her vision of reality. While I was planning my funeral in my head, she insisted I get retested, and after several tense days they came back, this time negative. According to the doctor, the first test had been a false positive. Thank fucking God.

Still, it served as one powerful fucking wake-up call. It was also the last time that I drank hard liquor.

"Do you know what's wrong with you?" Sharon asked.

"Tell me, darling," I said.

"You get up in the day," she said. "You exercise. And then it's fucking downhill from there. You go in the garden, see blue sky, the sun shining, and you go, 'I won't be happy until I find that black cloud.' You wait until that fucking dark cloud is in front of the sun."

She was right. After all these years together, Sharon had me pegged. The next time I hit the road would be the end of 1995. The name of that tour: *Retirement Sucks.*

Aimee: My parents moved us back to London again.

They were fed up with life in L.A.—earthquakes, riots, and music people who thought it was cool to give my dad drugs. And I had been begging my parents to send me to boarding school— I didn't like my L.A. school. I had a passion for dance. I was always twirling around and being theatrical. I had an audition for this school in England that was very hard to get into.

Sharon: Aimee was accepted into arts educational ballet school, which was run by the Royal Ballet. She had always danced, from two years of age. She had studied ballet and to get into this school was really a major thing. We were like, "Okay, let's go back," and that was the motivation.

It was easy—we had always kept a home, some sort of base there. And the kids had kept their friendships with their childhood friends going. So they were very excited about going back.

Kelly: We were like, "Yeah, we want to go back." We were excited because when we were kids we were very, very, very, very English. We didn't understand a lot of the American culture and a lot of people would make fun of us in school. When we were at home we were just like everyone else. We had missed English TV and English food.

But the only reason we moved back to England when I was in the second grade was so my sister could go to this dance school. We couldn't understand why she'd ever want to go to boarding school, but it didn't bother us. As long as I can remember, it was always me and Jack.

Aimee: You know, you trained, I would say, five hours a day of dance, and then you have three hours of school. I loved it. It was my whole life. I've always been a dancer. So that is what I was going to do. But then my mom took me out of that school and I was heartbroken, and she put me into a Christian all-girls' school closer to the house. I still wanted to board. She put me into boarding school. I was there till I was about thirteen. For three years, we were there. And then we moved back to Los Angeles.

Once again I was teased and gawked at, which made going to class feel like torture. I was Ozzy Osbourne's daughter. I heard, "Hey, there's the girl whose dad bit the head off a bat." And, "Can your dad get me cocaine?" Academics didn't interest me. Nothing did. I used to imagine how different my life would be if I'd been able to continue dancing in England.

Kelly: Suddenly we were in L.A. again. I don't even remember the whole moving process, to be honest. But we were excited. It was different now because we were at the beginning of our teen years. There was nothing to do where we lived in England—if we wanted to go to a movie theater or go shopping or go bowling, we would have to drive for forty-five minutes.

I didn't know what designer clothing was, I didn't know what money was, I didn't know what it was to be rich, I didn't know what it meant to have money—until we moved back to America. I was twelve years old, and I felt like I was learning a new language: Gucci, Dolce & Gabana, Neiman Marcus, and Armani. Here's a problem for a young girl: Why wasn't Saks Fifth Avenue on Fifth

Avenue? I couldn't believe that stores were open on Sundays; they weren't in England. Plus, it never rained. It was never cold. I could wear cotton T-shirts in the middle of winter.

Here's a picture that stands out for me as the ultimate coming-of-age moment of my childhood in L.A. I was about thirteen or fourteen, and I was at the Century City shopping mall with my best friend. She led me to a secret place where all the enormous industrial-size air conditioners blew out air. They were giant vents. We stood on top of the vents with the warm air blowing and got high. I felt like Marilyn Monroe in that famous picture where her dress is billowing up. That was my Marilyn moment.

My gripe was school. I hated it. Actually, I hated my first school, a private Christian school where they told Jack and me that we were satanic. They slapped our hands and ridiculed us unmercifully, and for no reason other than we were the children of Ozzy Osbourne. It was awful. Then I transferred to Hawthorne, a public school in Beverly Hills, and I liked it better because I could sit back, not do any work, and no one said anything to me. I fell way behind and then I stopped going every day.

At sixteen, I dropped out. No one seemed too concerned. Of course when you come from a family of dyslexics—all of us inherited it—school is a complicated issue.

𝕵𝖆𝖈𝖐: It had always been kind of apparent. Dad knew he had dyslexia and he kind of figured that I might. Kelly has it. We all have it, really.

I don't see letters backward like (concerned voice), "Oh, isn't that what dyslexia is?" It's not. I'll look at stuff but it just won't register. I know the word, but sometimes it will just take a lot longer for it to kind of click in my head as to what that word *means*. It's not like I'm distracted—it's more like the wiring is a little off. I can sit there and look at a word and be like, "Uhh . . ." but I completely see the word. I'm a slow reader because of it. I have problems with doing math.

I liked some subjects, like history, but my disability was overwhelming. Like my father, I dreaded having to read or write in front of the class, and homework was always a struggle.

I went to a special school for like four years. They just kind of teach you how to bear with it and kind of cope with it and stuff.

Ozzy: I think the kids have had the best education around. They were traveling from the moment they were born. They were in the fucking bus, man. They have seen more of the United States—of the world—than any of their friends.

Kelly: My father would say, "You've been around the world ten times. You got a different kind of education." My mother was always realistic about it, too. "Make the most of every day," she told us. "Be the best you can be. Whether you're an A or a B or a C student, try to do your best." That's what matters. But going there and wasting the time of the teacher and others trying to learn is fucking pointless."

Sharon: Do I wish that I had been stricter and insisted they stay? Probably, in reflection, yeah. Jack, I think, wishes he'd have stayed on at school and I *know* that Aimee wishes that, too.

I've thought about this so much, again and again. I'm glad I left school at fifteen—and I'm glad that I worked the way that I did. My parents weren't of the generation to push me to stay; they didn't know that you could be a biologist or a doctor. You learned to read and write and that gave you the skills to go out into the world.

But I say you can always go back. I'm not saying that to cover a mistake that I made by allowing them to leave when they did. Education is something that doesn't stop at any age. It's a constant thing. They're still so young that if they really want to do it, they're in a position where they can take time out to do it and pay their way through.

Jack: I don't think anyone was surprised or disappointed when I quit school in my junior year. I spent most nights out at clubs, scouting bands, and I'd be going to bed at four or five in the morning and sleeping till late afternoon. I couldn't get up for school. I missed the social aspect of being at school, but I knew it wasn't for me.

One day I stopped going. Melinda came in to wake me up, and I said definitively, "I am not going." I might've said, "Fuck off, I'm not going." I can't remember. Later, though, I spoke to my parents about it. I saw my mother's disappointment. But she is above all else a realist. "If you feel confident you can go through life without a high school diploma, I'm not going to argue with you," she said.

The thing is, I'm planning on getting my GED. I have to. I know that. You can't go through life without a high school diploma.

Aimee: I miss England every day. I really do. We were normal, countryside English kids that Mom wanted to send to finishing school when we were eighteen. Sometimes I wish that none of this would have happened and I would have finished school and gone to college and done that whole bit. Then at the same time, too, I don't believe in regretting things that you have or have not done because it gets you nowhere. You know you are where you are for a reason.

Kelly: I think you're born with everything already planned out for you, and I think it's fate what you do. I don't know. I think if something happens in life, it's meant to happen.

XIV

Sweet Leaf

---

*. . . Straight people don't know what you're
about.*

—"Sweet Leaf," Black Sabbath

Aimee: It was mostly my mom who spoke to me about drugs. But I knew. I never needed them to tell me, because they showed me. I had firsthand experience with that and what it can do to you.

Kelly: "Just tell me everything you do," my mom would say. "I won't be mad. I want to know. I don't ever want you to lie."

My mother tried to prepare us for the time when drugs would enter our lives. She knew we'd had an education from watching our father and everyone around him, and she knew we'd have to make our own decisions. She always emphasized openness. Like a fucking idiot, I believed her.

First, let me clarify something. Unlike Jack, I'm not a pot smoker. I've had really bad experiences with it. I'm not sure if I have a bad allergy or what, but whenever I've done pot I have gotten really violent and hit people. Or I've gotten itchy and my eyes have swelled. It's not my thing.

But oh my God, the first time I smoked pot. That's something I won't forget, and it wasn't because of my reaction to it. It was a nice afternoon, and I was with friends. We went to Venice Beach and smoked a joint. On the way home I told my friends that I was going to tell my mom about my getting stoned. They were shocked. "No, no, don't get freaked out," I said. "My mom's cool. She's always said I can tell her anything and she won't be mad." They thought that was cool—as did I.

Then I got home and told her. And guess what? She went fucking nuts. She went fucking crazy.

"Kelly! What the fuck did you do?"

"I tried pot, Mom."

"That is so fucking stupid! That's so fucked-up!"

She went ballistic.

Then she got out the school roster and telephoned the parents of every kid that I knew. I was so embarrassed the next day at school because she phoned this one kid's parents and blamed him

163

for giving me pot. Unfortunately, it wasn't the right kid. Not that she even cared. She wouldn't stop. She kept saying, "I can't believe it. How dare you, Kelly."

Finally, I was like, "Oh, for fuck sake." It wasn't even fun anymore.

Actually, I don't remember if it was ever fun. But I do know that it was completely different for Jack. He fucking smokes pot every day. I smoked pot once and got into so much trouble. They treated me differently because they know I have a mouth on me, and they know I get into trouble, so I was the one who had to be home at ten every night, and had to be asleep by 10:30. If I wasn't, I'd be in trouble.

𝕵𝖆𝖈𝖐: Poor Kelly. Everyone feels so bad for her. I'm the one that ended up in fucking rehab!

The first time I got high was when I was around thirteen. I was hanging out at a friend's apartment in Hollywood. He was a lot older than me and when he asked me if I wanted to try a hit, I said, "Yeah, all right." But I didn't just take a little hit. I took a massive, lung-bursting bong hit. It was like taking a drag off an exhaust pipe spewing toxic clouds. I inhaled the absolute most amount of smoke possible, and before I knew it I was just fucking ripped, baked beyond belief.

Everything started turning surreal, and all I could do was watch it all unfold from the sofa and try not to lose it. My friend had these superbig dogs running around the room. And this guy down the hall, he was in this band where everyone played organs. They were all jamming on these synthesizers and shit, and I could hear it all so clearly even though the music was far away. Then for some reason my friend's next-door neighbor was talking on her phone and every word of her conversation echoed through my head. Everything was just coming at me at a hundred million miles per hour. It was beyond weird.

But despite all that chaos, the one thing I didn't do was come home all tweaked like Kelly and start chirping, "Guess what, Mom? I'm so fucked-up."

Of course, it came out later, and she didn't like it too much. But it wasn't a huge deal.

I never worried about my appetite for weed. I always felt like, "Yeah, I could quit. But I don't want to quit just now because I'm having fun. I'm not hurting anyone. I'm not hurting myself. I'm getting my shit done." On the other hand, I got pretty wild and felt the burn of partying too much. One night I walked into the kitchen and told my mom that I was taking a few weeks off from partying. I needed it.

She was like, "Good. I'm proud of you."

As for alcohol, I've always gone through stages of more and less. I first started drinking when I was about thirteen. I'd have a beer or something every now and then. No, now that I think about it, when I was even younger, we'd go for Chinese food and I'd get a sake. I'd have a little bit. But I had to sneak it when I was older. Then one day my mom said she had no problem with us drinking. She didn't approve, but she didn't want her children lying about it.

By the time I was sixteen, she knew I was drinking and had friends who drank and she didn't want me driving or getting in a car with anyone who had been drinking. I tried to honor that, and I'm fortunate to have survived the few times I didn't pay more attention to the promise I made her.

Did I abuse drugs and alcohol? I didn't think so.

Of course, in retrospect, I fucked up. I thought I could handle everything I was doing, but then, as these stories go, it ended up handling me.

Aimee: I've just always been antidrugs. I don't want to end up an addict. I've lived with the fear I might have that so-called addict gene, whatever the fuck that is. I imagine it's like one sip or one snort and you trigger a reaction that changes you forever. No thanks. With my family history, why risk it? It's like playing Russian roulette.

That's why I probably never needed a lecture. I knew about

drugs and alcohol before I ever got the talk from my mother. Like her, I hate the taste of alcohol. I don't have a tolerance for it. I've never smoked a joint in my entire life. Could that get me kicked out of the Osbournes? I don't know. That's a thought.

Kelly: I'm not really a drinker, but I got drunk on my seventeenth birthday. We were on holiday in Hawaii, having this cool beach party. I had one shot of vodka and that's all it took. I was drunk. I'd never been drunk before in my life. Oh, I'd done stuff where I'd had one Bacardi Breezer and pretended to be drunk, but this was different. This time, though, I was fucking drunk. One fucking shot. That's all I had and I was out of my head. It was great for about two minutes, then I suddenly didn't feel well. I remember saying, "Jack, what do I do? What do I do?"

So, he took me back to the hotel room. I didn't say anything to anyone because I was trying to figure out what I was feeling. It was weird. Then I woke up the next morning really sick. I didn't like the feeling one bit. That's why I'm more of a social drinker. One drink every few months, and I'm fine.

Sharon: My kids are underage and they drink. Does that make me happy? No. Does that make me different than most other mothers of teenagers? No. They get sick, and then they feel like idiots. But there's only so much you can say, only so many times you can say, "Don't drink. Don't let your guard down." Ultimately, as Ozzy says, they're going to do it. I just want to know when they're doing it. Which is easier than it seems, because no one knows you like your mother. I can tell by their faces exactly what they've been doing.

I believe more in advice than rules. I explain the outcomes and consequences of their actions. I want them to be educated and aware of the effects of what they put into their body, to know what could happen to them if they use Ecstasy or acid. I want them to know they can go to jail if they use cocaine and to understand that drugs can kill them. I want them to know there's new research sugesting use of some drugs might actually cause diseases like MS or Parkinson's. If they're well informed, they can make good decisions—or so I hope.

We've been just as open about sex. When they were little, they wanted to know why Jack had a willy and the girls didn't. They also wanted to know where babies came from. My mother, quite seriously, told me that the stork had dropped me down the chimney. That's as much information as I got from my parents. I never said that to my kids. I told them where they came from, that Mom and Dad loved each other, and we wanted to have babies we could love as much as we did each other.

Ozzy: I have strong opinions about drinking, drugs, and sex. They nearly fucking killed me. I don't know of a better example for my kids than my fucked-up past. But then I think back to when I caught my father with a cigarette in his mouth and he said, "Ozzy, if I ever catch you smoking, I'll break your fucking arm." And, of course, I spent the next thirty fucking years smoking like a chimney. Kids always do the opposite of whatever parents tell them. That's a fact of fucking life, man.

My kids know how I feel about drugs and booze. Let me put it this way: There's a good possibility one of my children could be an alcoholic-addict if they would just take a drink or smoke a joint. I know my son has a bit of pot and a bit of booze, but I had no idea he could be an addict. When I took my first alcoholic drink, I loved the effect it had on me. It put me in another world. I didn't drink for the taste. I drank to get fucked-up. I knew instantaneously it was my fucking medicine. I needed it to survive. I don't see my kids desperate to, you know, drink a vat of fucking vodka or snort a bucket of coke the way I did. Now in my old age, having gone in and out of rehab, I believe in moderation. Everything in fucking moderation— booze, drugs, sex, and war. I wish the kids wouldn't do anything, but they're kids.

But, given our track record, there's no way they can pull anything over on us. We pretty well always know what they're up to.

Sharon and I know the tricks. For instance, the other night Jack comes in and he's all bubbly and sparkly. Sharon asks him, "How much have you drunk tonight?"

He says, "Mom, I've had nothing to drink, I swear."

She says, "Okay," and lets him carry on for five minutes. Then she says, "Okay, Jack, how many beers have you had tonight?"

He says, "Okay, Mom, two beers."

She lets him go on talking and then says, "Are you sure it's two beers?"

He goes, "Okay, it's been four beers and one vodka."

The next time it's five beers and one vodka and she tells him, "Okay, go to bed."

Trying to pull one over on Sharon is fucking stupid. We've been there and done it ourselves way too many times. Not that Jack doesn't try. The other day he tried throwing statistics at me, telling me that since 80 percent of the U.S. population has smoked pot, it must be okay. So I say to him, "Eighty percent of the population probably poke themselves in the eye every Wednesday morning. You planning on fucking doing that, also?"

I've also done my best to be honest about the facts of life. I put the facts straight out there. I tell the kids, "In my day, everyone got fucked. You got it as often as you wanted. There were even two chicks that made plaster casts of rock stars' dicks and put them on their bookshelves. There was also the chick in Texas who was famous for giving everyone head before they went onstage. You can't even begin to fathom the fucked-up crap that went on." At the end of the day, though, I got sick and tired of the nameless, faceless creatures. Plus, these days if you fuck around, you have to consider the double whammy. Not only do you have to worry about the clap, now there's AIDS. You don't want to fuck around with that. You can die from that shit. Period.

Honestly, the more I think about it, the less I know what to tell my kids. Maybe it's best to fucking whack off until you fall in love.

Talk about safe sex. It doesn't get any safer than whacking off.

𝕵𝖆𝖈𝖐: At eight, I discovered girls were more than my sisters and their friends. Actually, I was with one of my sister Aimee's friends when she turned and kissed me. I kissed her back. Nothing as fun, exciting, or pleasurable had ever happened to me.

Others followed. And not just with my sister's girlfriends. I've always had this way with the ladies. For the record, I lost my virginity when I was fourteen. It's nobody's fucking business, really. It wasn't magical or anything. I met a girl and it happened. I wish it had been more magical. Fireworks and all that shit.

But I wasn't all that impressed by the experience. It wasn't anything to e-mail home about. It was what it was.

There are more stories, but I won't tell them. As soon as I hit my teens, my mom lectured me about not being one of those guys who talk about the girls I've been with. She's totally right. I'd hate it if someone turned the tables on me. I know what it's like to be the focus of gossip. It's usually fucked-up.

Suffice it to say teenage sex is real and happening in Hollywood. Sex is so casual it's ridiculous. On any given day, I'll call up a buddy and ask what he did the night before and he'll nonchalantly mumble, "Well, you know, went to a club, got fucked-up, and went home with this chick." It's very hollow. It's no longer about love-making. It's become the act of fucking. It's not a big deal anymore.

Is that a good thing? No. It's emotionally polluted. I've never been in love, the adult, deep, meaningful kind of love. I'm looking forward to it. I can see myself in a relationship like that, marrying someday and having children. But at seventeen or eighteen years old, people my age aren't thinking about a deep experience. It's more about pleasure, excitement, the thrill of doing it, and the satisfaction of knowing you've done it. Don't get me wrong. I'm merely reporting on the situation. I'd like to be in love. But I'm neither a saint nor a hypocrite. If I'm at a club, meet a girl, and she wants to come back to my house and do the deed, am I supposed to say, "No thanks, I really need to be in love"? No, I don't think Jack Osbourne says that.

Sharon: I've spent a lot of time speaking to my kids about safe sex. I'm emphatic about drilling it into their heads. It's normal when the kids go out for me to say, "Have fun. Don't drink and drive. And wear a condom. Or make sure the sex is safe." Beyond that, I've told my girls to keep their dignity when it comes to sex. I don't want them to have their first sexual experience in the back of a car. That's horrible. I don't know any girl who has enjoyed her first sexual experience. They always do it because they're afraid they'll lose their guy if they don't. It's done more out of fear than anything else. They're scared they'll lose him to another girl.

I've tried to make my girls understand that there's a huge difference between infatuation and love, especially puppy love. Those kinds of feelings only last for such a fleeting moment, and once you give yourself to that sort of person, you've squandered a priceless gift. It's over in about two minutes. There are no fireworks. The experience means absolutely nothing. Inevitably, people talk about you and most of the time he won't talk to you. I've really tried to let my girls know that the most precious thing they can ever give any man is their body.

As for my son . . . I'm tough but realistic. I tell him to treat his girlfriends with dignity and respect. I hate it when you get a bunch of guys together and they're like, "Oh, she gave me head," or "I fucked her up the ass." I don't like that. If you've been with someone, you don't get brownie points by talking about it. I've always told Jack, "Just keep your mouth shut. Don't brag or humiliate the girl by telling your friends. That's not cool." The one thing I want my kids to learn is respect—respect yourself, respect your body, respect other people.

Something else I try to explain to them is that the hardest thing in the world, at least where sex is concerned, is to fight the urge to get caught up in the moment. Unfortunately, probably just about everyone has woken up on one morning of their lives, rolled over, and said, "Oh my God, did I really fuck him or her?" I don't think it happened too many times to me, but I had the unfortunate experience of waking up, looking next to me, and thinking, Oh my God, who is he? Where am I? What did I do? We all do things we regret. But if we're lucky, we learn by our mistakes.

The other thing I tell my kids is to bring everybody home. Do what you want, but do it at home. I want them here. It's their home, too. Yeah, I have my rules, and if I had my way the phone wouldn't ring at three in the morning, but I like knowing where they are. And I want to meet their friends.

Jack: They are really kind of modern parents. They are not like, "Heaven forbid, having a girl in your room!"

Kelly: When I don't have a boyfriend, my whole life revolves around the family. But when I have a boyfriend, I'll go places and do things with him. My mom tends to get upset and complain that I'm not around much. In fact, my parents seem to hate everyone I date. Like my first boyfriend. He was in a band in L.A. and had just gotten signed to a big record company. I was sixteen and he was eighteen. I really liked him. Everything was going great, then one day he just never called again. I thought it was something I'd said or done. I didn't really know what was happening. That really hurt me. I was crushed. In a way, though, I owe him some thanks. He made me a lot smarter.

Then there was the singer for another band.

Sharon: Piece of shit.

Ozzy: He was okay.

Jack: Hated him.

Kelly: We met backstage at Ozzfest in the summer of 2002. We talked and joked and traded numbers. When Ozzfest came to L.A. we went drinking and dancing on our first date at some club, and got along really well. I liked the music his band played, and like so many girls I was a sucker for a lead singer. Then word about us leaked out—*People* magazine even ran pictures of us.

Jack really didn't like him, which bothered me. And he didn't like my brother, either—so I was kind of in the middle. It all ended anyway on Valentine's Day 2003 when he broke up with me. Something about how he didn't feel like it was a good time for him to have a girlfriend.

A while after we broke up he called and said I should apologize to him. Excuse me? I was like, "You know what, I'm sorry if I ever hurt you. 'K? You happy now? 'Bye."

Aimee: Serious? Well, yes—I had my first boyfriend when I was seventeen, and the guy was twenty-two. We clicked, I think, because we had a lot in common. He's a good person and he's had some serious family problems. And he was trying to establish himself as a manager. We're still great friends and talk every day. That's about it—oh, he's someone I hope to be friends with always.

Kelly: My mom would probably meet more of my friends if my dad didn't walk around the house in his underwear. A few months ago, he'd just woken up from a nap or something and was heading toward the kitchen and his balls were hanging out. I was like, "Oh my God, there's something definitely not right with this picture."

She thinks it's cute.

Jack: This isn't the kind of house where you just stop by with your friends for a sandwich and a beer. One afternoon I had a friend over and Mom strolled into the kitchen. She lifted up her skirt and shouted, "Do you think I'm sexy?"

I'm standing there, watching all this, thinking, Oh my God. That's my mother. I think I might die right now. I'm convinced that someday I'll bring a girlfriend home and I'll hear my mom ask, "Hello. How's Jack's willy treating you?"

XV

Breakin' All the Rules
(A Valentine to Sharon Arden Osbourne)

───── ✦ ─────

Who else but Sharon Osbourne would throw a fellow
manager down a flight of stairs or pull the plug on a
show by the hottest band [Limp Bizkit] in the land?
In a business long dominated by men, Osbourne's
no-nonsense style is as legendary as her business
acumen. . . .

—*BILLBOARD*, DECEMBER 2, 2000

Ozzy: This is a typical "Ozzy puts his foot in his mouth" story. We were at some party and Sharon was trying to sing. It came out as this huge sound—it sounded like a wildebeest in heat.

I said, "What really amazes me about you is you've been doing this show business thing all your life, and bears have to commit suicide when you start singing . . . you really can't sing!" She looked me straight in the eye and goes, "Shit. You've been in the music business all *your* life, and you don't understand a contract from the back of a two-cent stamp. . . ."

Oh yeah, I thought, good one. Thank you. I mean, everything I've done since Sabbath—all the albums, the tours, the collaborations, the TV—I cannot take credit for. Because, as they say, behind every great man is a great woman. I feel like I got the greatest one on the face of this earth.

Sharon: In the mid-nineties all these music festival tours started to come up, and Lollapalooza was the one that was the cutting-edge, hip festival to be on. They had a huge cross section of artists—Living Colour, Jane's Addiction, Body Count, Pavement, Hole, Sonic Youth. I wanted Ozzy to be on it—I mean, every other fucker was on it! But they were like, "No way, no way. It doesn't fit."

Lollapalooza's booking was influenced by a lot of journalists who are just musical snobs. Ozzy's music is working-class music, he's a working-class hero. Of course, he didn't fit for their hip, cutting-edge, tight-ass mentality.

Now, you've got to remember that back in the eighties we did Monsters of Rock—this huge stadium tour with Van Halen, Metallica, and the Scorpions, and whomever. That was meant to be a vehicle for Ozzy. But I had to take it into stadiums, and at that time Ozzy wasn't popular enough to headline a stadium so it needed Van Halen. And their manager took control and I had to make a choice—and Van Halen got the headline slot.

Lollapalooza saying no gave me the push to finally do it. I was so pissed off with their attitude I just said, "Well, all right. I'll do my own."

Jack: I remember them saying, "Oh, he's not relevant. Who wants to go see Ozzy?" wallowing in their ignorance. Mom was like, "Well, fuck you. I'm going to do my own tour. Then I'll show you."

That first year in '96 we did two. Like a test. The first show was in Phoenix, and fucking just sold out in like two seconds. Then Mom and Dad both realized, "Wow, this could actually work!"

Kelly: It was still just an experiment. No one thought that it was going to be a big thing and then it ended up being huge. It sold out shows. Everyone had such a good time. It got amazing reviews. And because of that first year Ozzfest got budgeted for a whole tour the next year. And every year it gets bigger and bigger.

Sharon: I was never of the mentality of creating something where we're going to plant trees and I'm going to give you free food and I'm going to have twenty singing monks and then you're going to see a rock band. That's not what I do. I'm more basic. I'm not putting that down, but that's not what I do. I'm not a "save the world" person. I'm a caring person, but I try and give the public what they want.

It's a simple formula: two stages, an area for food and drinks and other stuff called Village of the Damned. Fourteen hours of music at a great ticket price, which we keep down because we have to pay all the main stage bands but Ozzy—who could drop bands X, Y, and Z and just keep it all to himself and probably comes out with the least money of anybody on the festival.

Kelly: Ozzfest is for the music. That's why my dad will take less money so that they'll give more money to another band to be on it. So the fans get to see more music. And so they can have better catering and food supplies and medical staff on the premises.

Sharon: Ozzfest originally, and still is, something where we give a chance for new music to be heard with a large audience and where it's all for harder-edge music.

Jack: It's definitely a gateway for a lot of bands to get their foot in the door. Ozzfest has done that for so many—Disturbed, Chevelle, Limp Bizkit, believe it or not. Incubus, Drowning Pool . . .

Kelly: . . . Slipknot, P.O.D., Queens of the Stone Age. Every major rock band that you can think of today has been on Ozzfest. System of a Down, Linkin Park, Tool, Rob Zombie, Marilyn Manson . . .

Jack: We're still good friends with all of them. This is Disturbed's third year on the tour. Chevelle's second. A lot of them are really humble to the fact that the tour that they were on before they actually got big was Ozzfest.

Kelly: I was ten when I first met Jonathan Davis in Korn. It was so weird. They were on tour with my dad, then suddenly they were like the hugest thing ever.

Jack: So eight years later and it's still going strong. In '97 we did fifteen dates. Then from '98 until now, we've been doing thirty to thirty-two dates a year.

Aimee: In the nineties, Ozzfest was like my summer camp every year. Being with friends and having fun with all the bands and getting to know everyone and traveling around.

I definitely think my mom's broken all the rules and proven everybody wrong. She's a role model for myself and a lot of other people. People tell me all the time, "Oh, we love your mom! She's so brave! She's this and that." I think that's what every great businessman or woman aspires to do in many ways. Any type of business—not just the music industry.

Kelly: I think she's a role model for any woman—or any man.

Jack: She's actually getting recognized as a strong leader in the music industry. Before it was, you know, "She's a woman trying to play in a man's game." And there still is that bigotry.

Sharon: I don't feel any sexism—not now. I'm at the stage where the guys that are up-and-coming in the business now could never, ever have the years of knowledge and experience that I have had.

Looking back at the way I've behaved and conducted myself in certain situations, it was because I had to fight harder than the guy next to me to even get heard, let alone accepted—trying to get accepted and *then* trying to earn your respect. I learned that you can't buy respect. You have to earn it. It's something that comes over time.

I just do my thing. I try not to think about it.

Jack: My mom has a hard time with no. If people don't listen to her she makes them listen. You know, for a long time my mom was like—still kind of is—like ugly-feared because she was known to go into someone's office and trash it. Even though she despised her father for the longest time, she learned a lot of things from him.

Like she knows how to make an entrance and a departure. My mom always has to have the last word on things and it's always the finishing word. You can't top it. Like when she stopped being the Smashing Pumpkins' manager, her line in the press release was "I've resigned from Smashing Pumpkins management due to medical conditions. Billy Corgan makes me sick."

Sharon: I actually stole it from Ozzy—he had used it before. I just kind of twisted it into what was going on with myself and Billy. But I've managed so many other acts, as well: Lita Ford, Gary Moore, London Quireboys. I can honestly say that I've never passed on working with a great band. I haven't passed on any Beatles. But I have made terrible fuckups business-wise. Huge.

You know what's best? To be able to work in a field that you have a passion for and then get a great check at the end of the year. It's like, "*Yes!* This is good!"

Kelly: I didn't look at her as like, "Oh my God! My mother is a top businesswoman and she thinks amazing in her views on things and she's so creative and she did this." I just see her as my mom.

She's actually managing me now, you know. Sometimes it's very hard. When I don't want to do something, she gets really upset and so do I. Still, in my situation I would say it's a good thing because no one knows me better than she does. She knows what I'm capable of doing and what I'm not capable of doing.

Aimee: Absolutely not. I would never jeopardize my mother-daughter relationship for a business deal or a disagreement over a photo shoot or this or that. Not only because we are very different and we don't necessarily agree all the time, but because I've seen the amount of stress that could just so easily be avoided. I've seen it affect Kelly's relationship with her. I've seen it reflected in my father's relationship with her.

Ozzy: There's not a shadow of a doubt in my mind that I wouldn't be sitting today in a house in Malibu—that I own—if it weren't for my wife Sharon. She kicked my ass around the country, she got my life and my shit together.

Put it this way: One day we were driving down the M-1 motorway in London, she was speeding, and this cop stops the car and says to Sharon, "Can I see your license?"

She says, "Yeah, it's on the backseat. . . ."

It's raining.

"Will you get out of the car and get it?"

"Fuck you—I'm not getting out of the car to get it. Do you think I'm fucking mad?"

I'm going, "Whooooaaaa!" and he says, "I beg your pardon?"

"Fuck off—I happen to be having a very bad period and I'm not in the mood."

Pause.

"No trouble, ma'am. Please drive on."

The marriage contract can be the most heaviest contract you are probably signing in your life.

XVI

You're No Different

STOMACH BANDING APPROVED IN THE U.S.
Despite its high rate of problems, the stomach band
device for the management of obesity has been
given regulatory approval for use in the U.S. The
device is an inflatable tube that surrounds the upper
stomach producing a small pouch . . . while it can be
effective, side effects are common. Ninety percent
reported side effects including nausea, vomiting,
heartburn, or abdominal pain. . . .

—U.S. FOOD AND DRUG ADMINISTRATION, 2001

Ozzy: When I first knew Sharon we would bang everywhere you could fucking think. We would do it in the street. It was sexy and it was fucking nuts. I couldn't get enough of her.

As a matter of taste, I actually like a woman to have a little heft and not look like a fucking cadaver like the models today. I love my wife whether she's fat, thin, fucking square, round, fucking oblong shape. She's the greatest lover I've ever had. She's the greatest lover, period. I don't think people know that.

My wife never knew whether she should be fat or thin. It didn't matter to me. At fucking fifty it's a bit late in the fucking day to want to become slim, young, and attractive. But yet, I get it, because she had a mother's diet. She ate the food the kids ate.

But no one asked what I thought. She just decided to do it.

Sharon: There comes a point when a woman has taken care of her husband, raised the children, fed the dog, and finally decides it's time to get her own ass in shape. That was the fall of 1999. I was about to have a meeting with a record executive whose office was done in hip minimalist decor. I was in the reception area looking through magazines, and I had somehow wedged my fat ass—at the time I weighed around 225 pounds—into one of the narrow little chairs that no doubt cost a fortune. When the time came for me to get up and go into the guy's office, my ass was stuck. His assistant had to pull me up.

I was forty-seven, a successful businesswoman at the top. Ozzy's records sold in the millions, we'd launched Ozzfest, and he was on shows like *Sesame Street* and *South Park*. The kids were doing their thing. Everyone was doing well except for me. Getting stuck in that fucking chair was the turning point.

My whole life I've been addicted to food. Whenever I was stressed, I'd eat—sandwiches, cakes, everything. I don't like fancy restaurants. I'm a connoisseur of junk. When Ozzy and I were younger, we'd wander around New York and try all the hot dogs. I

was also a professional dieter. I'd lost weight over the years, sometimes fifty pounds, sometimes seventy-five.

When I was skinny in the eighties guys hit on me all the time.
They'd go out of their way to make conversation with me. They'd
offer to put my bags in the overhead compartment on planes. When
I weighed 107 pounds, they'd be fighting over each other to help
me at the baggage claim. They'd ask to share a taxi.

But once I got a hundred pounds heavier, I'd be dragging my
suitcase across the airport, sweating, my dress sticking to me, and
nobody would lift a finger. I enjoyed the attention of being skinny,
but it was bittersweet. I'd think to myself, You fucking jerks. When
I'm fat, you don't give me the time of day.

It's no fun to be fat. In fact, it's terrible. You lie in bed, especially in the summer, and you're uncomfortable. I'd wake up in the
morning and my back would be killing me. When you're as over-
weight as I was, your legs rub together at the top. I also had this
belly that hung over and I'd get sores underneath it. On top of that,
I perspired more and my feet would spread, which meant that I
needed bigger shoes. And forget about heels; there was no way I
could wear them.

Once in Minneapolis, a girl tapped me on the shoulder and
asked if I was Ozzy's mother. I went crazy at her. In the midst of my
rage, I knew I shouldn't be screaming at her, but I was trying to
cover up my own embarrassment.

Someone I knew was detoxing at an L.A. hospital. While visiting
him, I heard some people talking about a new procedure that was
being developed, a gastric bypass operation. I won't even describe
it other than to say I quickly learned that it was still highly experi-
mental. The doctor performing it was trying to get the procedure
passed by the Food and Drug Administration. He needed some
guinea pigs and he impressed me when we spoke. Because I fell
into the correct weight and age bracket, I was chosen to be one of
forty guinea pigs, as well as the first woman, to undergo the
surgery.

After my medical exam, a nurse asked if I minded saying a few words on video, confirming that I understood the different risks associated with the surgery. Like so many women, I was desperate to be skinny. That's all I wanted. Risks? Fuck 'em. The next thing I knew they escorted me into a tiny white room, where I stood in front of a camera. The nurse handed me a piece of paper and asked me to read the printed statement. I looked at the paper and started reading the words.

But when I heard myself read, "I realize that people can die from this operation, and I realize and accept the risks," I looked up nervous and uncertain at the nurse, who smiled and nodded reassuringly. When I got to the end, she asked me to re-read the death part. "Just to make sure I have you on tape," she said.

That's when I put on the brakes. I made up some excuse, drove home, and told my husband everything. He went mad.

𝕺zzy: I was pissed off. I'm her husband, she's my wife, and if I was going to have something done as drastic as that, I'd say, "Do you think it's a good idea?"

𝕶elly: After I found out what she nearly did, I didn't talk to her for two weeks. It was one of the most disgusting things I'd ever heard in my life. Imagine going on videotape and saying, "Please try to make me skinny. By the way, it's okay if I die in the process. Tell my family I just wanted to lose weight." I was so glad she realized the stupidity of what she was doing before it was too late.

𝕾haron: I decided not to have the surgery, but I was still set on losing weight and changing the way I looked. There had to be another, safer way.

My doctor found out about a physician who was doing gastric banding, an operation that involved placing a tiny band around the entrance to the stomach and making it smaller so you can't eat so much. You get full sooner. It was a new operation, noninvasive. Much less of an ordeal than the one I'd been considering. Nothing cut or removed. If you don't lose enough weight, they can go back in and tighten the band. If you lose too much, they can loosen it so you can eat more.

It sounded safe to me, a cure for a problem I'd had all my life. Without telling Ozzy, who would've gone crazy with worry, I had it done. The procedure was simple—four little incisions—and within a few hours, I was fine. I went home the same day, broke the news to the family, and then spent the next four days in bed. Then, before I knew it, I was bursting with amazing energy. I still ate all the shit food I loved, like McDonald's. The difference was I could only eat little bits of all the junk.

In less than ten months I had lost almost one hundred pounds. I felt like it was the best thing I'd ever done for myself.

Ozzy: I still get mad thinking about the fucking balls Sharon had, going in and having a fucking band wrapped around her stomach without telling me. It bothered me. Especially after the other close call. Something could've happened. If she'd died, I would've killed her.

Kelly: I think it was one of the most selfish things my mom has done. She didn't realize how scared we got when we heard she went into surgery. My mom still thinks of herself as a fat person. Maybe she has phantom fat like people think they still have an arm when they don't.

Sharon: I decided to have plastic surgery, something I never thought I'd ever do. My God, if you would've told me that one day I'd have my fucking legs lifted. But when you're five foot two, hiding behind 225 pounds, *then* lose half of your weight, things hang and sag. I had my legs lifted, my ass lifted, my face lifted . . . everything lifted. Whatever was left I had liposuctioned. By the time I got out of the hospital, I was feeling the way I always dreamed of feeling. I didn't become gorgeous, but I felt comfortable with myself.

Jack: My mom's decision to get all that plastic surgery kind of pissed me off. I was convinced that she'd become her own joke.

But the more I thought about it, I realized that if it made her happy, it made me happy. I could tell that she felt more confident every day she got up and checked herself on the scale. She became this sexy mom. She was one of *People* magazine's fifty most beautiful people!

Kelly: Don't even get me started on that crap. I loved my mom when she was fat. She was so cuddly. After she lost all that weight, I'd always get something bony digging in me whenever we cuddled.

Dude, in high school I was the fat kid. *I* didn't think of myself like that, but I was always the one that all the guys wanted to be friends with because I was more like a boy and none of them ever liked me that way. I didn't care that I wasn't skinny and blonde. Well, I was blonde but I never got wrapped into that.

I'm not going to starve myself or work out. I'm not going to smoke cigarettes to keep myself from eating like so many girls in L.A. do. I'm not going to take diet pills. I don't even count calories.

I'm not fat. I don't see myself as being fat. I'm five foot two and weigh around 120 pounds. I'm fucking normal. Girls come up to me and tell me that I've made them feel better about themselves. A while ago, one girl wrote to tell me that I helped give her the confidence to stop being bulimic.

Fuck the whole weight thing. If you feel good, leave it. Don't push the issue.

Aimee: I know it's a sickness. I think I definitely did. Especially growing up in Los Angeles and going to high school here. Everyone has to be skinny. I thought it was just me who had a weight problem a little bit. But it was the pressure of our culture, more than an eating disorder. I just tried to eat healthy, and slowly but surely got comfortable with that.

I would say to girls that you can choose a life of battling with yourself, battling with how you should look, or you can choose acceptance and you can choose being healthy and confident. The more you battle yourself to look perfect, the more you'll make yourself miserable.

I'm just not impressed by pop culture's definition of beauty. There's a beauty to people who are truthful and at peace within themselves. Cate Blanchett is beautiful to me. She seems so at peace with herself and with who she is. She's so talented.

Ozzy: I think the Osbourne family is beautiful. I really fucking do.

Sharon: I've only had two addictions in my whole life—eating and shopping. Shopping just makes me feel good. It's my drug. I've always adored beautiful things.

Aimee: My mom used to drag me along to go shopping, and I'd just sit there and cry, wondering, Why am I here? This is so boring. I can't stand this. I like to shop, but I don't feel happy when I spend a lot of money. I feel guilty. My mom is a compulsive spender. If I go to a store and I see a shirt I like, I buy my favorite color. My mom will buy every color.

Ozzy: All that shopping of hers has cultured me in a lot of ways. For instance, a few months ago she spent $50,000 on a fucking vase. I still can't see paying $50,000 for a fucking vase. It's now worth something like $80,000. I mean, I'm willing to learn a thing or two. I just hope I don't fucking stumble into the damn thing and smash it.

Still, I can't say that everything Sharon buys makes fucking sense. One afternoon she wakes me up and says, "I just bought this table and mirror for ten thousand dollars." I thought the thing would be covered in gold. Then a couple of guys deliver it to the house and it looked like something that had been left outside a building site for about twenty years. The next thing I know, she's telling me how it's three hundred years old and how incredible it is that all these pieces had stayed together for all these years.

I hate fucking antiques.

𝕾𝖍𝖆𝖗𝖔𝖓: In 2001, we bought this incredible Mediterranean home in Beverly Hills for $4.5 million. Ozzfest was one of the most successful summer rock tours in the business. And it was like, "All right, Ozzy. It's great to keep making records and touring and selling millions of T-shirts, but we've got to go someplace else." I always knew he was the funniest guy ever and also one of the most extraordinary men I've ever met in my life. So I wanted other people en masse to see that.

XVII

Cable Ready

———— ⌁ ————

It started as a great idea, but now it's like the MTV *channel*. They have *game* shows and when you watch three hours of one type of music, you lose your fucking mind. *Headbanger's Ball?* I watched it the other night and had to turn it off.

—Ozzy Osbourne, December 1989

Sharon: I'd been trying to get Ozzy into TV in one shape or form since '93. It was the next stage of his career. Movies can't compete—nothing competes with TV. I'm really from the old school of variety entertainment—if you are an artist you did a bit of everything. I was always kind of an oddball: working with an old-time variety background in the genre of heavy metal.

I was like, "How do I do this? How do I do this?" I'd come up with different ideas and was approached by different companies for the usual, awful sitcom of the aging rock star who tries to settle down. I mean, how many times have we heard that this is being made with Gene Simmons or Michael Des Barres or some other ex-rocker. We were approached by a lot of those types of ideas and thought, Well, get your foot in the door and come up with an idea! But I could never quite convince people to take it to another place. It never worked. I couldn't allow Ozzy to be put into a show that was too cheesy. Or too hokey. Or too lame.

Ozzy and I did the Howard Stern radio show together. Howard told us, "You two have to get on TV. You're hilarious. You should have your own show."

"But what the hell would we do?" I asked.

"I don't know, be yourselves."

Aimee: I remember my mom wanting to do a show since I was thirteen, not necessarily a reality show, but some type of show. We met with people, and for a while it was going to be a scripted type of thing. It always seemed like a big mistake—my dad does not know how to learn lines. Then, finally MTV gave her the deal that she wanted and she took it and ran.

Sharon: MTV called. They wanted us to be part of this show *Cribs*. Stars in their homes. What's it like on the other side of the hedges. So we did *Cribs* and it was well received. In fact, it was the most requested episode they'd ever had.

I'm like, "Jesus. Come on, guys. We've got to do something here." So for almost eighteen months we were going back and forth: "What do we do? Okay, we have something, but what do we do with you?" I said, "Just make a long *Cribs*—that's all you have to do!"

Next came a meeting with MTV executives in L.A. At the time, we were in between houses, living in a rental in Malibu. "You can start the cameras when we move into our new place," I told them. After that, things came together fast. More meetings were held with MTV. I asked the children to attend, and they got more and more involved in the creative discussions. Everything remained very conceptual. I wanted the kids to make up their own minds before signing off. This wasn't something they had to do. Ozzy was off on tour, so he left it all up to me. And I left it up to the kids.

Jack: The show turned into a fucking emotional roller coaster before any camera crews moved into our house. My dad was off on tour, and I was in the studio with Incubus. The show kept getting pushed back because we hadn't moved into our new house yet. The more time I spent thinking about the show, the more freaked-out I got. One night I walked into my parents' room. My mom was in bed. "I don't want to be famous," I told her. She understood, I think. Later, my dad agreed with me. The more he heard about it, the less he wanted any part of this show. Aimee absolutely hated the idea from day one. So that was that.

Aimee: The shit that goes on in my house I think is so embarrassing and so disgusting and wrong, and the idea that millions of people would watch it horrified me.

I really remember I was just adamant from day one that I was not going to have anything to do with this. I just knew that it wasn't for me, knowing the suffering that I had gone through, having people film at that time wouldn't have been right. Me and my mom battled and battled for a year about this. Finally, my dad said, "Just leave her alone. She doesn't want to do it."

I don't like a lot of drama. I don't like a lot of chaos. I was eighteen years old then, trying to figure out what I wanted to do, organize my life and build some kind of a future for myself. Being on a reality TV show about your family, it wouldn't have been the wisest thing for me to do. I don't think that any eighteen-year-old girl wants to be remembered for the rest of her life as being yelled at or yelling at, you know, her family, so I just didn't—I didn't really believe that would benefit my life in a positive way.

Kelly: I remember Aimee sat in the living room with my parents and said, "You're a joke. This is going to ruin our family and destroy me." My mom almost pulled everything right then and there. Then my parents were like, "Look, what do we have to lose?"

Sharon: We had nothing to lose and nothing to live up to. If the show wasn't a hit, who cared? It wasn't like we were actors looking for another gig. We didn't have to worry that no one would give us another show.

Ozzy: Sharon's original idea was brilliant. She has good instincts.

Kelly: We finally moved from Malibu to our new house in Beverly Hills. We were that much closer to the show becoming reality because we'd agreed that MTV could shoot us in our new place for three weeks, starting in October 2001.

Sharon: Then the cameras came in. Then the three weeks turned into three months and then six months and then it just kind of went on and on. At first we thought we'd get three or four shows out of three weeks' worth of footage.

Jack: Once the MTV crew showed up at our house, whenever I opened my mouth, I was always thinking, What the fuck am I saying? I don't want to say this. I don't want to sound like this.

After a couple of days, I ignored everything as best I could. Nothing sucks as badly as waking up, kind of opening my eyes for the first time, and suddenly remembering, "Oh Christ, they're in my room. They've been watching me sleep on their secret camera and now there's a camera in my face." My one single rule was, "If you see I'm not awake, stay the fuck out of my room. It will just piss me off."

Ozzy: There were rules. No cameras in the bathroom, number one. No acting—I was just going to be myself. I didn't have to pretend to be Ozzy Osbourne. I am Ozzy Osbourne. I knew what to do.

Jack: I never wanted the cameras around when I was drunk, or when I was high. If I had girls over, they couldn't come around. They would try and I would freak out.

Kelly: I didn't think the world needed to know everything. I hated the way they taped our phone conversations. They didn't tell us they were listening, but you'd hear a click and suddenly the crew would appear with their cameras and mics. That really pissed me off.

My mom tried to change Aimee's mind. She'd say, "Aimee, please."

"No, I'm not doing it."

"Are you sure?"

"I'm not doing it."

On and on.

Aimee: More than once, they put me on tape and I'd tell them, "You guys are wasting your time." I reminded the producer that I'd never signed their agreement.

One afternoon my mom said, "Why are you doing this? They're going to have to edit you out. The show's not going to be successful because you're in prime footage and now they can't use it."

"Mom, I'm sure they'll make do."

It was time to move into my own place.

Sharon: I helped Aimee find an apartment and we decorated it. She was eighteen, and it was time. I still cried.

Aimee: Oh, it was very dramatic. My mom was crying, she didn't want me to leave, and my dad was scared for me. But I loved having my own space—I was so relieved. They're a cluttered mess. I like things neat. It's not like I have obsessive-compulsive urges in the middle of the night to organize my CDs or anything.

My family calls me the head mistress. Do you know what I mean? Do you see why?

I'd still come by the house. I was just so curious to see the humiliation, see exactly what was going to be taped.

"Why are you here? You don't live here" was my welcome back.

"Oh, fuck off . . ." was my reply.

Sharon: Once the taping started, I felt very self-conscious. I felt like I played to the cameras at first. After a few weeks, I got used to the crew and just went about my business.

For the longest time, we just didn't know what to think. At one point, the producers and executives from MTV came to the house and checked out the action. They'd seen the footage. We hadn't. They didn't want us to look at anything until they'd taped everything they needed.

I later found out that all of us would ask different people on the crew how it was turning out. Everyone loved it. They'd say things like, "It's fantastic," "It's incredible." I remember the producers, Greg Johnston and J.T. Taylor telling me they thought this was a breakthrough show. They were especially complimentary about Ozzy. They said he was hysterical, which I'd always known.

Then suddenly my brother, David—whom I had a big falling out with when Ozzy and I were married—called.

Four years ago, he had called to tell me he'd quit working for my father and wanted to get together. I spoke to Ozzy; he advised me to let go of the past and see him. David flew to L.A. and we had dinner at our house. Although the first few hours were strained, we eventually found a comfort zone, and kept in touch. Then my mother had died in 1998. Her funeral was held in London without me. It was sad, but it didn't change my life.

Now my brother was calling about our father: "He wants to see you," he said. "He's starting to suffer from Alzheimer's and is asking for you."

I had fully intended on allowing the MTV crews access to our lives, but this was too emotional. I knew there was no way I could let them tape this.

Ozzy: I was the one that said to Sharon, "Look, when you're dead, you're fucking gone. As much as you dislike what your father's done, when he's gone you can't say 'sorry.' When he's gone you can't say 'I love you.' When he's gone you can't say 'fuck you.' Your father is getting older." I said, "Do the right thing, Sharon. Phone your fucking dad."

So she phoned him. She hadn't spoken to him for twenty years.

Sharon: My brother brought my dad to L.A. a few weeks later. We met in the bar at the Four Seasons Hotel in Beverly Hills, a place my brother selected because my father was familiar with it. The place was empty except for the two of us. My father was in khakis, a blue button-down shirt, and a brown sport coat. His hair was white and thin, and he had a neatly trimmed beard. He looked like a proper English gentleman.

The initial moment proved horribly awkward. Neither of us said a word. We didn't hug or kiss. I said hello quietly. He did the same. He looked so frail. Clearly, he hadn't been doing well.

"You old bastard," I said. "What have you been doing?"

"Can we sit?" he asked.

We talked for the next three hours, until the sky turned dark and the bar filled up. The next day, my dad visited us at the house.

He wanted to see his grandchildren. Talk about weird. I told the kids that they could choose whether or not they wanted to let him into their lives.

Kelly: I told my mom that if she needed him in her life, I'd support her and meet him. I can't ever say "I love you" to him, but I don't think that matters.

Jack: I'm real passive about things, so I was like, "Okay." I had never met him before, so there was nothing that meant anything to me about him. And he just seemed like a weird, goofy old guy.

In his day, he was like the original Suge Knight times ten. I remember hearing that someone fucked with my granddad in the wrong way and he decided—I don't know if he did it himself or had someone do it—to hang some guy over the balcony and give him an earful. Mom was like, "Yeah, Suge Knight's got nothing on him." That's pretty hardcore.

My mom has him back in her life, and they're really close again. I just think it's sad for mom's father, because she just started getting close with him and he doesn't have too many years left.

Aimee: I didn't want to meet him. If he is as sick as my mom says he is, then there is no point. I think the reason he is so sick and suffered so much is because he was so cruel to everyone his entire life. I think that what goes around comes around.

I remember hearing my mom's side of things—that her father was delusional and a very angry person, and that she didn't want us being hurt by him. That he once sued us for everything we had. It concerns me because my mom is so sensitive and she's really protective of her family. I don't want anyone taking advantage of that.

Sharon: My father returned home, and a few weeks later Ozzy and I flew to England on business and helped my brother find my dad a good cardiologist. While we were there, he had a pacemaker inserted in his chest. The surgeon told us his prognosis was great, so Ozzy and I flew home the next day.

My life's usually gut-wrenching chaos, so happy endings seem weird—this situation with my dad seemed that way, for the most part. He recovered and I arranged for both he and my brother to move to L.A. I know so many people who are old and lonely because they've fucked up their relationships with their kids or their parents, and it's sad. At the end of the day, the most important people in your life are your family.

XVIII

Changes

———— ⌇ ————

They argue and aren't formal.
The children are hormonal.
They're altogether normal.
THE OSBOURNE FAMILY!

—*TV GUIDE* COVER, FEBRUARY 23, 2002

Jack: We survived Thanksgiving and Christmas with the cameras following us, and we began to wonder if they'd ever get enough footage. My dad was annoyed by his lack of privacy. He was drinking more and hiding out in his room. Kelly was saying that she wanted to go back to her normal life. I liked the guys in the crew, but I also wanted our privacy back.

A little after Christmas, one of the producers let it slip that they'd edited a rough cut of the first episode. That changed everything. After months of having everything we did recorded on tape, we wanted to see it. We were all like, "Show us! Show us!"

I constantly bugged J.T., one of the main producers. My mom was working her magic on him. He didn't stand a chance. Finally, he handed her a tape and made her swear to watch it by herself and not allow anyone else to see it. He had three concerns: 1) We would hate it and begin behaving self-consciously in front of the cameras; 2) We would hate it and sue to get out of the deal; and 3) We would hate it and kill the entire crew.

My mom laughed, told him not to worry, and gave him her word that, no matter what she thought, she wouldn't cancel her deal with MTV. And she promised not to let anyone see it.

I found the tape. I ran into my room and locked the door. A few friends were over. "Guess was this is?" I said. I played the tape. My friends whooped and laughed and hollered. It was very cool by them.

My reaction? After all the anticipation, it was anticlimactic. I didn't think the show was anything special. But then, it was my fucking family. One of my friends got mad at me for not being more pumped. "Dude, this is so fucking funny," one said.

"Really?"

"I have one word," another friend said.

"What?"

"Ka-ching!"

Kelly: I actually saw it with a whole bunch of people—my parents and the crew—in my dad's TV room. I was like, "So what?" After all the drama, I just didn't care anymore. I didn't think people were going to get it. I thought it was going to disappear without any noise. It wasn't a big deal.

Aimee: My parents got the first tapes, and I watched the first series at their place. When I saw the way they edited it and made my dad look like a clown, I wanted to cry. They made him out to look like this totally incapable human being. I repeated what I'd said before: "They're going to make so much fun of you guys." I hated it.

Kelly: One thing my dad taught me. It doesn't matter if they're laughing at you or they're laughing with you, so long as they're laughing. As long as you know you're a good person, it doesn't matter. My dad had nothing to worry about.

Jack: That's the way my dad acts. I think everyone else's dads are fucked-up, not mine.

Ozzy: I didn't like the show, but I'll tell you what: The editing was fucking genius.

Sharon: I finally saw that first tape and I was pleased and excited. The editing had a certain genius to it. I'd never seen anything quite like it. Despite all the screaming and cursing we did, I think people could see that we honestly loved one another very much. Not only that, but we love to be with one another. That's something not a lot of families with children who are as old as my kids—sixteen, seventeen, and eighteen—can claim. And in many ways, we're the same as everybody else. We have to deal with the same issues and problems, and speak our minds.

Jack: It was kind of funny because . . . well, this is how MTV edited stuff. You know that episode where it shows a girl in my room? That was my friend Jackie. The "next morning" wasn't really the same fucking time. When they asked, "Why was your door locked, Jack?"—that was three weeks later! Then Kelly said I had a girl in the room, which I didn't that day. Plus Jackie had been sleeping on the couch. . . .

Aimee: There were a couple of episodes where I'm mentioned very negatively, that I don't agree with. And I told them that I did not want to be mentioned. I mean, my sister and I don't get along. We're different personalities. I don't want to put her down, but she tends to, not really storytell, but she tends to indulge in dramatics whether they be positive or negative. I was like, "How necessary is this?" Now I will be known as the schizo sister, do you know what I mean? I didn't really care at that point, but it bothered me.

Sharon: When the show debuted on March 5, 2002, the initial rush of having cameras around had long faded. We were all off in our own worlds. Ozzy was out on the road. The kids and I were in L.A., doing different things. Jack was involved with his bands. A few days after that first show, I took Aimee and Kelly to Venice Beach for the afternoon. We were playing in a drum circle, just pounding skins and laughing. Suddenly, a dozen or so people, maybe more, were staring at us. I heard a few of them whisper, "That's them. . . ."

I asked the girls, "Who's here? Who are they talking about?"

They were pointing at us.

"But the show only aired three days ago," Kelly said.

We talked to some of them for a few seconds, but more people started coming. We had to leave.

A few days later, we met Ozzy in New York City. He was oblivious to the impact that show was having until we went for a walk down Madison Avenue. We'd only covered a few blocks when suddenly we heard the wailing of a siren. When we glanced over, we saw that an ambulance had slowed. The driver and his partner were waving. Over the loudspeaker they shouted, "Ozzy! We love you!"

Jack: Until the show aired, the only people who ever talked with me were guys from my dad's shows or regulars at the Rainbow, a Sunset Strip club where I hung out. But suddenly people were gnawing at me on the street. Little kids and grandmas asked for autographs. Things really started getting warped when we went to the Emmy Awards. Brad Pitt strolled up to me just to tell me what he thought of the show.

All I could do was stand there. What the fuck is going on here? That was Brad Pitt, and he came up to me to say he loved the show.

Not long afterward, I was at a club and Britney Spears asked me to come over and say hi. Drew Barrymore came up to me. It was all just totally insane. Not only that, the girls have been completely amazing. Now . . . oh God.

Aimee: I thought I could avoid all the warped, crazy fallout from the show by refusing to appear on the show. The media was fascinated with me. I became "the mystery Osbourne." My phone rang all the time with people asking for interviews. I refused everything. I'd be sitting in a restaurant, and a reporter from some English newspaper would hand me a card and say, "We'd like to do an exclusive with you on why you didn't want to do the show." I always tried to stay polite. I'd always say, "No thank you." But God, it was hard.

Kelly: Literally overnight, millions of people want to know everything about you. You have a publicist. She asks you about interviews. Various reporters want to know what you eat for breakfast, why you dropped out of school, do you do drugs, what makes you cry. Strangers come up to you all day long and say, "Hi, Kelly."

You wonder, Do they know me? Then you remember. You're on TV.

That's instant fame. It's not good or bad. It's just weird.

𝒜imee: "Oh, you're the missing link. You're the missing link!" I got that a lot. I also get, "I have a lot of respect for you for not doing the show." You know, it was never my intention to be like, "I'm not going to do it and be cool." But a lot of people think that. I also get a lot of shit for not doing it, like, "Oh, you think you're better than they are, blah, blah, blah, what's wrong with *you*?"

I just tell them that your question is answered—you just need to watch the show. I mean, it *is* real. There is nothing staged about it. Of course, consciously or subconsciously someone's going to act a certain way when they know that they are being filmed. But for the most part that's pretty much how my family is.

Jack: The critics loved the show, and everyone made such a big deal about our cursing. But in my family, saying "fuck" is no big deal. Now I don't even think about it.

The first time I swore was at a friend's house. He was swearing, and I imitated him. When I mentioned what had happened to my parents, they didn't like it. My mom told me that she preferred I not swear in public. But there are very few words in our language as fun, descriptive, and versatile as "fuck."

Ozzy: After a while, I started to wonder if my pants were unzipped or someone's tits were showing. The magnitude of this fucking thing was totally unexpected. It was an experiment that exploded on us. The only thing I can't understand is how everyone thinks we always go, "Good fucking morning. . . . It's fucking good to see you. . . . Pass me the fucking butter. . . . How the fuck are you?" Maybe we use the F-word a lot on the show, but it's just an expression. I curse, so I can't very well expect my kids not to do the same thing.

Kelly: Why'd the show click with so many people? The dialogue is funny. Especially our use of four-letter words, which is something we've been practicing since as far back as I can remember. Growing up, my mom made us say "poop" instead of "shit." We could say the F-word, though.

Sharon: I think children can say "poop" and it sounds cute. "Shit," on the other hand, sounds a bit cruder. I was definitely shocked by the amount of swearing that we used on the show. The degree to which it made up our vocabulary didn't become apparent to me until I watched a few episodes. Afterward, I just went, "Jesus." I suppose I was immune to it. But when you get down to it, I think that's one of the reasons why kids identified with my kids, and quite possibly why parents enjoyed the way Ozzy and I reacted to the kids. As crude as it sounded, it was completely real. There are things you do in your own home that you don't do in public—or you don't think you do. Swearing is definitely one of them. The average person doesn't sit down at the end of the day and analyze everything they've done and said. You don't go, "My goodness, I said the F-word fifty-seven times today. I'd like to cut down on that by at least fifty percent."

After the show exploded, everyone wanted to know us. The Osbournes were the new flavor of the month. We suddenly got all these requests for talk shows and interviews. It hit us like a blizzard, but I didn't lose my head. I knew exactly why they were calling. The Osbournes were hot.

The best example was *Rolling Stone.* The summer before the show was released I met with the magazine's editor about putting Ozzy on the cover. They told me he was too old. They didn't want old people on the cover. They wanted to put Staind on the cover, saying they were more relevant than Ozzy. I didn't want to belittle them, but they were a faceless band. The editor didn't disagree. He just explained that Ozzy was too old. I was so sick and angry after that lunch meeting.

A year later, who comes asking for Ozzy to be on the cover? But they didn't just want Ozzy, they wanted all of us.

A few years ago, back when we were normal people, I bought some tickets to Elton John's annual Oscar party. The event, one of the major parties following the Academy Awards, benefits AIDS, and I supported the charity. I also thought it would be fun for the children to attend. I got them dressed up and sent them off. But the party was so full, they turned people away, even those with tickets.

Aimee, Kelly, and Jack got to the door and were told that only celebrities could get in. Neither Ozzy nor I was there, though I don't know if that would've helped since we weren't famous in a Hollywood way. When the children realized they were getting the boot, they said, "But we bought tickets."

"You don't get it," the doorman told them. "We're only letting celebrities inside."

Now cut to the present. Not only is the whole family invited to the party, Elton wants us to sit at his table.

The point is, no matter how famous you get, always be yourself. Don't ever change just because you've achieved some level of notoriety. I think that's one of the reasons why so many people related to our show. In a world of phoniness, it was real. And it certainly hasn't done anything to diminish the way Ozzy's fans feel about him. They always knew Ozzy was funny. Now they're sharing the joke with everyone else. Many years ago we released a DVD on him. You could see Ozzy in all various states. He was drunk. He was crying. He was laughing. He was sober. That was the real Ozzy. We never tried to hide him. The popular media simply didn't care about him the way they did once the show came on.

And think: What kind of shocking revelations can the tabloids possibly say about Ozzy that hasn't already been said? It's all old news.

Aimee: My mom won the argument. She got her point across. She might have won the fact that the show became more successful than we all would have thought, but she didn't win the fact that my dad's laughed at every day. Now he's like a laughingstock and known as a stuttering alcoholic. After all his years of hard work and touring, this is how he's being remembered and appreciated.

Jack: That's the thing that kind of pissed me off about the show. They didn't really show my dad for who he really is. They never showed my dad's career, his creative side. You only saw him, like, stumbling around mumbling.

Ozzy: I'm in show business, man. What's the fucking problem?

XIX

A-List

[Networks] package dysfunctional people like the Osbournes, giggle at their coarseness and the crimes, and sink lower for higher ratings.

—BOB DOLE TO BILL CLINTON, *60 MINUTES*,
MAY 4, 2003

Sharon: One day after the show's debut, the telephone rang. It was Fox News host Greta Van Susteren, calling to ask for an interview with Ozzy and me. It impressed me that she made the call herself. We spoke for a few moments, and she seemed so pleasant and down-to-earth that we agreed to be interviewed by her.

She flew out to Los Angeles with her husband and crew. We all instantly hit it off. She was easy to talk to. About three weeks later, she telephoned again. This time she said that there was this annual press event with the president in Washington, D.C., the White House correspondents dinner. She asked us to be her guests, and we instantly accepted.

We flew to Washington.

Ozzy: The whole correspondents press dinner turned weird shortly after we arrived at our hotel in Washington, D.C. It felt like Beatlemania. Everywhere I looked, people were screaming, grabbing, pulling, and holding on to us. Sheer fucking madness. I thought Sharon was going to be trampled. I started to freak out, trying to imagine the fucking security that would be in place once the president arrived. I imagined that we'd be going through metal detectors, undergo a round of body-cavity searches and full-body scans.

But it wasn't anything like that. Even my assistant, Tony, didn't have to bother with security. We all got right through. By the time I got to the red carpet, everything turned into fucking pandemonium. The entire U.S. government appeared to be standing in the receiving line, *and they knew me.*

Sharon: We arrived at the event and we were definitely the oddballs of the night, unless you count the politicians. Everyone seemed to know Ozzy. It reminded me of being at one of Ozzy's concerts. Throughout the evening, we kept meeting famous newspeople, like Wolf Blitzer and the other anchormen and reporters we see every day on TV.

We met the balding guy—Ari Fleischer, the president's press secretary—and we grew excited. Talking to him was a real gas.

One after another, all these important people lined up to meet him and have their picture taken with him—congressmen, Republicans, Democrats, born-again conservatives, you name it. I just kept thinking, This is truly surreal. It can't be happening.

Ozzy did his best to keep it together. Every time he walked past Wolf Blitzer, he'd say, "You're Wolf Blitzer." Finally, Wolf Blitzer replied, "Ozzy, you've said that five times. I know who I am."

Then the president got up and said a few words. "We have actors and actresses here, and we have Ozzy Osbourne!" Everyone cheered when they heard that. All I could think was, Oh my God, he knows his name. I turned to Ozzy and said, "Can you believe it?"

Ozzy: When President Bush mentioned my name, I couldn't believe it. The only time I'd ever been to Washington, D.C., was for a few gigs. To the best of my memory, no president of the United States ever showed up at any of them.

Sharon: The night ended with us back at our hotel, thanking Greta and her husband, and then climbing out of the limo. It was a few minutes after midnight and we were still dressed in our fancy clothes. But it quickly felt as if our car had turned back into a pumpkin and we'd been transformed back into regular ol' Ozzy and Sharon. The next morning I left for London and Ozzy flew home.

I called him from Heathrow the minute the plane touched down. "Wasn't that just amazing?" I asked.

"It was, Sharon," he said. "It was like a dream."

Jack: I was so happy for him. I really was. It was like a dream totally came true. I watched a tape of the event, and I'd never seen anything so weird in all my life. I was like, "The fucking president is talking about my dad." It was cool.

When I saw that, it finally got to me how big the TV show was. I mean, I was always getting told how big it was, but unless you have an outside perspective, then you can't see it. I guess when the president speaks directly to your father . . . this was more than big. This was ridiculous.

Aimee: Amid all the fuss around the MTV show, there were opportunities for lots of other spin-off projects, including a sound track album. Everyone wanted to make a record. My parents knew about my music and hassled me to do a song for it, but I refused. I was like, "I'm not in the show."

Ozzy: She's got the most amazing singing voice you have ever heard. She's got Aimee's style—her own vibe, man. She is so unique, but she don't do anything with it.

Aimee: I play a little bit of piano and I do write. Lyrics, journals—I have books and books of stuff. That's basically how I got through my miserable years. I'd sleep all day and be up all night writing. And I'd be recording demos—all different kinds of music.

But I was not ready. I wasn't going to put myself out there and become part of the Osbourne hysteria right then. I decided I was going to wait until it cools down a little bit.

I mean, my music is something that's very precious to me. It's very personal. I'm truthful and very honest with my lyrics. It's not like the churned-out, pop machine type. I'm very influenced by female singers who have some sort of doom to their voice—Billie Holiday, Ella Fitzgerald. Of course, I also love Kate Bush, Prince, the Beatles, Queen. I like a lot of Missy Elliott's stuff. I think she's a great producer.

I'm not so sure that I would really want whatever label to get their hands on my music and make it marketable and pop culture–friendly, so to speak.

Ozzy: She totally reminds me of myself. But she's worse than I am. She probably overthinks it, you know. Thinks herself into doing nothing.

Aimee: I said, "Papa, why don't you have Kelly sing 'Papa Don't Preach'?" Okay. The next day it was done, and she's all over everything.

Kelly: It wasn't the easiest decision, following my dad into the music business and doing for my first song a cover of a pop classic by Madonna.

Did I want to sing? Was I up to the challenge? Was I any good at all?

"Oh, just do it, Kelly," my mom said.

"Why the fuck not?" Jack said.

What did I have to lose? Nothing.

So I recorded the single and I liked the way it came out. It sounded raw, energetic, and different enough from the original where I didn't have to worry.

To be perfectly honest, I didn't think the single would do anything. I went in, recorded it, no big deal. Then a few days later everyone started saying, "You have to sing at the MTV Music Awards." MTV is genius at the cross promotion of its shows, and the idea took on a momentum of its own and nothing could stop it.

In all honestly, I didn't want to do the awards show. My mom was the real force behind it. As smart as MTV is at creating new projects, my mother is smarter. Somewhere inside her conniving mind was a vision of using the success of the series to launch me into my own career. I think she also wanted to prove a point to all those critics who gave me shit.

Sharon: I wish somebody had blown my brains out on the night of the MTV Music Awards. My nerves were so absolutely shot I wanted to throw up. Sony president Tommy Mottola kept telling me that letting Kelly perform in front of everyone was going to destroy my child: "She's going to need a psychiatrist after this is all done." He convinced me for a while that I'd made a terrible mistake. So many people thought it was just entirely too much pressure to put on a child. But in my gut, I knew she wasn't just going to do fine, she was going to love it.

Getting up in front of that audience that evening took more than just courage. She had to believe in herself. I give her all the credit in the world for doing that. It wasn't your normal audience. The place was packed full of really big-time Hollywood celebrities like Nicole Kidman, Ben Affleck, Eminem, Vin Diesel, Paul Walker, Sarah Michelle Gellar, Jack Black. . . .

𝕶𝖊𝖑𝖑𝖞: I didn't care about the things critics said about me singing at the show. I don't feel I have to prove shit to anyone. I never have.

"Jack, I'm going to piss my pants," I told my brother.

Really, there was no limit to my nervousness. Yes, I knew the lyrics and had only the best people behind me. But how can you prepare for making your performing debut in front of Hollywood's biggest stars and millions of people on live television? I breezed through the rehearsal. But on the day of the show I didn't know what would happen when my turn came. I tried not to think about it. I hid from everyone. As soon as I got to the Shrine Auditorium, I was surrounded by people brushing my hair and doing makeup and fixing my clothes and telling me what to do.

Finally, I snapped.

"Don't fucking touch me, please!"

Everybody backed off and gave me my space. Just before I went on, though, I started freaking out over the huge set of stairs I had to walk down to reach the stage. I was absolutely convinced I'd some-how trip and fall. I stood there for what seemed like eternity and stared at those steps, watching myself fall.

Finally, a producer pointed at me and began the countdown. "Five, four, three, two, and one . . ."

I was like, Fuck it, I'll just run down the fucking stairs.

A moment later, I was on the stage in front of millions of people. I hardly recall anything. No, I remember two things. There was a teenage boy in the front laughing at me, and I wanted to clobber his head with the microphone. I also saw my sister waving her arms and cheering for me. That was really nice. Everything else flew by, and then suddenly it was all over.

Ozzy: I freaked out when I saw Kelly sing "Papa Don't Preach." Put it this way: My first gig was at a fucking fire station clubhouse in Birmingham, in front of three drunk firemen, and I was as nervous as fuck. She did her first gig in front of the entire world. I was shitting myself for her.

Sharon: What a glorious night! I was so happy for Kelly that I couldn't stop crying.

Kelly: Backstage, Eminem and the White Stripes were the first to offer congratulations, and I told everyone giving me hugs and high-fives that I loved them. I was drained, completely drained. Someone asked how I felt. Truthfully, I felt like sobbing. I wanted to sit in a chair and cry.

Of course, they would be tears of joy. I'd pulled off the improbable with flying colors. After I caught my breath, I floated around backstage, partying with the other celebrities and enjoying the feeling that I'd surpassed expectations. At some point, though, I pooped out. Two security guys carried me out to the limo, where I leaned half-asleep against my mother while Jack and Aimee gossiped about the show. At home, my mom and dad tucked me into bed like they did when I was a little kid.

As I drifted off to sleep, it felt like I'd dreamed the whole thing. The next morning, though, as I rehashed the night with my family, I realized it had been a dream come true. Luckily for me, I'd discovered a brand-new passion. I'd unlocked a part of myself I didn't know existed.

Aimee: Everything now revolved around Kelly. She'd always give these interviews and say things like, "My sister is so jealous of me." Or, "I'd be jealous, too, if I was her."

I'd read these articles and just moan. "Oh, please, Kelly. Stop it." There's absolutely no denying that she did a great job. I was just so proud of my little sister. So proud.

Ozzy: There was just too much good shit happening to us so quickly. I mean, I was fifty-three and all of a sudden this fucking television tycoon. Suddenly, the Osbournes are America's favorite family. Which is kind of interesting, to say the least, because we're British.

Then I was asked to perform at Queen Elizabeth's Golden Jubilee Concert at Buckingham Palace in June. Actually, when I first heard about the invitation, I thought Sharon was playing a joke on me.

"Ozzy," she said, "it's for real."

Sharon: It was real, and it was royal. Ozzy was going to be playing alongside such proper rock stars as *Sirs* Paul McCartney and Elton John, Eric Clapton, and Rod Stewart. Good for him, I thought. I was thrilled to see him up among his peers. Others might have been worried, considering his well-known history with bats and doves. Asked about the proper wardrobe and protocol for the event, one of the producer's assistants half-jokingly said, "I think I can guarantee he will be kept away from the queen's corgis."

We'd never done anything like the Queen's Jubilee. There'd been some big tours, but never anything involving the queen. For people like Ozzy and me, being invited to a function at Buckingham Palace is unbelievable. The queen has a home in Windsor—the Windsor Castle—and half of it's open to the public. Because of my perpetual intrigue with the royal family, I used to take the kids there when they were little. I'd walk around the place with my eyes wide open, trying to soak everything up. When Ozzy got invited to perform, all I could think about was that I got to go to Buckingham Palace and walk around without having to follow all those bloody ropes. Which is exactly what I did. I got to see what the place is really like inside. I walked through the garden, pinching myself. Ever since I was a little girl I'd dreamed of strolling through the palace. Every girl in England daydreams about the same thing, and there I was.

Unfortunately, Ozzy and I didn't see too much of each other that day. I was busy hosting the event for VH-1, and he was with all the other artists, rehearsing, visiting, resting, and gearing up for the big performance. Come to think of it, I didn't even get to meet the fucking queen. Ozzy did.

I barely noticed. I was having so much fun. The weather was perfect. Everywhere you turned, people were having street parties and picnics. And it seemed like every time you looked up in the sky, the Royal Air Force was performing flyovers. Incredible music was being played everywhere. The mood was upbeat and the air was stuffed full of joy. Every single person I met was happy.

No one was happier than Ozzy. He was among a select group of rock 'n' roll legends invited to perform at the gig. Brian May opened the show on top of the palace roof with a rendition of "God Save the Queen." Other big names included Brian Wilson, Ray Davies, Eric Clapton, Joe Cocker, Annie Lennox, Phil Collins, and Sir Paul McCartney. Ozzy performed the Sabbath classic "Paranoid."

Ozzy: I didn't want to get tossed in the fucking Tower of London for the rest of my life, so I was on my best behavior for the whole night. At the end, Paul McCartney walked onstage and played some Beatles songs—"All You Need Is Love," "Sgt. Pepper's Lonely Hearts Club Band," and "Hey Jude." You know, I was in heaven. I sang on "Hey Jude."

Getting onstage and singing with Paul fulfilled a lifelong dream for me. In all honesty, it was one of the greatest moments in my life. No fucking joke.

Sharon: Ozzy jumped up and down onstage. He was so excited he couldn't control himself. Then backstage, he hung on every word Paul said to him. It was adorable. Later, I saw him sitting in a chair, quiet, absorbing everything that had happened. I asked how he felt, and he said, "This just doesn't happen to normal people."

Ozzy: I love Paul McCartney. I love John Lennon. I love the Beatles. Most times in my life when I've met someone I've admired, I've ended up disappointed. They turn out to be boring or they're assholes. People probably feel that way about me. After meeting me, they say, "He's not so fucking crazy. He's not killing shit or fucked-up." But Paul McCartney was absolutely great, completely incredible—a really nice dude. I was in heaven when I got to sing with him, and then later I talked to him backstage and he was a gentleman. I was like a typical fucking fan. I told him the Beatles had been very important to me when I was a kid, and he was very cool about it. He exceeded all my expectations.

After singing with Paul McCartney, I walked offstage and thought I must be the luckiest guy in the world. I thought, If I was to drop dead right now, don't anyone fucking feel sorry for me because I had the best life. It's been, you know, rock 'n' roll up and down. If I had to go back and change, I don't think I would. Right now I feel on top of the world!

Jack: Oh, he was freaking. It was like the greatest day of his life.

Aimee: In a way, the experience that night was therapeutic. My dad had come so far in his life, and it had all started when he fell in love with the Beatles—especially Paul McCartney—and decided music would be his ticket out of a miserable life. That dream became real. Not only did he get to meet Paul McCartney, he got onstage and sang with him. He couldn't go back and re-create a less painful childhood. But his love of the Beatles was a good, positive part of his childhood, and I think it allowed him to see he'd made it.

Sharon: Later, we met Prince Charles and his lady friend, Camilla Parker Bowles. Everybody was so gracious. Charles was so nice to Ozzy. He made him feel very comfortable. I was fond of Camilla. In the receiving line, I said, "I think you're fucking great. I admire you."

As much as I loved Diana, I wanted Camilla to know I thought she was amazing. You know she's not beautiful. She's taken so much bad press because of it. And Charles still loves her. Just how many years can someone endure that kind of shit? Ten? Twenty? Thirty? It's not your fault if you fall in love with somebody, even if they're married and have children. I know from firsthand experience. It just happens. You fall in love. There's no explanation. People do stupid things all the time. Sometimes falling in love is one of them.

"You've gotten such a bad rap, and you've never said a word," I told her. "I think you're great."

But I'll tell you who's really great: the two princes, William and Harry. They were wonderful. Not one bit of attitude. Absolutely charming. They knew our names and were so gracious and nice. And they were even better looking in person, which I felt compelled to tell them. They were gorgeous.

"I have got a daughter for you," I told them.

They both laughed.

"Actually, I have a daughter for each of you."

Kelly: Finally, a boyfriend she'd like.

Sharon: I'd love for Kelly to marry one of the princes.

Jack: Kelly's already a princess. Maybe they're related.

XX

Reality

— ·~ —

Fuck Cancer

      —Fan banner at an Ozzy concert, 2002

Ozzy: I remember looking at Sharon on the grounds at Buckingham Palace. She didn't look right.

We were standing there just the two of us. The world seemed absolutely perfect. Nothing but good existed at that moment. Then I had this fucking thought that something bad was on the verge of happening. I whispered, "You know what, Sharon? I don't believe this fucking thing. I mean, everything we've done went quadruple platinum. Not platinum—fucking plutonium."

I was worried. You can't have the good without the bad. Something big and ugly is going to happen. Nothing becomes this successful without coming down with a fucking bang.

I remember saying to her on the grounds of Buckingham Palace, "You know what, as high as you go, you're going to come down the fucking same."

Sharon stared at me and just shook her head.

Sharon: Robert Marcato, one of Kelly's friends from school, worked in our office, and he was going through a hard time. I saw him hanging around the house at night, and he had a worried look in his eyes. About a year or so earlier, his mother, Reagan, a restaurant manager, had been diagnosed with colon cancer. I'd met her through the kids' school. She was a very nice, proud, and extremely private woman. Her prognosis for recovery had been fairly good. After Robert graduated, I gave him a job in the office, which kept him busy and gave him some spending money.

With the show about to start, it was a frantic time in our house. When I learned the reason Robert looked so bothered I arranged to visit his mother. He had been living with her surgeries and her gradual decline for a long time. He was shouldering the weight of all this because his mother had reached the point where the disease made it impossible for her to work, which meant she no longer had any income or health insurance. She was so private, she did not want anyone to know. These were real-life problems.

227

I'm at my best when there are problems to be solved. I brought Ozzy along with me, and we told her not to worry about money. We had plenty of money, enough to share with her and her son. Money can't solve all of life's problems, but it can alleviate some burdens. I joked with her, "No one is better at spending it than me." We would ensure she was as comfortable as possible and receiving the finest care available. The same with Robert. She didn't have to worry.

The kids were all supportive about respecting Robert and his mother's desire for privacy—even after the TV show exploded. Then everything about our lives became public—the family arguments, the cursing, Kelly's tattoo, Jack's pot smoking, Ozzy's shakes, and my fiery temper—going so far as to toss a ham into the neighbor's backyard. Only Robert's situation and my contact with my father were not put out in front of the public.

By late June, Ozzy was in rehearsals for another Ozzfest, which Jack was helping to shape. He planned on periodic visits from Kelly, who was moving to New York for the next three months to write and record her first album. Even Aimee had agreed to take a baby step into the public eye by doing a photo shoot for *Vogue* magazine.

I had only one complaint. My life was so full I literally had to schedule sleep.

Ozzy: I don't know if it was the situation in England, or the fucking stars or anything else around, but I do get these predictions, you know. And I felt that my wife is sick. And so I went for the colonoscopy first. Because Sharon would never go for a fucking exam, if her fucking life depended on it.

Sharon: My husband was after me to schedule a full-scale medical exam, something I hadn't had since my stomach operation three years before. Ozzy obsessed over that. The only thing he thought about as much was his own health. He's a world-class hypochondriac. Ozzy goes for physicals every six months. Ozzy loved the relief he got from hearing his medical tests were okay. He used to joke that he loved being told, "It's pure Bolivian." Now in his fifties, he just wanted to hear, "It's benign."

Ozzy: I'd never had a colonoscopy before. I'd heard about it from Katie Couric on the *Today* show—at fifty, you should get one every year. Sharon, who was turning fifty later in the year, refused to make an appointment for herself.

"I've been fucked in the ass enough times in business," she said.

She hates doctors. She's doctor phobic. She won't even put a fucking vitamin down her throat. I pestered her about the test. She said, "For fuck's sake, Ozzy. Don't ask me again."

I signed up for one and got a good report. God must've given me a liver and kidneys that are made of fucking titanium. A few hours later, he said they had found a small polyp in my colon and I got nervous.

"Is it going to kill me?"

"No, it's benign."

My thoughts returned to Sharon.

Kelly: She wasn't her normal self. My mom would always be very pale and get tired really quickly. Then she'd be a little grumpy and was always getting headaches. Everyone kind of noticed her fading a little bit. My dad noticed it the most and said, "You know, it's time for you to go to the doctor." We thought that she was just working too much.

Jack: I want to say, "Yes, I saw something," but I wasn't even aware. I thought it was just stress—you could tell that my mom was a little worried about something.

Aimee: I knew there was something wrong with my mom. I don't know why I knew it, but I did. I could see it in her face. I would call her doctors and I would try and make her come in. We got into huge fights. She would ask me what was wrong with *me*. I'd say,

"You need to go to the doctor, there's something wrong with you." She'd be like, "I'm fine. But I'm worried about you." We wouldn't talk for weeks. Dad knew something was wrong with her, as well.

Ozzy: I kept bugging her. If Sharon says no to something, you might as well set off a fucking bomb because she ain't going to budge. I might possibly be the only person on the planet who can get her to change her mind. My way is to drive her absolutely mad.

Sharon: I decided to give in and go to the doctor. I made an appointment. Nobody said a word out of fear I'd lose my nerve and cancel. I went to our personal physician, who's gentle and understanding. And familiar. He knew our family—he joins in our family joke in calling Ozzy the world's best patient. I made no attempt at hiding my feelings. "I'm sorry, but I hate fucking doctors."

We started with my medical history, which was good. Any surgeries? Just my stomach band. Eating habits? Shitty—the more a food is battered and fried, the better. Family history? Other than my mother, who died of cancer, none I knew about. Any addictions? I said yes. "Chocolate and shopping."

He began the exam, listening to my heart and lungs and checking my reflexes.

He looked in my eyes and my ears. Then he asked if I was tired.

"I've been tired all my life," I said, laughing.

He asked again.

"I'm always tired," I said.

"Do you get enough sleep?" he asked.

"When I can. There's so little time."

"How many hours a night?"

"Six. Eight. Some days I take a nap."

"And still tired?"

"Always. Just kind of dragging."

He made a notation on my chart and scheduled some tests right away. They did an upper endoscopy, sticking a tube with a camera attached down my throat, and looked inside my stomach. Then they put me out and did a colonoscopy.

When I woke up, my doctor told me they found two small growths. I was so woozy from the anesthesia, I can't recall if they described them as tumors, growths, cysts, polyps. All I knew is they'd found these two things and sent them to be biopsied.

I took the news calmly. I didn't ask any major questions. I did not know what questions to ask. I assumed what I had were like Ozzy's—no big deal—and I left it at that.

He said the results from the lab would not be available for between a week and ten days. I was like, "Okay, fine."

Jack: My mom mentioned going to the doctor and they found some polyps. I was like, "Don't they find polyps all the time?" She was like, "Yeah, I guess." I was like, "Okay."

Sharon: I left the hospital. I'd been told to carry on as normal, and that's just what I did. The schedule at the end of June called for everyone to go to New York, except Ozzy, who had rehearsals in L.A. Kelly was going to start recording her album. Melinda and I were moving her into her own apartment in the Trump Tower. Aimee was doing a shoot with *Harper's Bazaar.* Jack had show-related interviews set up. I was meeting with television executives about hosting my own chat show. Our schedule was crammed full.

Aimee: I visited my friend Dina in New York. She introduced me to one of her friends, who worked at *Harper's Bazaar* magazine, which was doing a story about natural hair. My hair was very long at the time—I didn't color, straighten, or do anything to my hair. When Dina's friend found this out she arranged for me to meet with the editors about participating in the piece. They thought I was perfect, and *then* they found out who I was.

I agreed to the photo shoot because I heard the photographer was to be Francesco Scavullo, who's legendary in the fashion world. I'm such a huge fan of his work. I said I'd be back in June with my mother, who was thrilled when I told her the news.

We checked into the Trump Tower Hotel in midtown Manhattan; my mom took me to my *Harper's* photo shoot at a studio in SoHo. Scavullo was amazing. He met me before I had my hair washed or any makeup, and then he had me sit on a stool while he took pictures. It was all so quiet and sedentary.

A few hours later, all of us were back in the hotel, hanging out in my mom's room and making plans. My mom had phone calls, one after the other, and Kelly and Jack were there, too. At some point my mother came upon the photos from her colonoscopy and held them up so everyone could see.

"Look what's up my ass!"

All of us knew they'd found two growths. We just weren't talking about it.

"It's not funny. That's poison in your body."

She quickly changed the subject. Then everyone went out into the city.

$\mathfrak{Sharon:}$ I went out to dinner with my friend at Sony Music, Michele Anthony. We talked business, gossiped, and celebrated the new deal I'd signed with MTV two weeks earlier. About 9:30 P.M., Michele dropped me back at the hotel. Kiss, kiss. I was exhausted, but as soon as I stepped inside the doorway, Melinda told me to please call the office in L.A. She said Michael in the office had been calling nonstop. "Like every fifteen minutes," she said in her Australian accent.

My assistant Michael answered on the first ring and said the doctor had left a message saying he needed to talk to me as soon as possible.

"I just came back from dinner," I said. "I'll call him in the morning."

"No, his message clearly said he wants to speak to you today."

That's when it first hit me. My stomach sunk to my toes and came back up again. When the doctor asks if you're sitting down and have a glass of water nearby, you know the news is not going to be good. The tests were back, he said, and the polyps were cancerous.

"You have to come back right away. We need to get the cancer out of you."

"I have to have surgery?"

"Yes."

I hung up the phone and looked toward the door—I didn't know what to do.

Jack: I'll never forget that moment. I had finished getting dressed and was about to head out to see my friend Franco and his band The Sexy Magazine when I heard my mother come back from dinner. I went down to her room to say good night before going out.

I walked in and found my mom, Aimee, and Melinda all sitting on the floor, all crying. My mom stared at me with bloodshot eyes and an expression I'd never seen on her before. She looked scared. She didn't look like my mother. I froze. My first thought was something happened to Dad. What happened? What's wrong?

"Nothing," said my mom, who got up, went upstairs with Aimee, and collapsed on her bed.

I asked Melinda. She stared back in silence. People tend to do that a lot around us. They're frightened of saying anything that will get them in trouble or jeopardize their job.

I was freaking out. I didn't know what to do. I went upstairs where my mom and Aimee were on the bed, holding each other and crying. They asked me to call Kelly and tell her to come back to the hotel.

That pissed me off. I was so scared and annoyed I finally screamed at the top of my lungs, "What the fuck is going on?"

My mom snapped out of her crying. She asked if I remembered the tests she had done. "I have colon cancer."

I could've reacted a thousand different ways. But when I'm scared or nervous I tend to crack a joke or say something inappropriate. That's what I did. I was like, "That's a pain in the ass."

My mom reached for me. We hugged very tight. That was so hard. I wanted to be strong. I wanted to cry.

"I'll call Kelly," I said.

I went into my room and pulled myself together. I called Kelly on her cell. She answered on the second ring. I could hear noise in the background. Ordinarily I would ask where she was, who she was with, and that shit. I just said, "Kelly, come home."

"I'm not coming home," she said.

"Come home, Kel."

"Fuck off. I'm not coming. . . . Jack, what is it? I'm at sushi, and I'm not leaving if it's something stupid."

"Kelly, I don't want to tell you on the phone. . . . It's Mom."

"Tell me what!?"

"Mom has cancer."

Kelly screamed and the phone disconnected.

Kelly: I suppose I went into shock. I know I screamed. I don't know how I would've managed if my friend Nicole Richie hadn't been with me. She got me into a car and brought me back to the hotel. I found my mom, Aimee, and Melinda crying together on the bed.

We were a giant ball, everyone hugging one another and crying. My sister kept saying, "I've been waiting for it to happen." My brother wouldn't cry. He was trying to be the man. I was a basket case. I was hysterical. I couldn't stop crying. I have a vague sense of my mom saying her doctor had said she had terminal cancer.

I went straight from hearing the word "cancer" to her funeral and the tears. I couldn't imagine life without my mom. All of us said that thousands of times. It was our nightmare. I held on to my mom and kept saying, "I love you, I love you, I love you," like that would prevent anything from happening to her.

Ozzy: When my Sharon got cancer, I freaked, because she is my brain, you know. I mean, I am totally fucked without her, and she is also totally fucked without me.

I always expected to be the one getting rushed to the hospital. How did I escape the damage of a lifetime of rock 'n' roll excess and not Sharon? This was a cosmic fucking joke. I told her to come home as fast as possible. She had already chartered a jet that night.

After we hung up, she called Tony on another line and asked how I was taking the news. As soon as I clicked off the phone, my head began to spin. I heard "cancer" and immediately went to the worst-case scenario.

Tony came into my room and said Sharon had asked him to get the doctor over to the house to give me a sedative. While we waited, I shared or more like babbled all my feelings for my wife, how Sharon is my world, my support, my lover, my wife, my pillar, my reason for living. I felt powerless and out of control. By the time the doctor arrived, I was in a state of shock. I got some relief when the shot he gave me knocked me on my ass for a couple of hours.

𝕾𝔥𝔞𝔯𝔬𝔫: We left all of our luggage at the hotel with Melinda, who was going to continue setting up Kelly's apartment. Aimee, Kelly, Jack, and I flew back to L.A. The flight on a private jet couldn't go fast enough. The four of us hugged and cried the entire six-hour trip. None of us could sleep. Several times the captain came back and said, "We'll be there soon."

Nothing happened fast enough for me. There was such urgency to everything, from wanting to meet with my doctors to seeing my husband, who was at home worrying himself to death. I looked at my babies, so big and beautiful and frightened. We had it all, and yet the clichés were suddenly true. Money can't buy the things that are most important—love, family, and . . . health.

I felt more scared than at any time in my life. I didn't know a thing about cancer. I drifted off into a semisleep and woke up moments before landing at the tiny Van Nuys Airport. Then I saw the cutest, most loving sight of my whole life. It was Ozzy. All dressed up, waiting for me on the runway, holding my two little dogs, Minnie and Maggie. I saw him and for the first time since getting the news, I felt at peace.

Aimee: My mom and dad were hugging, kissing, and crying. It was so romantic, so loving. And it was frightening. You know you don't have any control over life, you can go at any time, and you have to seize every moment you can.

Sharon: We went to bed and spent the night holding on to each other. We didn't want to let go. Ever since Ozzy and I had gotten together my life had been one long fight to change things. But lying together there in bed I realized the tide had turned. I didn't want anything to change.

If we slept it was in short fits between tears. Ozzy got up first and made coffee. At noon, we drove to Cedars-Sinai Medical Center and entered through the back door, as we'd been told by the hospital's security, in order to avoid any paparazzi that work the hospital beat looking for celebrity tragedy stories.

I liked my surgeon. His manner was matter-of-fact. He explained the diagnosis—two cancerous cysts in my colon. The operation he would perform—basically he was going to cut out a wide section of colon and check the lymph nodes most likely to be infected in case the cancer had spread. He patiently answered all of our questions—no, I was not going to shit in a bag. No, I was probably not going to die anytime soon.

I left feeling a bit of relief, but I continued to feel scared and unsure as I went for additional tests, all prep for the surgery. Walking down the hall, I glanced over at Ozzy, who was still having a difficult time, still drifting aimlessly through the nightmares being served up by his imagination.

"I'm scared to fucking death," he said.

I said, "Me, too, baby. Me, too."

Everything was methodical. I spent the rest of the day getting blood drawn and answering questions. Then I checked into the hospital. By the end of the day, I was spent. I went to my room, changed into hospital clothes, chatted with Ozzy and the kids until the sedative I'd been given took effect, and I faded into a deep sleep.

At the crack of dawn the next day, I was awakened by a nurse, prepped, and wheeled into surgery. I remember my doctor saying that if I had to have cancer the one I had was among the best. According to him, there was a 90 percent cure rate if the cancer was caught early enough, and mine appeared to have been detected early. Ozzy and I held hands until I was about to go into the operating room. Then we kissed.

My last thought before going out: Love and luck, I thought, would get me through this. Also the skill of some brilliant doctors and nurses. During the four-hour surgery, my surgeon removed twelve inches of my colon and half a dozen lymph nodes. Ozzy got the report in the waiting room and told the children. Several hours after the operation, I woke up in serious condition. Apparently I had lost an unusual amount of blood. My blood count went down so low they rushed me to intensive care and gave me massive amounts of blood. I woke up again the next day. It was July Fourth—our twentieth anniversary!

XXI

Anniversary

———— ⚬ ————

My husband is probably the only star I've met without an ego. He's just so open, and I've taken my lead
from him.

—SHARON OSBOURNE, *NEW YORK DAILY NEWS*,
JULY 14, 2003

Ozzy: Waiting for my wife to wake up in the ICU wasn't the way we'd planned to spend our twentieth. I was mildly sedated myself when I got the call she was up and went to see her. Sharon was screaming. She was having a fucking conniption about the transfusions she'd been given. "AIDS," she muttered. I understood. All of us did. She feared she might get AIDS from the blood. If not that, then something else.

"At least she's screaming," I told the doctor. "It's a good sign."

I couldn't stop thinking that Sharon was going to die. I went home and took a sleeping pill. The next day Sharon was better. She was weak, but her vital signs were all good, her blood pressure was on its way up, and I saw life in her eyes. The doctor warned me she was going to need plenty of rest before resuming any kind of schedule, and then she had chemo to look forward to. "Sharon's problem is that she never stops," I told the doctor. "She doesn't even stop to use the bathroom. She just runs by the toilet when she needs to take a piss."

"She's going to have to slow down," he said.

"Tell me, how do you turn a fucking hurricane into a breeze?"

By the third day, Sharon was strong enough to be moved to a private room. Both of us relished the chance to be together, talking, watching TV, and just being close, though Sharon at one point nearly ripped out her IV and clobbered me when I let my anxiety float freely and blathered on about how if my dear wife did unfortunately die I wouldn't likely remarry. "It's always been Ozzy and Sharon," I said. "Ozzy and Debbie wouldn't sound right. Neither would Ozzy and Jane. Or Ozzy and Tina."

"You know, Ozzy, you saved her life," the doctor said.

"What the fuck do you mean?"

"If you hadn't made her get checked, we never would have found out about the cancer until it was too late."

They'd cut out all the cancer, but the big question was the results of the lymph nodes that had been removed. They'd reveal if the cancer had spread.

"Have those tests come back?" Sharon asked.

They hadn't. Because of the Independence Day holiday, those results wouldn't be available for two more days. The wait was grueling.

On Monday, the results came back. Cancer had showed up in two lymph nodes. Sharon and I were fucking devastated.

I immediately thought about Robert Marcato's mother. She was failing fast. But the doctor talked us through the facts, explaining that every case was different, and that though cancer had spread beyond the colon, which wasn't necessarily good, we still didn't have to worry.

"We're still looking good," he said. "We caught it early. It's not in Sharon's liver or anywhere else. We can zap it with chemo—about three months of chemotherapy."

We scheduled chemotherapy for later in the month, and they told us the prep work Sharon would need before then. We began to realize the situation had turned in our favor from the shock of finding out about the cancer to being able to fight back.

"We're going to make it," I said.

Sharon squeezed my hand. "Right. Fuck this cancer. I'm not going anywhere yet."

Kelly: Our house was never as empty as when my mom was in the hospital. And she never sounded happier than when she called to say she was coming home from the hospital the next day. The doctors had told her everything would be fine. I cried like a baby seeing her walk up the stairs, saying, "My babies. It's so good to be home with my babies." Even the dogs were happier. Minnie curled by her side, and Maggie wouldn't budge from her feet.

She held court in her bedroom between naps. We filled her in on our lives, watched television, and caught up on the latest gossip as we paged through the tabloids together.

My dad was the most relieved to have her back. He was helpless without her and so happy to have her back home he didn't know what to do. He walked in and out of the bedroom every half hour or so, checking to make sure she was there. He had flowers delivered throughout the day. They were enormous arrangements, some as tall as me. My mom also received the most beautiful bouquets from Jay Leno, Adam Sandler, and friends and fans from around the world. Her room smelled like a flower store.

We tiptoed around, mindful not to bother her.

"Is this a fucking morgue around here? Did someone die?"

She had surprised us by coming down to the kitchen. She stood in the doorway, looking thin and pale, like a stick in a nightgown. But she was herself. "I'm not dead and I'm not planning to die anytime soon. Got it?"

She went out and had her hair washed, got a manicure and pedicure, and then had a snack in the Polo Lounge at the Beverly Hills Hotel. While waiting for her car after lunch, she heard a noise in the bushes, like a baby crying. She couldn't see anything without going into the bushes, which she wouldn't do. She got one of the valets to go in, and he came out with an adorable baby kitty. She brought it home. More trouble for my dad. "It's not enough we're dealing with cancer here," he said. "You have to bring in a homeless fucking cat."

My mother insisted that my dad join the Ozzfest tour. My dad was having a tough time, taking lots of medications, and relying on booze to keep him calm. He needed to be busier. She convinced me to go to New York to start on my album. "You have to get off your ass and quit worrying yourself into anxiety attacks," she said following one such episode when I couldn't catch my breath and my heart felt like it was going to explode. I didn't want to leave, but since Aimee was supervising her care, I let myself be talked into getting on a plane.

Aimee: I think my mom was in shock and very depressed. At the height of when she should be enjoying herself—what she had worked so hard to become—this was happening. That was her main concern. Not, Am I going to survive?

My father was freaking out all the time. He drank, which was obviously the way he chose to cope. My sister was in New York, my brother was doing his thing. There was a lot of avoidance and denial, but no one worse than my mother herself.

𝔖𝔥𝔞𝔯𝔬𝔫: Anyone who thinks I agreed to go through with the second season of the MTV show for the money is wrong. I wouldn't have gone ahead if I'd known about the cancer first, but I negotiated the deal two weeks before being diagnosed. Between the time I had surgery and started chemo I thought many times about backing out. Ozzy left the decision to me. At first I said no, not when I'm when going through chemotherapy, losing my hair and throwing up.

But I changed my mind. I thought if I'd have made the decision to get the cameras out of the house, they would have thought, Mommy's dying—it must be so bad! I didn't want them to go through that. So I said, "Fuck it. We'll carry on as normal, and if they want to film me taking my treatments, they can."

Before I could begin chemo, scheduled for July 29, I had to make myself stronger. I spent a couple of weeks eating to increase my red blood cell count, resting, and trying to avoid stress. MTV moved their crew in slowly, nothing like the first time when we went through the shock of a sudden invasion. This time they started by sending cameras out on the road with Ozzy and Kelly. Every time I tried to get involved from home, Ozzy turned into a Jewish mother. "It doesn't matter how much money you have if you don't have your health. . . ."

𝔎𝔢𝔩𝔩𝔶: I was working with a team of pros in New York. I got to the studio by eleven, recorded a song, ate lunch, watched *SpongeBob SquarePants* for an hour and a half, and then recorded again. It was fun.

I don't play an instrument, but all the songs were mine lyrically. How it works is I'll have a line or a melody line, you know? Sometimes, it can start just with one word. For example, "Shut Up" started that way. I'll hum something and then somebody who I'm with will play it on the guitar and then it will just go from there. It's a long process where you'll start out with something, but it will be completely different when it's done. I mean, that's how my dad does it. That's how I do it.

When I was a kid I used to sit there and watch him writing songs. It would always make me laugh because when he's in the middle of it he gets louder and louder and louder. He'll be like, "NO, NO, NO! IT SHOULD BE THIS INSTEAD OF LIKE THIS!!" You always know when he's writing because he gets really loud. He still does it to this day.

I just get really quiet because I have really bad concentration skills. In order for me to sit and be able to put my whole attention into something, it's very hard. So if I'm talking about something I won't be able to do it.

Looking back, I wish I could've expressed myself a little more honestly in terms of styles of music and made an album that rocked harder, but the record company wanted me to make a sassy pop album, which is what I did.

Aimee: Kelly's album just sounds like everything else on the radio, and I don't think it's an honest reflection of who she really is. I think it was done very much to feed into what's "in" right now and what we can get played on the radio. That's fine, because I do think one can use that mentality to a certain extent before one says, "Okay, this is not who I am. This is not what I originally wanted to record."

Kelly: I played all the tracks for my mom over the phone. I have no idea if she could really hear, but she encouraged me. My dad listened and said stuff like, "Kelly, darling, I'd be lying if I said it was my kind of music. But you're working hard and I'm very proud of you."

Public opinion ranged from one extreme to the other. "How can you give Kelly's album any more than one star? How can you even review it?" one asshole wrote on the Internet. "Kelly's album is awesome!" a girl said on another site. "It's the best album I have bought this year. I love her."

To me, it's a fun pop album, and that's all it was every supposed to be.

Ozzy: I respect what she's doing. My daughter Kelly has got such a wonderful work ethic.

Kelly: Robert's mother had taken a turn for the worse. It was very painful to watch my close friend going through that. None of us wanted to think of Robert losing his mother. None of us wanted to think about losing our mother, who had the same type of cancer.

My parents visited Reagan, and I remember my dad coming home bummed out.

Ozzy: The last time I saw Reagan it was very, very sad. What a courageous fucking woman. She was on morphine patches and fucking Dilaudid. She was so sick, the poor one. But she wouldn't stop living. There comes a point when you've got to let go, but she wouldn't let go.

Kelly: My mother sympathized deeply with Robert's mom. She promised her that she and my dad would take care of Robert, who was already spending all his spare time at our house.

Sharon: In mid-July I went to the hospital and had a small catheter implanted in my chest. That's where they'd connect the IV that would deliver the chemo into my body. The surgery was minor; I was out the next morning. A few days later, I toured the facility where I'd actually be receiving the chemo treatment. The staff worked behind a large desk, while the patients were in a large room filled with several rows of reclining chairs with IV poles next to them.

"That has to change when I'm there. I'm going to bring in music. Liven up the joint. Put some life into it."

But on July 29 I didn't feel like celebrating. Robert's mother passed away the same day I started the chemo. It was so sad. We welcomed Robert into the family, gave him his own space in the guest house near the backyard pool.

My goal was to stay focused and positive. I arrived for my first appointment with Ozzy, who sat next to me as I had a brief medical exam. But he fell apart when the nurse was preparing to prick my finger for a blood sugar level test.

I was like, "If he can't get past them pricking my finger, he's not going to survive the rest."

I had Tony take him home.

I went downstairs to the room with the chairs. Was it going to hurt? Was it going to burn? Was I going to feel sick right away?

I felt myself coming apart when Gabriel, the nurse who ended up helping me through the entire treatment, brought me into one of the two private rooms. He turned on the TV and said, "It'll be okay."

Gabriel turned out to be my angel. This young man was pleasant and patient. He talked me through every single step. He kept coming in the room asking if I needed anything. I was less scared. He told me, "Remember, this is the easy part. You'll feel the effects later."

I didn't feel anything when I was hooked up. But about twelve hours later I began to tingle. I literally felt the medication slowly coursing through my entire body. The sensation first made me feel weird; by the second day I was ill. I had the runs and the thought of eating made me sick. I was hypersensitive to everything. One of the dogs shit in my bedroom and as soon as I smelled it, I threw up. That began a chain reaction. I ran to the bathroom all night long. I had no control over the way I felt anymore.

I fell into a routine. Every Monday I saw my doctor at Cedars. If my white blood count was high enough I went downstairs, got myself hooked me up to chemo, and did paperwork while the cancer-killing toxins dripped into my body. Then I went home and waited. I felt sick within forty to forty-eight hours. Like clockwork. It came over me and stayed. By the end of the first month, I was in a dreadful state. My body was in shock. I lost twenty pounds and pulled out hair by the handful. I couldn't stay off the toilet. I kept a trash bin in front of me because I had it coming out both ends.

And I was scheduled for six months of treatment!

I remember Ozzy was on my back to eat more and stay off the phone. He would mention something about cancer being nothing compared to chemo. That's the shit that will kill you, he warned.

Ozzy: Common sense says that if Sharon is going to have surgery, and she's going to have fucking chemotherapy, the last thing she needs is a restriction to getting food. I mean, chemotherapy already fucks your taste buds. So before the surgery I kept going on and on about the fucking band on her stomach. I wanted the doctor to rip it out, but I guess I didn't win that battle.

I didn't think she'd make it through chemo. By the end of the first month she was so thin and frail. I badgered her to eat more and take care of herself and stop trying to manage the business the same as before.

Two days after Sharon completed her fourth chemo treatment, I finished a show in Denver and flew directly home, arriving home pretty late, around three in the morning. I found the nurse sitting at the kitchen table chatting to the security guard, having a nice cup of coffee. Sharon was in bed sleeping, the nurse said. She had taken a Sonata.

But I knew those sleeping pills wouldn't put a fucking fly to sleep. I went upstairs and looked in on Sharon, who was in bed, looking stiff, like someone lying too still and the muscles have locked into place. I lifted back her eyelids: nothing but the whites of her eyes. They weren't moving.

I remember very calmly, I got on the house intercom and told the nurse, "Get the fucking paramedics, she's dehydrated."

Sharon: I vaguely heard a voice say, "Get her up to intensive care." "No, do it here," one person said. "No, take her up there." I had brief moments of consciousness when I woke up and saw doctors and nurses rushing around. I had no strength. Nor could I move. At one point, I took a deep breath, closed my eyes, and thought, I guess this is it. I'm gone.

𝒪zzy: I had no idea how close we came to losing Sharon. No one told me. They knew I'd fall apart and then both of us would be in trouble.

But I could see she was struggling to hang on. She spent the next eleven days in the hospital trying to recover. She looked like a dying twig. She had no strength. She could barely move. She was frighteningly thin, and if her blood pressure fell any lower she would have died.

Sharon was pumped full of vitamins and given blood transfusions. I reminded the doctor that Sharon had had an allergic reaction to Dilaudid in the ICU during her first hospitalization. "She can't take any opiates," I said. "Not even a fucking Vicodin." The doctor thanked me.

I honest to God believe I had a nervous breakdown. Everything we'd experienced the past year suddenly got to me, topped by Sharon's cancer, which was like a piano crashing over my head.

𝒜imee: Still every day she was planning meetings and taking phone calls. I got pissed off at her and remember screaming at her, "What more needs to happen for you to realize you need to actually look after yourself for once?"

I took care of her as much as she would let me. I was scared. I saw weight loss, dehydration, hair loss. Her memory was terrible. We would get phone calls at 3:00 A.M. from her saying, "I remembered what I was going to tell you earlier. . . ."

𝒮haron: When I'd come out of the hospital, my eyelashes were gone. Most of my hair was falling out, too. I realized everything that was happening on the outside of my body—the hair falling out, the withering, the sickness—was also happening on the inside.

I'd been taking a liquid food supplement through an IV every night, but it was so vile I couldn't stand it any longer. Halfway through the treatment I had the band on my stomach loosened so I could eat more.

Jack: My mom's hospitalization worried me. After she got out, I waited a few days and then went into her room for a heart-to-heart. I'd just overheard her schedule a meeting for the TV talk show she planned to launch. That really made me angry. Why did she still feel she had to fight for something every day? How much bigger can you get? How much more money do you need?

I slid onto the bed next to her. "You're on a hit TV show," I said. "You're making millions of dollars. Dad's career is fine. Kelly's career is fine. You don't have to worry about me. What more can you do?"

"I don't know," my mom said.

"Then just stop."

"Oh, honey, it's not that easy."

"Well, if you want to see my twenty-first birthday, you're going to have to learn how."

Sharon: Solid food made me stronger. I also found strength in the place where I got chemo. I met Ava, a smart-looking woman who looked to be in her late thirties or early forties. She had a brown scarf over her head. After receiving her chemo, she came up to me. "My children adore your show. They won't believe I saw you."

"Thank you."

"I know you're having a tough time, but hang in there," she said. "If you make it this far, you can go all the way."

I found out she had had breast cancer three years earlier. The week before she'd been diagnosed with cancer in her spine.

"If you don't mind me asking, how do you feel?" I said.

"Shitty. But I have kids. I'd like to see them grow up."

Right on, I thought. Fuck the pain and discomfort. None of us wants to go before we have to, and we'll go to almost any length not to.

For a few months, I saw an older gentleman getting chemo nearly every Monday. He wasn't doing well. In fact, toward the end, he drifted in and out of consciousness as he took the treatment. I asked the nurse why he kept going, why he chose to keep up the fight.

"If he was able to live another month, he decided it was worth the try."

I had to keep thinking about living. I continued to make plans. I had missed my twentieth anniversary and I was too ill in October to celebrate turning fifty, so I planned a New Year's bash at which Ozzy and I would renew our wedding vows in front of our family and friends. Our first marriage had been a lovely enough ceremony on the beach in Maui, but none of our friends had been there. And Ozzy had passed out drunk.

XXII

𝕽enewal

―――――― ⟿ ―――――――

Ozzy: Six hundred people? You're kidding me.
Where was my consultation about this?
Sharon: It's a surprise for you.
Ozzy: I'm not good at surprises. . . .

—OZZY GETS THE NEWS ABOUT THE PARTY ON
GOOD MORNING AMERICA, NOVEMBER 25, 2002

Ozzy: My sisters and my brothers had never been to the United States—they all flew out for this fucking bash scene, this New Year's Eve fucking thing. I must confess, I wasn't that keen on it. I was still coming out of the hole at that point, you know. I was very shaky emotionally.

Aimee: My father was dead set against it. He said she wasn't strong enough to weather the stress of overseeing such an event. There was too much stress. I was also against it. At one point I saw my mother start to crumble. She thought about it and said, "Maybe you're right. If I have to cancel this party, I will."

But lots of money had been spent to reserve everything, from the hotel to the band. People had arranged to fly in from all over the world. MTV was taping it. And she was set on seeing it happen.

I saw she was dragging. A stranger wouldn't have known it by looking at her. She's amazing. We fought while getting dressing, which is typical. My mother loves to take shit out on me when she's stressed, but once the party started she was at her best.

Ozzy: Personally, I wanted to hold it off until Sharon had gotten over the fucking chemo, and got the green light to go. But then it was New Year's Eve . . .

Sharon: . . . 2003! Five hundred of our closest friends and family members filled an elegant ballroom at the Beverly Hills Hotel I'd had decorated with hundreds of giant red roses and soft candles. The mood was very romantic. I felt like a fairy-tale princess in an off-white gown and diamonds from Harry Winston. Ozzy looked dashing in a tux. The two of us held hands and cried while staring at our three children. Rabbi Steven Rubin presided as we exchanged vows—again.

"The love that sparkles between you is without question the greatest gift life has to offer."

"I'm privileged to be your wife," I told Ozzy. I was sniffling. "And thank you for my babies."

Ozzy: "I love you, Sharon," I said.

I was very lucky in falling in love with her. To say I love Sharon is not enough—I mean, she's great, she's fucking greater than great. She's given me everything I need. There's nothing else any-one can give me, apart from fucking venereal disease.

Jack: They are the old Jewish couple. They love each other—they literally can't go to the bathroom without each other!

Sharon: Everyone we wanted there showed up, including my father and brother, Ozzy's sisters and brothers, Aimee, Kelly, and Jack, Randy Rhoads's mother, plus friends like Justin Timberlake, Chris Rock, Jon Lovitz, and Marilyn Manson. There was more than enough champagne to wash down buffets of pasta, sushi, fish and chips, and chocolate goodies. At midnight, all of us cheered as bal-loons dropped and the Village People rocked in the new year.

Ozzy: I'm amazed so many people came. To be perfectly honest with you, I was just doing it for Sharon. I was back in bed by fuck-ing ten, fucking eleven.

Sharon: At the end of the evening—more like early morning—I wanted a nightcap, a kiss from my husband. I found him passed out on the sofa in our hotel suite. What could I expect? It was the same on our wedding night twenty years earlier. At least this time he made it into the room.

I went back out and partied the rest of the night.

Jack: Weddings are supposed to be white, but I looked around and Kelly was wearing black, Aimee was wearing black, I was wear-ing black, and so was Dad. That struck me as kind of funny—I guess we wear black at our weddings.

I got a little bit emotional, you know, I thought it was touching. I also got drunk—I don't remember anything from about 11:30 until 4:30. I know I got home around five.

𝕾𝔥𝔞𝔯𝔬𝔫: Doing something that grand was probably too much for me at that time. Certainly staying up all night pushed me beyond exhaustion. After a point, I was running on adrenaline. Should I have behaved like that? No. But at that moment in my life I was so weak and ill from the chemo that I didn't know if I was going to live or die, and so why not? I didn't know if I'd be around to do it again.

𝒜𝒾𝓂𝑒𝑒: Around seven or eight the next morning my mother woke me up by jumping on my bed. "Mom, what the hell are you doing?" I asked.

"I want to go play," she said.

It was light out. She didn't want the party to end. Few healthy people could've kept up with her, but my mother wasn't healthy. I got out of bed, escorted her back to her room, drew a bath, and sat while she bathed and recounted the party.

"Who won the raffle?" my mother asked.

Shortly after midnight there'd been a raffle, the grand prize being a lovely diamond necklace from Asprey. I didn't know the answer. An hour later, I had her changed into pajamas and tucked into bed. She promised to sleep, but she watched television all afternoon, and then went shopping with my cousins and out to lunch.

𝕾𝔥𝔞𝔯𝔬𝔫: I could've fixated on any number of incidents from the previous night's party, but as I got going the next day I wanted to know who ended up with the beautiful necklace. All I heard was that a young woman had won the raffle. No one knew her name. It shouldn't have been such a mystery, since all the invitees were family members or friends. Since MTV had taped the entire event and had the winner sign a release, I was able to find out she was Renee Tab.

Who was Renee Tab? She hadn't been on the list of invitees nor anyone's official guest. After some investigation, I found out she was a twenty-six-year-old agent at ICM and had been among a group who snuck in along with the girlfriend of one of Jack's buddies.

She got a hold of a raffle ticket and won. In my mind that was wrong. She chose to go in and have a good time. Fine. But don't walk away with a $15,000 diamond necklace when you aren't supposed to be there. Which is what I said to this gal when I called her up and explained that I thought the correct and most gracious thing to do would be to give the necklace back.

But she didn't want to hear it. She insisted that she had won it and was keeping it.

"Excuse me?" I said. I tried to remain as pleasant as possible. "I don't know you. You don't know anyone in my family. You weren't invited to this event. The necklace was meant for a member of my family or a friend. . . ."

No matter how nicely and clearly I explained the situation and asked for the necklace back, she refused.

"But I won it fairly," she said.

"No you didn't. You weren't even an invited guest."

Finally I had enough. I felt violated by her ignorance and selfishness. I lost my big fat temper.

"You fucking idiot," I said and the conversation went downhill from there.

Worse, I got worked up into such a state of anxiety and anger it affected my health. I spent the whole day and that night stewing and frothing about the incredible rudeness, wrongness, and my lack of recourse. I put out a press release and listened to agents and lawyers say I was making a mistake.

"In my opinion, this woman is hurting me more than chemo," I said.

Ozzy: It was two days after the party, and I was on my way out of the house to visit with my brother and sisters. It was real chaotic.

Sharon comes in while I'm getting ready and said, "What are you doing?" I said, "I'm going to see my sisters."

"Give me five minutes and I'll be with you."

She's like the fucking Eveready battery.

"Stay in fucking bed . . . please."

So I get into the car with Tony and go down to the Beverly Hills Hotel. Just as I took my foot out of the car, Tony's cell phone rang.

𝔍𝔞𝔠𝔨: I was the only one of us at home when my mom went into a seizure. One of the nurses taking care of her screamed for help, and after that it was pandemonium. Neither nurse on duty knew what to do for my mother, who went in and out of consciousness. She was shaking and her eyes rolled back in her head. One of the nurses finally called the paramedics, but before she finished giving the information a security guard scooped my mother up and carried her outside to his van. I was right next to them, followed by the nurses and an MTV sound guy.

The scene inside the van as it sped to the hospital was even more chaotic. One of the nurses was crying, the other was screaming, and I was so scared. I thought my mother was about to die. I got angry at her. I was like, "Fuck, how can you do this? There's something so wrong with you to leave me like this."

The drive took about fifteen minutes. Halfway there I lost it on the nurses. If my mom was going to die I figured she should have some classical music playing in the background. If not that, Dad's music. If not that, she should hear me talking to her. Anything but a couple of nurses freaking out. "Shut the fuck up!"

"Jack, calm down, dude," the security guard said. "Your mom doesn't need this."

I got myself together and held my mom's hand. I told her I loved her and to hang on, we were almost at the hospital. Just before we pulled into the emergency entrance, my mom looked up at me. Her eyes locked onto mine and she smiled. I thought, Okay, that's good, she's going to make it.

Kelly: I was out and checked my messages, including one from Jack, who simply said, "Mom is dead." Then he hung up. At first I thought he was playing a really mean joke, but then I called the house and heard she'd been rushed to the hospital after suffering another seizure. I tried to get a hold of someone. Finally I reached Uncle Tony, who told me she was all right. "She's in the hospital. She had a bad one. But she's going to be fine."

Ozzy: I sat in the hospital room, next to Sharon's bed, with one of those surgical masks. Sharon's doctor stood across from me. We'd finished talking and were just staring at each other. Both of us were fed up and at a loss as to what to do. Finally, I said, "If I wasn't so scared of losing her, I'd kill her myself."

That got a weak smile from Sharon.

I've always said that about my wife. What will kill my wife—will be my wife.

Aimee: I drove over to the hospital. I get there and she's had a seizure and my dad is hysterical. He says he can't take it anymore. This has got to stop. She was doing this to herself.

Sharon: I woke up. I thought I was in an airport lounge, waiting for a flight. I still laugh at that.

I spent four days in the hospital and insisted on going home the moment I felt better. I couldn't take time off. I had to make the various meetings I had scheduled and reschedule those I'd missed. I was unable to stop.

Aimee: We were driving her home, and I said, "Do you realize what you're doing to everyone, as well as yourself?"

"I've earned the right to be selfish," she said.

Sharon: A few weeks later I paid the price. In was in Las Vegas watching Ozzy do a show at one of the hotels and felt another

seizure coming on. With some help from security, I made it backstage from the soundboard before passing out. When I opened my
eyes, I was in the hospital, lying in a bed next to a man with a snaggletooth who was staring at me.

"I seen you on TV, right?" he asked.

"Yes," I said groggily.

"Aren't you the mother of the Osmonds?"

I called the nurses and demanded to be let out.

"I don't blame you," Snaggletooth said. "You Osmonds live in a
mother of a mansion. I seen it on TV."

I needed medical care, not commentary. I had my room
changed. I also had my L.A. doctor fly into town and oversee my
treatment until I was stable enough to go back home several days
later. I'd never been as happy to sleep in my own bed. I'd never
made so many people in my family angry at me all at once.

Kelly: I love my mother dearly, I just hated the way she was
ignoring her health. She didn't eat enough. She didn't drink enough
water. She didn't get enough sleep. Although she didn't feel well,
she refused to take any time off so she could rest. What does that
tell you about her? That she's a fucking idiot.

Aimee: And the MTV cameras were still at home!

I was more vocal than anyone else. Since the cameras weren't
allowed to follow me, I could talk to her honestly. I felt freer to let
her have it. The second morning she was back home I went into her
bedroom, expecting to curl up beside her and watch TV. Instead I
found her getting dressed for a meeting in Beverly Hills. I couldn't
believe it.

I said, "What are you doing? What more needs to happen to you
for you to realize that you need to stop and actually look after yourself for once?"

I get pissed off at her every second of the day.

Jack: If my mom could put up with the cameras and the crew living with us while going through chemo, I could, too. We finished the second season and they had shot enough for a third season, as well. My mom got the word they were finished. We were happy, but also a bit sad since we had all made friends with the production crews.

We had a mellow party at our house for the crew. It was like the last day of school: All of us traded numbers. We'd grown close to many of these people.

A few days later, MTV threw a wild party at a Hollywood nightclub. This was the blowout that everyone expected. A couple of hundred people showed up—more than three-quarters of whom I'd never met before as they worked behind the scenes, editing, supervising, doing the music. It was a great evening. People were peeling off their clothes, dancing, and drinking too much. And me, too.

𝕶𝖊𝖑𝖑𝖞: I got ill at the sight of all these women, not girls but grown women, going after Jack. A lot of incredibly weird things have happened to my family since the show began, but in my estimation the transformation of Jack Osbourne into Brad Pitt ranks among the most mind-boggling.

I slept late the next morning and then walked through the house without worrying that someone was going to poke a camera in my face and dangle a microphone over my head. It was my first break from *The Osbournes* after two years. What a pleasure.

𝕺zzy: The cameras were gone. We bought a new house on the beach in Malibu, something Sharon had wanted for years. I agreed to spend the money on one condition: no interviews or photographs there—ever. It's our sanctuary. I said, "If I find a hole in the wall or see a blinking red light on top of a camera lens, I'll go fucking crazy."

I wanted to be able to walk around naked in my own house and scratch my balls if I want to. Every guy should have that luxury. I even raised the subject of selling the house in Beverly Hills. We haven't put up a *For Sale* sign yet, but it's a possibility.

I suppose I'm now a big fucking expert on reality television.

One day I was picking up some T-shirts at Barneys in Beverly Hills when my assistant, Tony, came over, laughing. He warned me there was another star in the store.

"It's someone with a reality show," he said.

"Anna Nicole Smith?"

"No, even better—Roseanne Barr."

A crew was following Roseanne, who'd recently signed to do her own reality show. Somehow she heard I was in the store and wanted to get me on camera and ask me a few questions.

"No fucking way," I said.

We got stuck waiting outside for the valet to bring me my car. Sure enough, Roseanne zeroed in with her crew and shoved a mic in my face.

"What's it like? I'm doing this fucking TV reality show of my own and I want to know from you, what's it like to do it?"

"You know what it's like?" I said. "It's what we do."

"I don't get it," she said.

"We're like monkeys in a cage," I said. "Only I'm not in the cage anymore. Now it's your turn to let people watch you scratch your ass."

"Right," she said.

"Good luck."

XXIII

Afterglow

———— ⟿ ————

My kids aren't just normal sixteen-, seventeen-year-
olds. They have lawyers and business managers . . .
and I can't throw up on my own and Ozzy can't get
drunk on his own.

—Sharon Osbourne to Barbara Walters,
ABC News, November 2002

Ozzy: Why did the show work? You know what, to answer that is never-ending. It is the most difficult thing to say why it works, because I'm me—and we are the show. We don't act—we are.

Jack: I totally think it was because of 9/11 that the show did well. Because the show came out in March 2002—a couple of months after the shit hit the fan. I think at that point people were so depressed, were losing their jobs, there was no comfort. America was always on red alert. It's chaos, you know. And to have something come out that made people laugh and feel secure, yeah.

Aimee: I think most people will look back on *The Osbournes* as a laugh—good entertainment. That's not a bad thing, but everything I feared came true. I'm just glad I won't be remembered for yelling at my sister or fighting with my mother or walking out of the room when my dad had a beer. I still have my identity, as well as my privacy.

My mother's cancer was really the big event in our lives. It was a reality check—none of the other bullshit is important, except her health. The important thing is family—that's all you have.

Sharon: Ultimately without MTV we wouldn't even be speaking here today. Well, if we hadn't done the show I would still have had cancer—I probably wouldn't have seen that doctor because I might not have been so tired. Before the show Jack was still drinking and I often think, Well, would Jack have gone as far with drugs if we hadn't done the show? I think that Jack and Kelly were under huge pressures. *Huge* pressures.

Even though my kids—all of them—have probably grown ten years in two, the upside is still more than the downside.

Jack: I'm so against kid stars. Because it's fucked-up. At such a young age having all that attention coming toward you, getting all this recognition, where you are on the cover of *Rolling Stone* one week, *Entertainment Weekly* the next. It's stressful. I find people don't get that, how stressful it is, especially for kids. It screws with your head, it really does.

Aimee: It's completely warped. I find it very entertaining to see how it's changed my brother and my sister and my mom. They are crucial to every social gathering and awards ceremony in the world, you know. I think it's pretty silly. My mom is so busy she doesn't really have time for much. My dad is still the same person. He has dealt with fame before.

Sharon: My husband's always been famous and he'll never change. My husband's fame has never taken Ozzy through rock star mentality stages and diva stages and tantrum stages. He's always just been Ozzy. He's always handled it so well.

Ozzy: At fifty-three I suddenly went from being Ozzy to OZZY. I met the Queen of England. I met the president of the United States. And I'm still Ozzy, you know.

Sharon: I think that in the next season it will be good to see what happens to a family that a nation embraced and made famous. I mean, the people on the street made us famous—not a record company or a marketing company. It's interesting for those people to see, "What does fame do to this family?"

I think it'll also be interesting to see how Ozzy handles his kids and his old wife, who were always in the background and are suddenly all in the foreground.

Aimee: Well, I've really detached myself from all that. I let them do their thing and it really doesn't affect my life. I wish them well and I hope that it works for them. Whether I approve of it or not is irrelevant because it's not really my place to say.

Sharon: Whatever the kids want to do right now is open to them. Kelly's made her record, she's over in Europe on tour with Robbie Williams. Aimee's been offered film work. Jack's been offered a lot of work in television. I just look at it as an unbelievable opportunity for them to find their path in life. I don't know what they're going to end up doing, but they sure as hell have got the opportunity to try on all these different heads, see which one fits, and find where they belong.

Jack: I do care what the critics say, but then again, fuck it, I'm still going to get paid at the end of the day. I mean, I really don't care what they think. Make fun of me, but still give me my fucking check.

I know that when we're done with this show, financially I'm going to be stable for the rest of my life. And that's a really big security to have at seventeen.

Sharon: Of course, *The Osbournes* will come to an end. Everything does. The greatest shows that have ever been on TV have to come to an end. I'm not saying that we are one of those greatest TV shows, but everything comes to an end. The best we can hope for is that as organic as it was at the start, it will be that way to the end.

XXIV

Let's Talk

Sharon Osbourne says she'll be watching her language on her new talk show . . . "people come into my home (on MTV) and that's the way I choose to live my life . . . now I'm coming into their homes."

—ASSOCIATED PRESS, JULY 14, 2003

Sharon: One morning early in February 2003, not long after all the TV crews had packed and gone, I woke up feeling different. I felt it the second I opened my eyes, like a lightness. I laid in bed and thought about what might have possibly changed overnight. Then I knew. The cancer was gone from my body. I don't know how, but somehow I just knew it was gone.

A week later, I had a blood test and for the first time since that first exam, the results came back negative. I went through one last chemo treatment and was done. Ozzy and I celebrated by having matzoh ball soup and carrot cake from Jerry's Famous Deli, and champagne. Ozzy and I were alone in the house. The kids were all out. I didn't require any nurses. There weren't any camera crews.

"Do you hear that, baby?" I said.

"Hear what?" Ozzy said.

"Quiet. We're the only ones home."

We got in bed and watched TV. Ozzy tried to relax, but he fidgeted and tensed like a man in the dentist's chair.

"I don't know if I can get used to it," he said.

After spending the winter in L.A., my father went back to England with my brother. Almost immediately his Alzheimer's disease worsened to where he needed round-the-clock care. His decline was sudden, shocking, and quite sad. He's comfortable and receiving the best care. But I feel for those families who can't afford it. My father can't manage for himself, and his memory is shot. He's like a small child. I'm the only person he remembers at this stage. "Get me Sharon," he tells my brother. I wonder if he wonders where I am, or if he thinks I'm still fifteen and working as his receptionist.

After not speaking for twenty years, we talk almost daily.

Speaking of talk—it looks like my talk show idea is becoming a reality. More than three-quarters of the station owners across the country agreed to air a syndicated hour after meeting me at a television convention in New Orleans in January this year.

I'd dreamed of doing a talk show for the past ten years, but I had about as much expectation of doing it as I did of becoming a ballet dancer. But within the first month of *The Osbourne's* debut, I began to receive calls offering me a show.

"Yes, yes, yes. How did you know that's what I wanted to do?"

By March I was working daily with coaches and producers, developing the skills and techniques needed to carry an hour. The most important thing I learned is something that helps in every situation—be yourself. Don't pretend to be someone you're not. I can't be Diane Sawyer or Barbara Walters, both of whom are among my favorites. Oprah is also at the top of my list. I love Oprah. The woman is a genius. Such class and dignity and inspiration.

I only hope I'm good enough to do shows that entertain people and make them feel better about themselves. Hopefully, they might also learn a thing or two. Like every talk show host, I have a list of dream guests. Like Eminem. I'd love to ask what he really thinks about his mother. Brad Pitt is also on my list. I'd ask him to kiss me. I'd also love to have on Elizabeth Taylor, Liza Minelli, George Clooney—"Can I pinch your butt, George?"—and of course, Michael Jackson.

I like Michael. I feel badly for him. I worry that if someone doesn't rescue Michael and straighten out his life, he might not make it into old age. I can't see Michael Jackson living as a Hollywood has-been.

I can see that show. I'd sit Michael on the couch and say, "You are probably one of the most talented entertainers ever. But you fucked up. Get over it. Join the club. Everybody fucks up. We've all fucked up. The thing you have to learn is that there's nothing wrong with the truth. Telling the truth is always easier than telling lies. It will make your life so simple. So when I talk to you, you don't have to pretend. You don't have to tell fantastic stories. Just be yourself."

Come on Michael, let's talk.

Ozzy: I have no idea why Sharon wants to do a talk show. She doesn't have to work. She is always telling me to slow down, and I tell her the same thing. I think she's mad. But if doing a talk show makes her happy, then I'm all for it.

Will it be any good? It's either going to be the number one talk show or else it's going to be the number one turd on television.

I find Sharon fascinating. She could be her own best guest. She has an opinion about every fucking thing. She's funny. And she teaches you something important. Never let go of your dreams. She has spent her entire life turning the impossible into the possible.

If I'm home, I'll probably watch it.

Sharon: What I really like about *The Sharon Osbourne Show* is that it can tie in so well with our MTV show. Because the way they film *The Osbournes* won't change, only now the crews'll be following me to the Time-Warner studios and then home again. If the talk show was on another music channel then it would compete, but Time-Warner has nothing to do with MTV. They'll just be promoting each other's show . . . nice, huh?

I like collaborations like that. Just like the ones that Ozzy has done. You know—he's recorded with Was Not Was, DMX, Primus, Ringo Starr, Alice Cooper, Miss Piggy. It's something that I always encouraged him to do because I don't believe that because you're in one set genre of music that you shouldn't step out. It's like, "Hey, So-and-so wants you to go and sing on their song. Do you respect that person? Are you into that music?"

So go do it! Have fun with the Chemical Brothers . . . or with Old Dirty Bastard or Sweet Baby Jesus, or whatever his name is . . . or with Busta Rhymes. . . .

Ozzy: Sharon keeps me abreast of the times, you know. I'd never go, "Get me Busta Rhymes!" I didn't know who fucking Busta Rhymes was. But I went and did it and had such a blast doing it . . .

apart from all the fucking armory, the fucking bulletproof vests and that, you know.

Sharon: It's unbelievable how doors keep opening for us. So much has happened to us in such a short space of time. I still run Ozzy's career, on his own and when he's with Black Sabbath. I've added Kelly as a client, and I also run a small, boutique record label called Divine Recordings that has had about eight releases, including a great Sabbath tribute album, *N.I.B. II.*

In early April, I had a violent run-in with Renee Tab, the ICM agent who walked out of my New Year's party with a $15,000 necklace. I'd had my lawyers send her a letter, suggesting we settle our dispute by auctioning the necklace on eBay, with the money going to colon cancer research. After she refused, I felt like I had to let it go for my own well-being.

We literally bumped into each other at Koi, a hip sushi restaurant in West Hollywood. Ozzy, Jack, and I had gone there for a quiet Thursday-night dinner. I walked Jack out to the valet stand. On my way back, I bumped into Tab by the restroom.

Things went from bad to worse very quickly. Later, she would accuse me of spitting and screaming racial slurs at her.

It would've been like her calling me an English bitch. I'm from England, and I am a bitch. She would have been entitled to such an opinion.

Instead, this girl, who's built like a brick shithouse, punched me in the face, laying me out on the cement floor. That wasn't too hard to do, considering our weight differences. I ended the night in the emergency room at Cedars-Sinai Medical Center, where doctors treated me for a dislocated jaw, chipped teeth, and various bruises. Not long after, I heard Renee planned on suing me for $20 million and getting a restraining order against me. Unfortunately she never appeared in court, because I was like, "Please, God, do it so I don't ever have to see her face again."

Ozzy: I've always said violence achieves nothing. The real work in a fight is done by expensive lawyers. They do the most damage.

We had a more serious fight on our hands.

𝕽𝖊𝖑𝖑𝖞: No one wanted to believe Jack had a problem. I told my mom several times, but she didn't listen to me. The person in the biggest denial was Jack himself. One night I saw him in the kitchen and he was so fucked-up he either didn't care or didn't feel himself step on broken glass. He walked on it all night, despite blood everywhere.

At one point, I said, "Jack, you're bleeding." He looked at me with vacant, doped-up eyes and said, "Oh."

"Do you know you're fucking bleeding?" I asked.

He looked down at his foot, shrugged, and said, "So fucking what."

𝕵𝖆𝖈𝖐: I was out of it—just a bit.

I'd just had a party at the house in Malibu. Things got crazy. I was completely wasted on a whole bunch of things, walking around barefoot. I didn't even realize a glass had broken on the floor and I was walking through it. Kelly comes up to me and says, "Jack, your feet!" And I was like, "No, it's not." She says, "Look!" There was blood all through the house. She was like, "Go lie down."

𝕽𝖊𝖑𝖑𝖞: My brother can be rude, but he's not mean and nasty. Worried, I tried confronting him several times and always got shut down. "Fuck off," he'd say. "You don't know what the fuck you're talking about." He wasn't himself. One time, he invited twenty friends over to the house and some stupid fucking actor friend of his spilled some red wine all over a wall and the floor, which was a mess. I scrubbed my fucking hands to the bone because I didn't want my mother coming home to a shithole.

I was like, "Jack, please, if you drink something, put it away."

He said, "Fuck you, Kelly. You fucking bitch." He screamed one profanity after another, which startled me at first, and then I realized he was out of his mind. He was completely and totally fucked-up. "Jack," I said, "I haven't done anything to you. Calm down."

"Don't tell me to calm down," he said, and then he punched me in the face.

I was like, "Oh my God!" Knowing he wasn't right or safe for me to be around, I got my shit together and left. When I came back the next morning I found him sound asleep in the chair. I stood there and looked at him, feeling so scared that something really bad was happening to him and I couldn't help.

I prayed to God he'd wake up and realize he needed help. If not then, soon. And then I was so relieved to hear he'd confessed everything to my mom and was going to rehab. I knew it was the best thing for him. I knew he had to be there or else he might end up dead.

Ozzy: Jack kept his problem a secret for a few months, then he told Sharon. I was very proud he recognized that he was doing something bad to himself and needed help.

Good for him. At seventeen years old, I never would've gone to my folks and said, "Mom and Dad, I've got a drug problem. I need help."

Sharon: It was nighttime, and I was in bed when Jack came into my bedroom. I saw he was upset and struggling with something. He said he wanted to talk. Something about the combination of the tone of his voice and the look in his eyes told me that we needed to be alone. Leaving Ozzy to watch television by himself, I went into Jack's bedroom. By the time we sat down, I knew he had been drinking and I thought he was high. I thought something really bad had happened to him or one of his friends earlier that night.

I had no idea what was really going on until he told me. "Mom, I think I have a drug problem. I think I need help."

He started to cry. I asked if it was more than pot or alcohol, both of which I knew he'd been using for years. Jack nodded. Oh my God, I thought. My nightmare. How many times had Ozzy and I talked about the chances one or more of the kids might inherit his tendency for addiction?

Jack had been seeing this girl who had a nearly forty-year-old guardian who said he gave him a handful of Vicodin and also got him to sniff some ground-up OxyContin, a narcotic pain reliever. He tried it several times and soon found himself addicted. For months, he had been buying pills from friends. He thought at first he didn't have a problem, but then he realized he was in trouble.

"I tried so hard," he said. "But I couldn't stop."

I felt guilty for not being more aware. How could I not know?

Jack: I don't blame them. I mean, you know when my mother was walking around with cancer and Dad was telling her to go to the doctor? Now that I think about it, it's like, "Why didn't I notice?"

Sharon: I spent the night in Jack's room. He was like a boy who'd had a nightmare. He didn't want to be by himself.

We met with a therapist the next morning, and Jack told more of his story. He had tried to quit cold turkey and couldn't. Then he tried to cut down on the amount of pills, and he couldn't do that, either. Finally, he was using and trying to keep anyone from finding out.

I realized I didn't know anything about OxyContin. No one I knew did. I called Dr. Drew Pinsky, an expert in addiction, who told me about the drug and helped us in finding a bed at a rehab facility. It wasn't like checking into a hotel. Every facility in California was full.

The wait gave us time to pull together. His sisters were supportive and happy it was out in the open. Ozzy had a hard time at first, but got himself together and was stronger than I was. He quit drinking and pledged to stay sober as a way of supporting Jack. One night, he went off on the freeloaders and con artists who attach themselves to celebrities and provide drugs, to keep themselves on the inside. He blamed himself and struggled through those tough emotions.

Jack: He's told me that he doesn't even know how many friends of his died from using. You know, in a sense, he blames himself for those deaths. I don't know why.

Ozzy: It might also be genetic. It might be the ticking time bomb he inherited from me. You never know what drink or which drug is going to set it off.

Sharon: About a week after Jack asked for help, a bed opened up at Las Encinas, a small rehab on the grounds of a hospital in Pasadena. We snagged it for our Jackie boy. I was an emotional wreck by this time, so I stayed home while Ozzy and Tony took Jack. He spent several days detoxing in the hospital's psych ward before being moved into the rehab.

That put him in a terrible mood when we spoke on the phone at night. He asked to come home and we said no. Even after detoxing, he wanted to come home. Again, we said no. We visited him about ten days after he'd checked in, and he was very angry at us. "Fuck you for not taking me home," he said. "I was the one who wanted help and now I'm clean. You aren't listening to me, and so fuck off."

We visited again three days later and he was a different person.

"I know. I get it. I'm sorry about the way I spoke to you. I'm working on my first step. I'm with the program."

Ozzy: We moved Jack to another treatment place in Malibu after two weeks. He'd got a taste of the hard life in Pasadena, where he was around psycho kids. I know he didn't like that place. The rehab in Malibu was more comfortable. Still strict. He was on AA and doing the counseling sessions. I remember at the end of my second visit, one of the therapists said, "Jack feels like he's safe in here."

Jack: I had a group session with my dad. My mom was late. It was me and this counselor—the head therapist—and my dad. My dad started freaking out and getting all emotional. I was so moved by it. It just kind of dawned on me: I don't want to die.

And that was really where I had been going! I knew I couldn't go back there because it wasn't good and there was nothing good about it.

On Saturdays, I was allowed to leave for four hours with my parents. The first time they picked me up, we ate lunch at Nobu, my favorite sushi restaurant, and we followed that with a trip to the grocery store. I realized we were being followed by paparazzi. A whole team of them. It dawned on me that I was news, that people were watching me and talking about what I was going through. That freaked me out.

"Are people laughing at me? Do they think I'm a fuckup?"

"Jack, nobody's laughing. They respect you for getting help."

My dad told me, "Everybody fucks up. The smart ones learn from it." In July, I decided to just go public with it myself. I went on MTV and told the world:

"I don't want my life to be controlled by a drug."

Ozzy: This ordeal has brought Jack and me closer together. I know what my son is going through. I've been through rehab fourteen times.

In fact, this thing really turned my head around. When I was his age I never thought I'd be making public announcements against drugs. But after this fucking ordeal, I did—a week after Jack revealed his story, I spoke up.

"I used to think they should legalize pot, but you know what? They should ban the lot. One thing leads to another. When I found out the full depth of him getting into OxyContin, which is like hillbilly heroin, I was shocked and stunned. The thing that's amazing is how rapidly he went from smoking pot to doing hillbilly heroin."

Maybe that shocked and stunned some people into getting help. Or staying clean. I can only hope.

I know—all this from the guy who wrote "Sweet Leaf"? I'm a chronic, alcoholic, drug addict. Currently I'm not using or drinking. Will it stick? I can't answer that question.

All I know is today I'm not gonna pick up a drug or a drink.

XXV

The Osbourne Empire

———— ⌇ ————

The only thing left is *The Osbournes on Ice*.

—OZZY OSBOURNE, *MTV NEWS*, JULY 7, 2003

Sharon: I've never wanted to build an empire. I've always said that. My father built an empire and yes, it's great to make money on the way, but I've always had so much satisfaction out of working with people who are hugely talented.

Ozzy: I keep saying to Jack, "I would like you to go to drama school and become an actor." I think he's a natural actor. You've seen him on camera, he's very cool, very clear, very correct.

He said to me, "I don't want to be an actor." I said, "Well, be what you want, I'm just making a suggestion. I'm not saying that you *must* be an actor."

Sharon: Kids are changing all the time. Always, always, always. Jack's still on about how he wants to be a fireman. That's what he always wanted to be—a fireman. He's goes, "Well, what if I'm still interested in it?" And I go, "Why not?" It's fine.

Jack: [Picks up utensil] I mean, this fork has more musical talent than me at this point. Ideally, I'd like to kind of follow in my mom's footsteps even though the music business is a rapidly dying industry. I think right now an independent record label is where you'll be able to make any cash whatsoever. I think the industry is just going to resort back to small labels.

I'm not so much into the management game—I'm more into the finding of the bands. I do scouting for record companies. I've been doing that for coming on three years now. I think it's supersatisfactory to be like, "Yeah, I found *that* band."

I came close to that once, but it was a long story—a lot of drama. I'm not rushing into it. When I do it I kind of always want it to be under the radar. I don't want it to be like, "Jack Osbourne's band!" I want it be more about the music.

Ozzy: Kelly, I really don't know. I would like to see her . . . I don't mind what they do as long as they enjoy what they're doing.

Kelly: It's really been fun. I mean, on the road all through Europe, opening for Robbie Williams—I've had a great time. I think this opportunity to get out and be by myself away from everyone was good. You get a better perspective on things. And it's very weird: A lot of Americans think of me as an American, but a lot of people here see me as English.

You start to realize little things that you miss about America, like ice in foods and they put so much butter and mayonnaise and salt in everything here. But then again, the bread and the fruit and the vegetables are so much better over here.

What I find pathetic is that when you're on the road, and especially with other bands, they feel as though they have to act up and live out that whole sex, drugs, and rock 'n' roll lifestyle. It bugs me to see all these bands that go out there and are rude and trash dressing rooms and that's not what it's about anymore. That's such an eighties cocaine-and-booze lifestyle, and it isn't that anymore.

Most of my friends are in bands and to see how different they are from when they're on the road or just hanging out with me . . . it's ridiculous, because they live this, "We don't care about money, we do it for the music" lifestyle. Well, then why don't you care about that person that's going to have to clean up after you?!

I find it pathetic because it's not about that. It's just about getting up every day and doing what you love—making music and being able to perform.

Sharon: Kelly was honeymooned by Tommy Mottola, the former head of Sony Music. That's why her first album's with Sony. He said, "You know, this is a great opportunity—Kelly's got a great personality. I want to sign Kelly." He was very, very much a part of everything that Kelly did musically. At that time, I was on my deathbed. So Tommy took her by the hand and did everything for her. We loved everyone at Sony—all of them had seen Kelly grow up. One of the executives there is Kelly's godparent.

And Ozzy's been with Epic, which is part of Sony, for over twenty years. My husband made a fortune over the years for that company: Over twenty-three years selling platinum, Ozzy had a guaranteed audience. They were doing a very good job and over the years we had created a family-type atmosphere. In fact, for a guy that's been in the industry thirty-four years, he's only ever been on two labels—one with Sabbath and one by himself!

We stick—we like continuity.

When we knew that Tommy was leaving Sony last December, I said to Kelly, "We've got to watch it because God only knows what they're going to do with you."

My instinct was right.

Don Ienner came in and took over and didn't want anything to do with anything that Tommy was responsible for. And I get it, you know? I absolutely get it. I knew it instinctively that they would drop her, and they dropped her. Her godfather was the one who called me and told me it was over.

But Kelly's record was out only four months, okay? It had done extremely well, making great steps. Four months of promotion and then they decide to pull the plug. Four months in!

Jesus Christ. I know it's business—it's not personal. I get all of that. But yet, when it's your own child, you don't get it.

Ozzy: I told Sharon, "You know what? I ain't here, either. I'm out. They'll never get another record from me. They fucked my daughter, so they fucked me."

Sharon: I'll give them this much: Ozzy had a firm deal with them for three more records. They were very good by saying, "All right, Ozzy. Buy yourself out and you can go." They know it's unfixable.

In hindsight, maybe we were wrong by letting Kelly go there. If I had to do it again, maybe I wouldn't have put both Ozzy and her together in the same company.

One other thing, I think Kelly learned a huge lesson out of it—a *huge* fucking lesson: Nothing comes easy, nothing's a given, and you do have to work. There's great value in that.

Aimee: Do I think that Kelly is going to have a long career in music? That it is going to be as smooth as it started out? No. I hope that she'll grow up and really establish herself and work hard and find something that she really loves to do as opposed to just doing this to just doing this, to riding it out for all its worth, you know? But she's so young.

Ozzy: I am betting that Aimee is a late bloomer. I didn't start getting serious in my rock 'n' roll till I was twenty-one. Even then I was keeping on a day job, you know. But then I got serious with it. Aimee's only nineteen. She's got such an incredible persona, a vibe about her. She is fucking stunning.

Sharon: I always told them, you can make anything happen if that's what you want to do. You want to be an actor? Be an actor. Whatever it is you do, as long as you do it well, then I don't care.

Aimee: In the last few years, I didn't really think or necessarily want to become an actress. It came about when Lois Curren and Rod Aissa were developing this movie idea adapting Emily Brontë's *Wuthering Heights* for MTV. They asked me to read the script almost a year ago. I really enjoyed it, and they asked me to consider being a part of the project when it did start coming together.

I was kind of hesitant because I didn't want to be in some MTV teen movie, but I met the director, Suri Krishnamma from London, who is a great guy. He knew what was going on and wasn't into any petty industry bullshit. He was really direct with me and that's really what drew me in, to be honest—more than the material.

I wasn't doing anything. I was depressed. Nothing was really happening for me. So I thought, What the hell! I'm going to do it. I'm going to *enjoy* it. I'd be getting a chance not only to go away to a foreign place, but to meet people and experience something. So that's what I did, and it was one of the best things I've ever done.

But it's only one possible path for me. I don't think anyone should limit themselves to one creative outlet, whether it be acting, writing, singing. I think that a lot of the time if you can act then there's an 80 percent chance that you could be good at writing or directing or teaching or drawing. It all really is a package for me. It's not so much just one thing.

Sharon: There's music and talent on all sides of the kids' family tree.

Aimee: Louis Osbourne is great. He's a musician, too, you know? A deejay in England. Louis has really suffered—he hasn't had a nice childhood at all. And he really loves Dad a lot. I see that. He's very genuine.

Kelly: The only one I'll have anything to do with is Louis. I refuse to have anything to do with Jessica because she never treated me like a sister. And if she didn't want anything to do with us, then she should never ask for anything.

Ozzy: My daughter Jessica and I are not really on hunky-dory speaking terms. I have fallen out with her a bit. We keep our distance. But I have just recently become a fucking grandfather. She has just given me a granddaughter.

Aimee: My music? It's taken me a while, but I really think that I have found the right people that I want to work with, who understand me, who support me, who don't want to turn me into another moneymaker off this reality madness that's going on.

Kelly: You know what? I haven't heard my sister's music. And I think it's very sad, because she is so talented and so beautiful and she has the most amazing qualities about her and she can make anyone laugh. But she doesn't use any of her talents in the right way. I do think that she's depressed.

Aimee: I still battle depression. But at the same time I'm so sick of everyone telling me I need to take medication. I stopped. I don't want that poison in my body. I mean, it really would make me hyperactive or too mellow. I don't need it. I've learned to know myself well and to know what sets me off and to try to get myself out of that rut when I'm in it.

You can't keep playing the victim. There's a point when you have to accept the way things are and that your parents are the way they are. They're not going to change no matter what you say or no matter how much pain you try to express to them. You have to accept it and move on. I've learned to deal with that and I'm very happy where I am in my feelings toward my family. I think that everyone goes through that and *should* go through that to a certain degree.

Jack: Yeah, I have pretty bad depression. It had been diagnosed before. I just wasn't taking the medication regularly.

Ozzy: I've tried different antidepressants. All of a sudden, I couldn't say two words. Then my doctor put me on this new medication because I suffer from a hereditary problem: I have a tremor.

Anxiety is still very common for me. But I don't go, "Doctor, give me a Xanax, give me a Valium, give me a fucking OxyContin, or a shot of morphine." At the age of fifty-four, I'm beginning to own my problems. And when you own your problems a little bit, it gets a little bit better, you know. I must confess as I'm getting older, I'm getting a bit more sensible, and I appreciate love a little bit more.

Sharon: Everything with Ozzy is in excess. Ozzy can't take one of anything. Not one chocolate, not one grape, it has to be the lot.

Not that long ago, Ozzy tried Viagra. If it said take one, he'd take five. It's true. It made his face go all blotchy and sweaty. And he was perspiring and acting crazy. He was like, "These are great, I'm a new man."

Ozzy: I'm running fucking seven or eight miles a day, or every other day. Lifting weights. I've dropped nearly thirty pounds, my stomach is flat, my legs are strong. But there are people that haven't got the time, people that haven't got the willpower, people that just will not.

Sharon: Ozzy's finally succeeded. He'd been trying forever to quit. I've never smoked in my life. He'd try that gum and he would smoke and have the gum and still smoke cigars and cigarettes. And those patches were like the worst, because he would wake up to smoke, and he'd still have the patch on his arm and I'm like, "You're going to have a fucking heart attack!" Then he went through the phase with pipe smoking. Like, "What the hell are you doing?" That was disgusting!

Ozzy: I'll tell you: If you keep putting bad shit in your body, it is going to have a bad effect. How I quit smoking I will never fucking know. Smoking is right next to smack as far as addictions go.

Sharon: I've said this to you before—especially in America, it's more accepted to be a drug addict than it is to be fat. People do not take well to fat people. And it's really sad, because I've been fat and I've been thin, and the difference is like night and day.

Ozzy: I think I am a biological miracle. Obviously my time isn't up yet.

A friend of mine had a father who worked construction on a high-rise. One day he fell off the scaffolding on the seventeenth floor. On the way down, his armed jammed into a bucket, breaking his fall. He pulled himself up and avoided certain death. Three days later, he was driving, fell asleep, crashed, and died. The moral of the story? When your number's up, your number's up.

I am amazed that I can remember all this shit.

Sharon: Ozzy is a working-class hero and a true survivor. It's like they say when they drop the big one, there'll just be the roaches. Well, there'll be roaches and Ozzy. . . .

Ozzy: If I go dead right now, don't feel sorry for me, because I've had a great fucking fantastic journey. I mean, I'm not planning on going right now. But if my number is up—I'll have made it three times in my life, man: Black Sabbath, Ozzy Osbourne, now *The Osbournes* . . .

Sharon: The health issues have settled down, but I don't think that our lives will ever be mellow. That doesn't come with being an Osbourne. It just doesn't. There are still the projects and concerts and lawsuits out there. There's always drama with us. It will never be mellow.

Ozzy: Family means hard work. Family means dedication. Family means love. Family means I married her.

One thing I want to say about America: American families are either extremely functioning or extremely fucked-up. I truly believe that every single family is somewhat dysfunctional. Two families cannot do the same thing or be the same way. Kids are so unpredictable, and life is so unpredictable.

Sharon: Now it's a whole different thing for Ozzy and me. For the last eight, nine years it's no more Grammy Awards if he doesn't want. If he doesn't like it, if it doesn't feel right, we're not going there.

Ozzy wants to get back to the way that it was before the craziness.

Ozzy: I desperately want to go back to my roots, man. I want to fucking make a record, man. I want to have fun, you know. Having a camera crew behind me 24/7 is not what I mean.

I do not want to be the wealthiest man in the graveyard. You can't fucking take it with you.